APR 2 3 2020

D0583851

Academic Writing Skills for International Students

www.thestudyspace.com – the leading study skills website

Study Skills

Academic Success	Practical Criticism
Academic Writing Skills for International Students	Presentation Skills for Students (3rd edn)
Business Degree Success	The Principles of Writing in Psychology
The Business Student's Phrase Book	Professional Writing (3rd edn)
Career Skills	Researching Online
Cite Them Right (10th edn)	The Student Phrase Book
Critical Thinking and Persuasive Writing for Postgraduates	The Student's Guide to Writing (3rd edn)
e-Learning Skills (2nd edn)	Study Skills for International Postgraduates
The Employability Journal	Studying in English
Essentials of Essay Writing	Studying History (4th edn)
Get Sorted	Studying Law (4th edn)
Great Ways to Learn Anatomy and Physiology (2nd edn)	Studying Modern Drama (2nd edn)
How to Begin Studying English Literature (4th edn)	Studying Psychology (2nd edn)
How to Study Foreign Languages	Studying Physics
How to Study Linguistics (2nd edn)	Success in Academic Writing (2nd edn)
How to Use Your Reading in Your Essays (3rd edn)	Smart Thinking
How to Write Better Essays (4th edn)	Stand Out from the Crowd
How to Write Your Undergraduate Dissertation (2nd edn)	The Undergraduate Research Handbook (2nd edn)
Improve Your Grammar (2nd edn)	The Work-Based Learning Student Handbook (2nd edn)
Information Skills	Work Placements – A Survival Guide for Students
The International Student Handbook	Writing for Engineers (4th edn)
The Mature Student's Guide to Writing (3rd edn)	Writing History Essays (2nd edn)
The Mature Student's Handbook	Writing for Law
Mindfulness for Students	Writing for Nursing and Midwifery Students (3rd edn)
The Macmillan Student Planner	Write it Right (2nd edn)
The Personal Tutor's Handbook	Writing for Science Students

Pocket Study Skills

14 Days to Exam Success (2nd edn)	Posters and Presentations
Analyzing a Case Study	Reading and Making Notes (2nd edn)
Blogs, Wikis, Podcasts and More	Referencing and Understanding Plagiarism (2nd edn)
Brilliant Writing Tips for Students	Reflective Writing
Completing Your PhD	Report Writing (2nd edn)
Doing Research (2nd edn)	Science Study Skills
Getting Critical (2nd edn)	Studying with Dyslexia (2nd edn)
Managing Stress	Success in Groupwork
Planning Your Dissertation (2nd edn)	Time Management
Planning Your Essay (2nd edn)	Where's Your Argument?
Planning Your PhD	Writing for University (2nd edn)

Research Skills

Authoring a PhD	The PhD Viva
The Foundations of Research (2nd edn)	The PhD Writing Handbook
Getting to Grips with Doctoral Research	Planning Your Postgraduate Research
Getting Published	The Postgraduate Research Handbook (2nd edn)
The Good Supervisor (2nd edn)	The Professional Doctorate
The Lean PhD	Structuring Your Research Thesis
PhD by Published Work	

Career Skills

Excel at Graduate Interviews	Social Media for Your Student and Graduate Job Search
Graduate CVs and Covering Letters	
Graduate Entrepreneurship	The Graduate Career Guidebook
How to Succeed at Assessment Centres	Work Experience, Placements and Internships

For a complete listing of all our titles in this area please visit
www.macmillanihe.com/study-skills

Academic Writing Skills for International Students

Siew Hean Read

© Siew Hean Read, under exclusive licence to Springer Nature Limited 2019

All rights reserved. No reproduction, copy or transmission of this publication may be made without written permission.

No portion of this publication may be reproduced, copied or transmitted save with written permission or in accordance with the provisions of the Copyright, Designs and Patents Act 1988, or under the terms of any licence permitting limited copying issued by the Copyright Licensing Agency, Saffron House, 6–10 Kirby Street, London EC1N 8TS.

Any person who does any unauthorized act in relation to this publication may be liable to criminal prosecution and civil claims for damages.

The author has asserted her right to be identified as the author of this work in accordance with the Copyright, Designs and Patents Act 1988.

First published 2019 by
RED GLOBE PRESS

Red Globe Press in the UK is an imprint of Springer Nature Limited, registered in England, company number 785998, of 4 Crinan Street, London N1 9XW.

Red Globe Press® is a registered trademark in the United States, the United Kingdom, Europe and other countries.

ISBN 978–1–352–00375–8 paperback

This book is printed on paper suitable for recycling and made from fully managed and sustained forest sources. Logging, pulping and manufacturing processes are expected to conform to the environmental regulations of the country of origin.

A catalogue record for this book is available from the British Library.

A catalog record for this book is available from the Library of Congress.

Contents

Acknowledgments

I am very grateful to Neil Matheson from the University of Auckland for giving me access to his collection of more than 600 student assignments from a wide range of subject areas, which can be viewed on the university website, *https://awa.auckland.ac.nz.* Neil also read some earlier material and provided invaluable advice. I would also like to thank Colleen Bright, now retired from the University of Auckland, who worked with me on the initial proposal in 2016.

Extracts of academic writing from 22 subject areas are reproduced with permission from the individual writers. I would like to acknowledge their enthusiastic support of the project when it was just an idea, so thanks to Adam Holden, Adrian Katz, Annyssia Gonsalves, Bethan Powell, Catherine Lee, Ella Tunnicliffe-Glass, Emma Cavanagh, Giovan Widjaja, Grace Brebner, Hadassah Patchigalla, Hannah Feenstra, Imogen Allan, Isaac Hollis, Jerome de Vries, Jessica Lan, Jun Takamatsu, Kelly McMillan, Kerry Chooi, Lisa Brown-Bayliss, Mathijs Kros, Megan Iminitoff, Minkyung Kim, Nee Zhen Khoo, Olivia Salthouse, Stephanie Morton, Tim Harrison, Tricia Lawrence, Vanisha Patel, Victoria Silwood, and Wakana Matheson. I would also like to thank Mary McIntyre for letting me use one of her paintings as a basis for a visual analysis assignment.

Thank you most of all to Helen Caunce from Red Globe Press for believing in the project's potential and whose patient mentoring and constructive advice throughout the project got me across the finish line.

Finally, I want to thank my family for their moral support and help in many practical ways during the past year.

Introduction

Who is the book for?

The book is written for students who have mastered the language requirements for university entrance but are looking for guidance on how to improve and develop their academic writing skills. If you are enrolled in undergraduate study in an English-medium university, this book will give you the tools to write academic subject-matter with confidence. If you are a native speaker of English, you can also find techniques in the book to help you make a more successful transition to university writing. The contents and the skills addressed in the book are also appropriate for students in post-graduate studies in English and for tutors teaching Academic Writing courses.

What can you learn from the book?

University written assignments can vary across different subject areas. However, there are common skills and competencies that can be learnt, practised and applied to different types of writing. These skills are the central focus of the book. Specifically, you will learn techniques which will enable you to

- understand assignment questions and write a relevant response
- structure and organise ideas logically
- present a point of view and develop an argument
- use an appropriate academic writing style, including integrating and citing evidence in your writing.

How is the book organised?

The book is divided into **five parts**. Each part is further divided into separate units, with a focus on an aspect of writing.

PART I Essential features of academic writing introduces five key principles underlying good overall written communication in university contexts: appropriate writing style, conventions for using sources, clear structure and layout, coherent flow of ideas and accurate use of language.

PART II Types of university written assignments provides an overview of writing tasks from different subject areas. The structure and style of each type of writing are illustrated with examples of student writing.

PART III Developing your writing explores ways to advance ideas in the body of the essay or report, using different expansion techniques.

PART IV Presenting a point of view: argumentation addresses one of the most challenging types of writing at university. It requires you to examine an issue from different perspectives, present a point of view or thesis on it, justify it through systematic reasoning and arrive at a logical conclusion.

PART V Putting it all together presents a selection of full-length assignments with annotations to alert you to specific features of structure and style. More importantly, it provides an opportunity for you to review the principles of academic and assignment writing covered in the book.

What are the unique features of the book?

- The book uses techniques that <u>support</u> and <u>promote</u> independent learning. The support-promote model uses a three-step approach: It

SHOWS WHAT a particular aspect of writing skill involves.

EXPLAINS WHY it is especially challenging

SHOWS HOW you can master it and apply it to different writing tasks.

- Authentic examples of assignments from many subject areas provide models of good writing and also highlight particular problem areas. Notes in boxes in the right and left margins explain features of structure and style.

- Models and frameworks facilitate confident transfer of skills to different assignments.

- ⚠ This icon alerts you to an important point, such as exceptions to the rule and advises caution when applying a technique or principle of writing.

- Practice activities at the end of each stage of instruction enable you to **test** your understanding and learning. Answers to most activities, including some useful comments, are provided at the end of the book.

How to use this book

The book is structured in a way that progressively builds your writing skills, providing you with the tools to become a skilful and confident writer. Parts I to III form a logical sequence and cover essential principles of academic writing using shorter extracts of student writing. Parts IV and V examine how these principles come together in full-length assignments.

If you are in your first year of university or preparing to enter university, it would be advisable to work through the first three parts in the order they are presented to get an overview of what is expected. In Parts IV and V, references are made to the basic principles covered in the earlier parts of the book. However, if you wish to practise a particular skill, such as writing the introduction or thesis statement, you can locate it by consulting the index.

Part I

Essential Features of Academic Writing

Part I highlights five features which characterise all good academic written communication and practice.

Main units

Unit 1 Appropriate writing style
Unit 2 Correct conventions for using sources
Unit 3 Clear structure and layout
Unit 4 Coherent flow of ideas
Unit 5 Accurate use of language

These features may not have been emphasised at high school or college, depending on your previous experience of writing in English as an additional language. It is therefore useful to have a quick review of academic writing style and conventions at the start of your university study. These features are reinforced in Parts II, III, IV and V which look at longer extracts of student writing, including full-length essays.

As you work through each unit, you will begin to develop an effective academic writing style and quality that will give you a confident and successful start to university and during your degree.

Practice activities at the end of each unit allow you to test your understanding of each feature. Work through them carefully before checking your answers in Appendix A at the end of the book.

UNIT 1 Appropriate writing style

Key topics

1.1 Comparison between written and spoken styles
1.2 Strategies for developing an academic writing style

What is style?

The word 'style' refers to the particular way you use words and sentences to express ideas. At university, you are often communicating complex issues and facts. When you write, it is important to think about the most effective way to convey your message to the reader. Writing appropriately means using a writing style that is suitable or right for university contexts and the assignment you have been given.

1.1 Comparison between written and spoken styles

Academic written communication is a carefully considered activity. While you are writing, you do not have visual contact with your reader. You rely on the precise use of words, phrases and accurately constructed sentence structures to convey your message.

In general, academic writing style is **objective**. It is based on facts and evidence gathered from research or investigation. It conveys ideas through logical reasoning and analysis. It is **formal**. It follows conventions which are expected and used in university settings.

Spoken communication involves active participants in face-to-face conversation or discussion, as in a tutorial session at university. It relies on facial expressions and gestures, rephrasing and more repetition than is necessary in writing.

In general, a spoken style is **subjective**. It is influenced by personal feelings or opinions. It uses emotive language. These are words which indicate strong emotions such as *incredible, wonderful, unfortunately, sadly, remarkable*. It is **informal**. It uses words and sentence patterns found in friendly and relaxed conversations or situations.

Using speech sentence patterns and words in a written assignment gives it a conversational and casual quality, which is inappropriate in university contexts.

The table below summarises some common features of language use in both styles.

Written academic style	Spoken style
1. does not use personal pronouns or personal reference in formal writing (*Technology has changed the way people communicate.*)	uses personal pronouns and personal reference (*Personally, I think, technology has changed the way we communicate.*)
2. conveys ideas using non-emotive language, academic words and specialised vocabulary of a subject area (*a significant/substantial number, converse, communicate, address*)	conveys ideas using emotive language (*great, so many, huge, massive, wonderful, incredible!*) uses slang or conversational vocabulary (*kids, heaps, lots, get, chat*)
3. uses precise words (*The damage is extensive. Two-thirds of the land is submerged under two metres of water.*)	uses simpler, less specific, informal words (*Many things were turned upside-down by the storm. A lot of land is now under water.*)

4. constructs formal sentences (*In the current economic crisis, employment opportunities for new graduates are limited.*)	uses fragments or incomplete sentences (*Not a good time to look for a job these days. Not when the economy is in crisis. Especially for new graduates.*)
5. uses standard word order of formal sentences (*It is also; It can also; People use this method mainly; This method is mainly used to ...;*)	Uses non-standard word order (*Also, it is; It also can; Mainly, people use this method*)
6. uses different types of sentences: simple, compound and complex sentences (see Unit 5)	may use mainly simple and compound sentences
7. uses formal devices to link ideas (*in addition, however, similarly, by contrast, as a result, first of all, another* – see Unit 4)	uses simple connectors (*and, so, but, or, also*) and informal devices to link ideas (*like*)
8. uses full forms (*it is, for example, such as, that is*)	uses contracted or shortened forms and abbreviations (*it's, e.g., i.e., etc.*)

⚠ Some features of spoken communication are found in newspapers and magazines. These are inappropriate for most written academic assignments. Therefore, unless you are specifically asked to submit your writing as it would appear in a newspaper or magazine, avoid the style used in these publications. In some subject areas, shortened forms are acceptable. You may find a list of acceptable abbreviations used in your subject area in your course handbook.

PRACTICE ACTIVITY 1.1

Below is an extract from a 1st year Academic English essay about the value of a university degree. The writing style has many features of spoken communication.

<u>Test yourself</u>. How many features of spoken style can you identify?

> Actually, more and more jobs need a university degree these days. Like in China, also employers are always looking for university graduates for basic-level jobs. And not only that, for some specialised fields you need to get post-graduate qualifications. Like a Masters or a PhD. There's so much competition for jobs. Also, I think we face lots of pressure from society to keep providing proof of scholarship and skill. So, a university degree's a good investment for our future. Especially nowadays with more people chasing fewer jobs.

<u>Find examples of the following features</u>

informal words or slang	
emotive language	
contracted forms	
personal pronouns	
incomplete sentences	
sentences in wrong word order	
informal connectors	

Check your answer with the revision below. You will notice that personal pronouns, informal vocabulary and connectors have been replaced by more formal and academic words. Which other words from the text have been replaced? Fill in the blanks to show the numbered changes. The first one has been done as an example.

1. Today, a university qualification is essential for most 2. work. In China, 3. for example, 4. employers are also increasingly looking for university graduates for the basic-level work. 5. In addition, some specialised fields 6. require post-graduate qualifications 7. such as a Master's or a Doctoral degree. With 8. increasing competition, there is 9. considerable pressure from society to keep providing evidence of scholarship and skill. 10. Therefore, a university degree is an important investment for 11. the future, when 12. demand for work exceeds availability.	1. replaces _these days_ 2. replaces _____ 3. replaces _____ 4. replaces _____ 5. replaces _____ 6. replaces _____ 7. replaces _____ 8. replaces _____ 9. replaces _____ 10. replaces _____ 11. replaces _____ 12. replace _____

1.2 Strategies for developing an academic writing style

➡ Restrict the use of first (*I, we, my, our, us*) and second (*you, your*) personal pronouns

Most university writing requires your thesis or point of view on an issue. Some assignment instructions ask for your opinion in a direct way: '*Do you think ...?*'. When you write your essay, you might feel that it is necessary to respond with 'I think' or 'In my personal opinion' to let the reader know that it is your opinion.

This style is unnecessary and not effective in academic contexts. In fact, over-using personal pronouns can get in the way of the message, as the following example shows:

The following extract is from a 1st year Engineering Practical Work report. This part of the report requires the student to evaluate the work experience. Read the two versions describing the same experience. Which version describes the experience more effectively?

Version 1	My main task for each day was to complete the computational analysis. I also had to write a one-page report at the end of my day's work for my project leader. For me, the most valuable experience was that I had the opportunity to be involved in a real project and I could understand more clearly how theory informed practice.
Version 2	The main task was completing the computational analysis and writing a report for the project leader. The most valuable part of the three-month work experience was being involved in a real project and understand more clearly how theory informed practice.

⚠ Version 2 conveys the experience more clearly without the distraction caused by the overuse of personal pronouns. In some subject areas, such as Sociology and Language Teaching, reflective essays and journal writing assignments are often set to encourage self-reflection. Instructions for these types of writing may say that you can use 'I' and 'My' in your journal entries. In general, however, avoid excessive use of personal pronouns in academic written assignments.

Below are more examples to show how the same idea can be expressed using a more academic writing style and without the need for personal pronouns and personal reference:

✔ objective and impersonal

Education can be influential in shaping lives. This essay discusses three benefits of having a university degree: it can increase professional and personal opportunities, broaden knowledge and skills, and contribute to the advancement of society.

✖ overly personal (use of first person pronouns)

Personally, I think education can be influential in shaping our lives. In this essay, I will discuss three benefits of having a university degree: increasing our professional and personal opportunities, broadening our knowledge and skills, and enabling us to make a significant contribution for the advancement of our society.

✔ evidence from research

The pursuit of higher study can be vital for development. Pursuing university study could be the most important decision of a person's life. According to a study by Jones (2000) of graduates, 70 per cent of graduates reported that university study expanded their world view.

✖ personal experience as evidence

People say that higher study is vital for development. In my case, pursuing university study has been the most important decision of my life. I can say that university study has expanded my world view and I am a better person emotionally, intellectually and socially.

✔ third person referencing replaces 'chatting'

A university degree is essential for many people. With a university degree, they are in a better position to compete for the best jobs and improve their employment prospects.

✖ speaking to the reader (second person pronouns)

A university degree is essential for your life. If you have a university degree, you are in a better position to compete for the best jobs and improve your employment prospects.

➡ Expand your sentence range

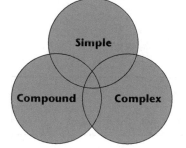

As a writer, you make choices about how you want to convey your ideas, which ideas to combine and which ideas to emphasise. Knowing how to write different types of sentences gives you more stylistic options for writing at university.

Principles of coordination and subordination

Understanding these two principles can help you combine sentences to make connections between ideas clearer and to add some complexity to the way you express ideas.

You can express ideas in simple sentences, as shown in the following sentences adapted from a Film, Television and Media Studies essay on the effect of digital technologies. Each simple sentence contains <u>one</u> main idea:

Digital cameras are portable.

Their 35 mm counterparts are more burdensome by nature.

Digital cameras provide more freedom to filmmakers.

Shooting a film becomes a spontaneous, flexible and creative process.

Coordination creates <u>compound sentences</u>. The ideas that are joined have the same status or rank in the sentence. It is usually signalled by a linking word, called a <u>coordinating conjunction</u> or coordinator (e.g. *and, but, or, so*), or by an adverbial at the start of the second sentence (e.g. *moreover, however, as a result*).

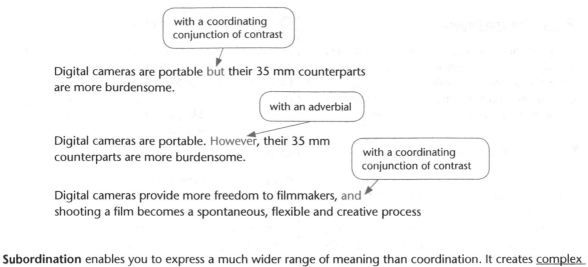

Digital cameras are portable but their 35 mm counterparts are more burdensome.

Digital cameras are portable. However, their 35 mm counterparts are more burdensome.

Digital cameras provide more freedom to filmmakers, and shooting a film becomes a spontaneous, flexible and creative process

Subordination enables you to express a much wider range of meaning than coordination. It creates <u>complex sentences</u>. The ideas that are joined do not have the same status. One idea is the main idea; the other is subordinate to it. This means it <u>depends</u> on the main idea to complete its meaning.

A word that introduces the subordinate idea is called a <u>subordinating conjunction</u> or subordinator (such as *although, while, since, if, unless*):

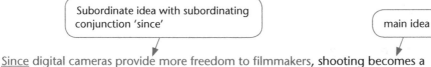

<u>Since</u> digital cameras provide more freedom to filmmakers, shooting becomes a more spontaneous, flexible and creative process.

The table below presents some common subordinators:

Meanings	Subordinators
Time	*after, as, before, since, until, when, while, until, as soon as, whenever*
Place	*where, wherever*
Condition	*if, unless*
Contrast	*while, whereas, although*
Reason	*because, since, as*
Purpose	*in order to, so as to, so that*
Result	*so, so that*
Preference	*rather than*

⚠ Subordination can also be signalled _without_ an explicit subordinator, as in the following complex sentence:

> This is a relative clause introduced by a wh-word instead of a subordinating conjunction.

Digital cameras, which are less burdensome than their 35 mm counterparts, have allowed shooting to be more spontaneous and flexible.

Relative clauses using _wh_-words (_who, which, whose_) are commonly used in scientific writing. Placed directly after the main subject, they provide descriptive detail or comment.

➲ Vary sentence starters

If you find that you often start with the <u>subject</u> of the sentence, or with 'The', 'There is' or 'It /This is', try varying sentence openings to add interest and variety, as shown below:

The new technologies are also having a significant impact on a global scale.
Variation: On a global scale, the new technologies are also having a significant impact.

The government is increasing the retirement age to delay superannuation payments.
Variation: To delay superannuation payments, the government is considering increasing the retirement age.

It is impossible to activate the alarm system without the C34 device.
Variations: Without the C34 device, it is impossible to activate the alarm system.
Activating the alarm system is impossible without the C34 device.

Robert Harris is an accomplished violinist who has performed all over the world.
Variation: An accomplished violinist, Robert Harris has performed all over the world.

There will be substantial benefits when the overhead rail is completed.
Variations: When the overhead rail is completed, there will be substantial benefits.
Once completed, the overhead rail will bring substantial benefits.

➲ Use academic and precise vocabulary

When you have an adequate academic vocabulary base, you are not restricted to the language of speech such as the following:

- simple, general or vague (non-specific) words e.g. _something, things, somewhat, interesting effects, great idea._

- slang or words common in conversation e.g. _lots, heaps, way better, cool, plenty._

- clichés, defined by the _New Oxford Dictionary of English_ as 'words and phrases that are over-used, tired and lacking in original thought'.

Example

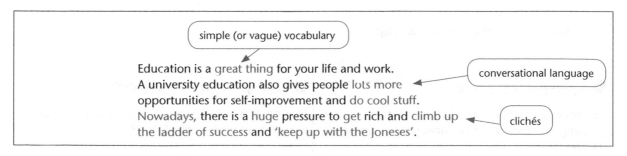

simple (or vague) vocabulary

Education is a great thing for your life and work.
A university education also gives people lots more opportunities for self-improvement and do cool stuff.
Nowadays, there is a huge pressure to get rich and climb up the ladder of success and 'keep up with the Joneses'.

conversational language

clichés

Revision: A more academic style and tone is achieved through the use of specific and academic vocabulary. Notice the highlighted changes.

> Education can have a significant impact on people's lives and their employment prospects. A university education can provide not only career advancement, but also opportunities for personal growth and vital skills development. Today, there is considerable pressure to accumulate wealth and status, often recognised by society as determinants or symbols of success.

 For an understanding of academic vocabulary and a useful list of academic words, visit this website: www.victoria.ac.nz/lals/resources/academicwordlist

Write with conviction and authority

Writing with conviction shows you have a firm belief in your ideas. Writing with authority shows you have adequate knowledge of the subject. These aspects of academic writing style are relevant in writing tasks that require you to present a point and view and justify it with reasoning and argumentation (see *Part IV Presenting a point of view*). However, it is also important to exercise caution and avoid sounding extreme or unreasonable.

Some ways to show caution

- Use **'hedging'** words (such as *generally, tend to, could, may, it could be said that*)

In terms of writing style, hedging means reducing the forcefulness of a statement. Hedging makes you sound more cautious and accurate. However, overuse of hedging can weaken your arguments. The opposite of hedging would be the use of these modal verbs (*will, must, need to, have to, should, ought to*):

✔ Uses hedging	✘ Uses no hedging
Future citizens of a society are generally expected to better themselves and society.	As future citizens of a society, we should strive to better ourselves and society. *(suggesting obligation)*
Pursuing a university degree can enhance people's ability to contribute to society as effective citizens.	Get a university degree and contribute to society as an effective citizen. *(giving instructions)*

- Make your point clearly and directly:

✔ Makes the point directly	✘ Poses questions (to the reader)
Literacy can help to create a better world and pursuing university study can have positive outcomes for everyone.	How can literacy help to create a better world? What are the benefits of a university degree?

• Use formal, non-emotive language. Emotive language is influenced by personal feelings and opinions:

✅ Uses <u>formal, non-emotive language</u>	❌ Uses <u>informal, emotive language</u>
In Chinese culture, a university degree is widely *viewed* as a significant achievement. *In fact*, it is *not uncommon* to find at least one graduate in every family. More than 90 per cent of Chinese families are one-child families and the parents *tend to* expend all their energy, time and finances on their only child.	4. In Chinese culture, having a university degree is a remarkable achievement. Sadly, more than 90 per cent of Chinese families are one-child families and parents spend all their energy and time (even their entire fortune) on their children. There is at least one graduate in the family!

emotive language

inappropriate punctuation

PRACTICE ACTIVITY 1.2

A Use the subordinators (in *italics*) to combine each set of simple sentences. They are adapted from a Geography essay exploring the differences between the terms *gender* and *sex*.

1. a. The words 'gender' and 'sex' are often considered to be interchangeable.
    b. They refer to two different phenomena.

    → *Although* _____, _____.

2. a. Sex refers to the biological differences of male and female.
    b. Gender refers to the social identities of masculinity and femininity.

    → *Whereas* _____, _____.

3. a. Gender is generally based on biological differences.
    b. Gender is assumed to be 'natural' rather than a socially constructed discourse.

    → *Because* _____, _____.

4. a. People are born with a particular sex.
    b. Gender identity is something gained over time as a result of socially constructed psychological influences.

    → _____ *while* _____.

5. a. The feminine identity is considered to be more nurturing and caring.
    b. It is often the expectation that women stay at home with the children and perform domestic chores.

    → *Since* _____, _____.

B Rewrite each of the following sentences using more formal sentences and academic words. The first one has been done as an example:

a) Resources are running out.   *Resources are being depleted.*

b) Maybe there'll be a change in policy.   _____

c) It is a worrying issue.   _____

d) We must tackle the problem head on.   _____

e) The role of a manager is to keep an eye on
    things to make sure everything is going well. _____

C Use the hints in the margins to help you find features of spoken communication and replace them with precise and academic words and formal sentences:

> vague words

> phrasal verbs-verb +preposition

> personal pronouns

> personal experience as evidence

> informal words, slang

One benefit of overseas university study is you get the opportunity to try out new experiences. Especially if the university has special services for international students. Like at this university, there're so many different kinds of club activities for international students to enjoy. Not only that, but also you get to know the local culture and make new friends. Like, you can join the Canoe club which organises an activity every weekend. Also, if you're a member, you can hire all the canoeing gear cheaply, which makes things so affordable for us students especially. Other clubs, e.g. rock climbing, scuba diving, and surfing etc. are just as great. I come from a country where clubs are really out of the reach of ordinary people. But here, since I joined the Rock Climbing club, I've discovered amazing stuff and learnt heaps of new things. We were asked what we thought in a survey by the University's International Students' Centre and joining clubs got the highest rating!

> contracted forms, abbreviations

> emotive language

> non-standard word order

> incomplete sentences

> informal linking words

UNIT 2 Correct conventions for using sources

Key topics

2.1 Referencing: commonly asked questions
2.2 Using quotations: some DOs and DON'Ts
2.3 Paraphrasing and summarising: some strategies

At university, you are expected to read other people's research findings and ideas and use them to support your arguments. You may use

- a direct <u>quotation</u> (exact words enclosed in inverted commas)
- a <u>paraphrase</u> of the quotation (rephrase of the quotation in your own words)
- a <u>summary</u> of the text (shortened version with just the main ideas).

Quotations, paraphrases and summaries are drawn from other sources and must be referenced. You must tell the reader the source of your information and document it accurately in your essay or report, using standard referencing conventions.

2.1 Referencing: commonly asked questions

⑦ Why should I reference?

When you reference, you demonstrate good academic practice by avoiding <u>plagiarism</u>. Plagiarism is the practice of taking someone else's work and presenting it as your own. By referencing, you also show the amount of research you have undertaken to answer the assignment question.

⑦ What should I reference?

You must reference all published academic material used in your assignment, except for widely-known or undisputed facts (the notion of 'common knowledge' or 'expert knowledge'). Facts like the following do not need referencing:

> Water boils at 100 degrees Celsius.
> Bangkok is the capital of Thailand.
> Taylor's Scientific Management principles are still relevant today.

⑦ What referencing style should I use?

You will soon become familiar with some of these referencing styles: American Psychological Association (APA), Harvard, Modern Language Association (MLA), and Chicago. The latest editions of these and other styles are readily available via the internet. Use a style appropriate to your discipline or as recommended by your faculty. Once you have selected a style for a particular subject area, use the format consistently and accurately throughout the assignment. **Do not mix and match styles**.

⑦ How should I reference?

There are two main ways:

- as an **in-text citation.** This acknowledges the source of your ideas <u>in the essay</u> itself. In-text citation styles vary depending on the referencing style used in the assignment.

- as a **list of references.** This list is placed <u>at the end</u> of the essay or report on a new page with the heading 'References'. It is a list of <u>all</u> the sources you have referred to in your essay or report. It provides full bibliographic details in alphabetical order by surname.

⚠ Different referencing styles may have their own use citation systems. Consult the official referencing guides provided by your department or check in your course handbook.

The table below illustrates some of these differences:

Style	System	In-text citation for a quotation	Bibliographic details
APA Harvard	author-year-page	In his Harm Principle, Mill (1956) states that 'the only purpose for which power is …' (p. 13).	Mill, J.S. (1956). *On Liberty.* Indianapolis, Ind.: The Bobbs-Merrill Company, Inc.
MLA	author-page	In his Harm Principle, Mill states that 'the only purpose for which power …' (13)	Mill, John Stuart. *On Liberty.* The Bobbs-Merrill Company, Inc.
Chicago	Footnote/numeric	In his Harm Principle, Mill[1] states that 'the only purpose for which power is …'. 1. John S. Mill, *On Liberty* (Indianapolis, IN: The Bobbs-Merrill Company, Inc., 1956), 13.	Mill, John Stuart. *On Liberty.* Indianapolis, Ind.: The Bobbs-Merrill Company, Inc. 1956.

? How does it work?

The following example uses the APA referencing style ('author-year-page' system):

Example (1st year Business, using APA referencing style – 'author-year-page' system)

In-text citations

There are two competing theories about the definition of entrepreneurship Proponents of the behaviourist theory believe that entrepreneurs are individuals who are naturally more creative, more extroverted, more confident and more optimistic than the average person (Fisher & Koch, 2008). However, there are some scholars who argue that a behaviour is a behaviour as opposed to a set of innate personality traits. For example, Spinelli and Adams (2012) defined entrepreneurship as 'a way of thinking, reasoning, and acting that is opportunity observed, holistic in approach, and leadership balanced for the purposes of value creation and capture' (p. 87).

in-text citations (author, year, page)

Note also the different ways of introducing sources

References

Fisher, J., & Koch, J. (2008). *Born, not made: The entrepreneurial personality.* Retrieved from http://web.b.ebscohost.com.

Spinelli, S., & Adams, R. (Eds.). (2012). *New venture creation: Entrepreneurships for the 21st century* (9th ed.). New York, NY: McGraw-Hill.

List of sources in alphabetical order by surname

? If I use ideas from the same source in the same paragraph, do I need to cite the source again?

You do, but use some variation to integrate the source into your text.

Example (1st year Anthropology, discussing early European settlements)

The in-text citations are for the same source and they are all at the end of the sentence:

> Most sites were situated along a coastal route (Curtis, 2003) and many were open-air sites with a preference for showing cave occupations along the upper Paleolithic glacial 25-12kya (Curtis, 2003). Settlement was relatively predictable within this period with logical settlement patterns around resource-rich areas and local specialised sites for the manufacture of hunting tools. Such bases were regularly by Cro-Magnon (early modern humans) and Neanderthal (Curtis, 2003).

> The source is cited without any variation.

Revision

> This introduces the source and blends it into the sentence.

> This indicates that you are still using the same source.

> According to Curtis (2003), most sites were situated along a coastal route and many were open-air sites with a preference for showing cave occupations during along the upper Paleolithic glacial 25-12kya. Curtis also points to archaeological evidence which showed that settlement was relatively predictable within this period, with logical settlement patterns around resource-rich areas and local specialised sites for the manufacture of hunting tools. This evidence further confirmed that these bases were used regularly by Cro-Magnon (early modern humans) and Neanderthal.

> This phrase refers to the evidence mentioned in the previous sentence. There is no need to repeat the citation.

2.2 Using quotations: some DOs and DON'Ts

? What and when should I quote?

In general, use quotations sparingly; paraphrase or summarise. A quotation is a kind of evidence to back up something you have already stated. Use a quotation only if it:

• conveys a powerful meaning or point of view	**Example** (1st year Art History) Manet was not interested in depicting a false reality, preferring to focus on themes, social commentary and the painterly qualities of art. Such painterly qualities are exemplified by Manet's application of paint, for as Gardener mentions, he used 'art to call attention to art'[1].
• provides a new perspective and supports your own thesis	**Example** (1st year Business) Spineli and Adams (2012) reject the traditional approach of defining entrepreneurship ... They defined entrepreneurship as 'a way of thinking, reasoning, and acting that is opportunity obsessed, holistic in approach, and leadership balanced for the purposes of value creation and capture' (p. 87).
• states an important principle or law on which your discussion is based	**Example** (1st year Philosophy) In this principle, Mill (1956) states that 'the only purpose for which power can be rightfully exercised over any member of a civilized community, against his will, is to prevent harm to others. His own good, either physical or moral, is not sufficient warrant' (p. 13).

Examples of ineffective use of quotations

- **Unnecessary quotation**

The two quotations in the following extract from an Anthropology essay could easily be paraphrased. The first quotation is not very useful unless the reader understands what 'African savannah' is. The second quotation is too commonplace to have much impact:

Unnecessary quotation	Paraphrase
European settlement was perhaps much later because the Middle East and Asia were more favourable environments at the time being 'more comparable to African savannah' (Roebroek, 1994, p. 303) unlike Europe which was a 'heavily forested' (Roebroek, 1994, p. 303) environment.	Roebroek (1994) argues that settlement in Europe came much later because settlers from Africa in particular were probably drawn to the open grassy plains of the Middle East and Asia. Europe's dense vegetation, however, was seen as a less favourable environment for settlement (p. 303).

- **Too many quotations in the same paragraph**

Using quotations to build an entire paragraph does not show the reader that you have understood the issues. In general, it is not good practice to begin with a quotation.

The two quotations in this short introduction are too close together. At least one of the quotations could have been paraphrased:

In his essay *On Liberty,* John Stewart Mill poses the question: 'what restrictions are legitimate, or morally justifiable, and what ones are unwarranted interference in the freedom of individuals to act as they wish to?' (Dare, 2010). Mill proposed an answer to his question in the form of the harm principle. In this principle, he states 'the only purpose for which power can be rightfully exercised over any member of a civilized community, against his will, is to prevent harm to others. His own good, either physical or moral, is not sufficient warrant' (Mill, 1956, p. 13). In this essay, I will discuss …

[?] How can I integrate quotations into my text?

Introduce the quotation to provide a smooth transition from the previous sentence to the next.

Example (1st year Anthropology, using MLA author-page citation style)

Quotation not introduced	Quotation introduced and integrated into text
Settlement in Asia happened much earlier than in Europe. 'The spread out of Africa most probably was eastward first via Ubeidiya in Israel and Dmanisi, Georgia' (Roeboek 20).	Settlement in Asia happened much earlier than in Europe. Evidence from one study showed that 'the spread out of Africa most probably was eastward first via Ubeidiya in Israel and Dmanisi, Georgia' (Roeboek 20). OR use an author tag with a reporting verb Roebeck suggests that "the spread out of Africa was probably eastward first" (20).

[?] If I use only some words or change words from the quotation sequence, how can I indicate these changes?

The following example shows how to indicate changes made to the original quotation using APA referencing style. Your chosen referencing style may have other guidelines.

Example You wish to quote parts of this source text: Saul, J.R. (2005). *The collapse of globalism and the reinvention of the world.* Camberwell: Viking.

> To believe in the possibility of change is something very precise. That there are choices. That we have the power to choose in the hope of altering society for the greater good. It means we believe in the reality of choice.

Indicating changes to the quotation (dots and square brackets)

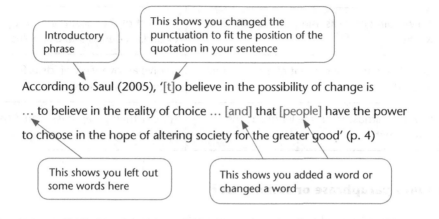

2.3 Paraphrasing and summarising: some strategies

Paraphrasing and summarising allows you to include other people's ideas in your assignment using your own words. They are effective alternatives to direct quotations and over-quoting. When you paraphrase or summarise, you also demonstrate to the reader that you have understood what you have read. In general, paraphrases and summaries are used more than quotations to develop ideas in paragraphs.

The following extract shows how quotations, paraphrases and summaries (in-text citations highlighted here) are used with the student's introductory comments and thesis to build a paragraph.

Example (1st year Business on whether entrepreneurship can be taught)

There are two competing theories about the definition of entrepreneurship. Traditionally, entrepreneurship is defined in terms of the personal characteristics that distinguish entrepreneurs from non-entrepreneurs.	Student's introduction
Proponents of this theory believe that entrepreneurs are individuals who are more creative, more extroverted, more confident, and more optimistic than the average population (Fisher & Koch, 2008, p. 1).	Paraphrase/summary
Those who were not born with these so-called entrepreneurial traits simply cannot become an entrepreneur, even if they have been trained to think and behave like an entrepreneur (Thompson, 2004, p. 246).	Paraphrase/summary
There are, however, some scholars who reject the traditional approach of defining entrepreneurship. Instead, these scholars believe that entrepreneurship is a behaviour as opposed to a set of innate personality traits. For example, Spinelli and Adams (2012) defined entrepreneurship as 'a way of thinking, reasoning, and acting that is opportunity obsessed, holistic in approach, and leadership balanced for the purposes of value creation and capture' (p. 87).	Quotation
Proponents of the behavioural approach of defining entrepreneurship believe that anyone can learn to become an entrepreneur, regardless of their personality traits, because it is possible to teach individuals to act and think entrepreneurially (Drucker, 1985, p. 23; Spinelli & Adams, 2012, p. 42).	Paraphrase/summary
To this day, there is still no consensus on the definition of entrepreneurship. However, although the theory that entrepreneurs owe their success to a set of innate personality traits still remains widely-accepted, some aspects of entrepreneurship can be taught through education.	Student's thesis

Commonly asked questions

❓ How is a paraphrase different from a summary?

The following table summarises the main differences:

Aspects	Paraphrase	Summary
Definition	a rewording of ideas using own or different words	a report of the most important points excluding details and examples
Purpose	to rephrase the full content of a source text or most of it	to give an overview of ideas from a single source or multiple sources
Length	could be almost the same length as the source text	shorter than paraphrase; could be less than a third of original

❓ When should I paraphrase or summarise?

- Paraphrase or summarise overly long quotations (especially if you have many of them in your essay)
- Paraphrase wordy quotations

Example 1 (1st year Anthropology, discussing whether gender is biologically determined)

This 2103-word essay has 7 quotations, ranging in length from 39 words to 120 words.

This quotation consists of 120 words. It describes a gender upbringing practised in an indigenous community in Canada. (NOTE: Conventions require long quotations to be indented, as shown in this extract):

> Stewart (2002) describes a *kipijuituq* upbringing thus:
>
> > Male infants judged to be kipijuituq become socially female: they are dressed in female clothing, expected to act as girls, and are referred to by female kinship terminology. They do not, however, take on all elements of culturally defined feminine gender roles. That is, a kipijuituq may play with dolls and otherwise behave in a feminine manner but is not taught sewing, cooking, and other traditionally feminine activities. In the event that an infant is judged to be kipijuituq, that judgment must be obeyed by the child, its parents, and kinspeople. It is (was) believed that if that judgment were ignored, the infant and its kinspeople would be visited by misfortune, such as a hunting accident or a poor catch (p. 15).

Paraphrase (rephrases the whole quotation; 88 words – closer to original length)

Stewart (2002, p. 15) explains that in a *kipijuituq* upbringing, male children who are deemed to be feminine by the community have to grow up wearing women's clothes and behaving like women. However, they are not required to learn household tasks which are traditionally performed by women. Once labelled as a kipijuituq by the community, these children and their families have to abide by the decision. Failure to do so could bring ill luck to the children and their families or some serious mishap could happen to them.

Summary (provides overview or main points only; 46 words – about a third of the original length)

Stewart (2002, p.15) explains that male children judged to be feminine wear women's clothes and behave like women, but do not perform tasks traditionally done by women. Failure to abide by the community's decision could have serious consequences for the children and their families.

Example 2 (1st year Art History on Manet's painting style)

This quotation has many abstract noun phrases (underlined here). In addition, the integration of the wordy quotation into the sentence creates an over-long complex sentence:

This shows Manet's views on the <u>true nature of the social relationships</u> forged by the middle-class in these new situations as '[h]is reserve toward <u>representation of emotion</u> and his <u>immersion in the aesthetic side of social life</u> can be taken as <u>examples of modern detachment</u> paralleling that of the protagonists in many of his works.'

> What is Manet's view exactly?

(?) How can I paraphrase and summarise successfully?

There are two challenges to successful paraphrasing and summarising. The first challenge is to identify quickly and accurately other people's ideas. This requires effective reading skills. The second challenge is to express the ideas in your own words. This requires an adequate vocabulary base.

A strategy for effective reading

This strategy improves concentration and understanding and helps you to paraphrase or summarise accurately:

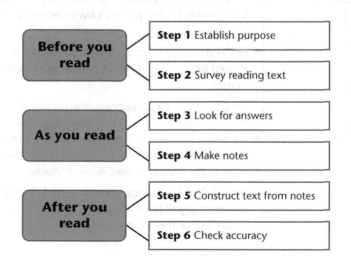

Before you read	**Step 1** Establish purpose
	Step 2 Survey reading text
As you read	**Step 3** Look for answers
	Step 4 Make notes
After you read	**Step 5** Construct text from notes
	Step 6 Check accuracy

<u>Explanation of steps</u>

Step 1 Establish the purpose for reading

The purpose gives you a focus for reading and helps you to anticipate meaning relationships, sentence structures and vocabulary. Ask Wh-questions (e.g. What, Who, Why, How) to check understanding.

Step 2 Survey the reading text

Surveying gives you a general idea of the main content and organisation of the reading text. Look quickly at words in the title, sub-headings, captions under images. Circle words that match your own from Step 1. Look at the first and last sentences of paragraphs to help you identify the topic focus of each paragraph or section.

Step 3 Look for answers to your questions from Step 1

In this step, you are not reading everything. You can adjust your reading speed – slowing down for a relevant point and moving quickly over unnecessary details.

Step 4 Make notes as you read

When you make notes, you are actively processing the content as you read using different words to express the same meaning. Use a note-making style that you are comfortable with.

Step 5 Construct your paraphrase or summary from notes

When you construct sentences from notes, you are less reliant on the sentence structures of the source text. Your paraphrase or summary is also more likely to have a different text structure from the original.

Step 6 Check accuracy of content and language use

Read your summary or paraphrase to make sure it accurately represents the author's ideas and opinions and not your own.

? How does the strategy work?

Paraphrasing a quotation

Example (1st year Philosophy)

In this principle, he states "the only purpose for which power can be rightfully exercised over any member of a civilized community, against his will, is to prevent harm to others. His own good, either physical or moral, is not sufficient warrant" (Mill, 1956, p. 13).

Step 1 Establish purpose: to rephrase a quotation

Step 2 Survey for general idea of quotation:
→ *Harm Principle – Q: when to intervene to stop a person from acting in a certain way*

Step 3 Look for answers
→ intervention to protect general public – justified; intervention for the person's own sake – x justified

Step 4 Make notes
→ condition for intervention/control – public at risk; cannot intervene to protect person from hurting himself

Step 5 Construct paraphrase from notes →
In this principle, Mill (1956) states that a necessary condition for intervening in a person's actions is if the general public is put at risk. Control of any kind to protect the person himself is unjustifiable.

Step 6 Check accuracy: review Steps 1, 2 and 4 to ensure that you have accurately reflected the content of the source text in your own words.

Summarising a longer text

Step 1 Establish purpose: You are responding to this question: 'Using sweatshops as an example, examine the associated geographies of production and consumption' (Geography).

Your questions: Why do sweatshops exist? How do sweatshops demonstrate processes of production and consumption?

The annotations in the article below show active reading in action: Steps 2, 3 and 4.

Blood, sweat and tears: the emergence of sweatshops

M R Reid   2017

In modern societies, globalised production has become the norm due to the increased links between nations. The change in the geographies of space and place are extremely important in relation to the production processes of brands utilising sweatshops.

Driven by capitalism

In Western capitalist societies, the aim of production is to maximise profit. Wage labour is an important part of the capitalist system and sweatshops are viewed as easy ways for companies to gain profit by driving down the cost of production. Generally characterised by low wages, long hours and poor working conditions, sweatshops illustrate two important features of the geographies of production. Firstly, Western corporations can significantly lower their production costs by utilising the cheaper labour of developing countries, thereby increasing their margin of profitability. This is now recognised as a global division of labour with management being carried out in the West and production being carried out in developing states. In the clothing sweatshops in Bangladesh and Nike's contract factories in Hansae, Vietnam, many identical products are produced in this environment through the efficiency of the division of labour. Secondly, the notion of the 'shrunken world' means that fewer resources are needed to transport commodities back to the Western world due to technological improvements. This reinforces the idea of place in the development of commodities, where production is carried out in the developing world and management in the developed world.

Consumer sovereignty

Consumer sovereignty drives production and the prevalence of sweatshops. Heintz (2004) believes the increased consumption of the West has meant an increase in production has had to take place. Heintz argues that this process has allowed many citizens of developing countries to be employed in sweatshops. Indeed, many corporations realise the effects that decreased consumption would have on production and attempt to conceal the poor conditions of many sweatshops. Timmerman (2009b) examines the large numbers of sweatshops that have guards, as well as strict procedures around entering their premises.

The culturist perspective

This perspective argues that society has a culture through trends and people purchase products to uphold this identity. Corporations will continue to use sweatshops to extend and influence this culture. This concept can be shown through the corporation of Nike and its sweatshops. Nike's manufactured shoes were originally targeted at the American hip-hop trend, but its sweatshops in Hansae, Vietnam exploit this culture of buying trends and brands.

STEP 2 Survey title headings and key words (highlighted here)

STEP 3 Look for answers to questions from step 1:
What does 'geographies of space and place' mean?
Why do sweatshops exist?
How are consumption and production connected?

STEP 4 Make notes on highlighted parts

Sweatshops – hard work for low returns, cheap available

Production in Asia; management and consumption in West

Sweatshops for maximum profit – main aim of prod in capitalist economy

Sweatshops – on-going enterprise – produce branded goods – fuelled by consumption patterns in the West

Step 5 Construct summary from notes. The length of a summary depends on <u>how</u> you want to use the article in the essay. A long summary is usually about a third of the original length.

Example summary

> In an article entitled *Blood, sweat and tears*, Reid (2017) alludes to the exploitation of sweatshops and changes to the geographies of production and consumption in a capitalist economic regime. With sweatshops located in poor developing countries in Asia, mass production costs can be significantly reduced, thus maximising profit returns to the corporations. Sweatshop workers are viewed as a cheap and available work-force that enables large Western corporations to produce branded goods quickly and in bulk. Sweatshops are an on-going enterprise for large corporations to meet the demand for goods by people in wealthier countries efficiently and cheaply. Reid argues that the reality is that sweatshops will continue as long as people in wealthier countries are willing to buy brands.

[?] What is an acceptable paraphrase or summary?

The following diagram summarises <u>five</u> criteria for constructing an acceptable paraphrase or summary:

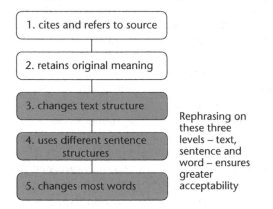

1. cites and refers to source

2. retains original meaning

3. changes text structure

4. uses different sentence structures

5. changes most words

Rephrasing on these three levels – text, sentence and word – ensures greater acceptability

Criterion 1 Cites and refers to the source

- <u>Citing the source:</u> You do not need to enclose a paraphrase or summary within quotation marks but you do need to provide proper references to show that the ideas are not your ideas. Some referencing styles do not require full in-text citations for a paraphrase or summary. If you are unsure, include them or check with your faculty.

  The following table shows three ways to cite and refer to the source according to the referencing style used. (Note in particular the variations in the reporting verbs, placement of commas and full-stops.)

Referencing style	At end of paraphrase or summary to emphasise the idea	At start of paraphrase or summary to emphasise the author using different reporting verbs	At start of paraphrase or summary to refer to both work and author
APA (author, year)	… (Mill, 1956).	Mill (1956) states that …	In his essay, *On Liberty*, Mill (1956) states that …
Harvard (author, year)	… (Mill, 1956).	Mill (1956) argues that …	In his essay, *On Liberty*, Mill (1956) argues that …
MLA (authors page)	… (Mill 13).	Mill points out that … (13).	In his essay, *On Liberty*, Mill (13) points out that …
Chicago (numeric/footnote)	…[1]	Mill suggests that …[1]	In his essay, *On Liberty*, Mill suggests that …[1]

- Referring to the source: This involves the use of **reporting verbs**. Although they are not always needed, reporting verbs can add variety to the way you introduce in-text citations. More importantly, they demonstrate your understanding of the author's purpose and the ideas expressed. Used in a summary of research (as in a literature review), these verbs can guide the reader through the review. In addition, they enable you to blend a quotation or paraphrase smoothly into your writing.

Below is a classification of reporting verbs according to purpose or function. (Note: The tense of the verb could vary depending on the time frame of the research you are reporting):

Reporting purpose (usually in the present tense). See the note below.	Reporting methodology (usually in the past tense)	Reporting results	Reporting point of view or position of author. The tense may vary (see the note below).
aims to	analysed	confirmed	argues that
considers	compared	demonstrated	claims that
is concerned with	conducted	identified	concludes that
defines	drew on, used	found that	challenges
describes	investigated	highlighted	holds the view that
explains	interviewed	mentioned	is critical of
gives, provides	measured	established	notes that
presents	surveyed	reported that	proposes, suggests
states	used	showed	questions

⚠ **Tense changes in reporting verbs.** In general, use the present tense when summarising or paraphrasing and if the content or opinion is still relevant (even though the publication is not current). Use the past tense if you are reporting the author's findings of a specific study completed in the past. If the author's opinions about that study are still relevant, use the present tense. If they have changed since the last study, use the present perfect tense. Tense shifts like these are common in literature reviews (see *Part II, Unit 4*; see the chart of English tenses in *Appendix B*).

Example 1 No use of reporting verbs

In the following extract, no reporting verbs are used to guide the reader. It is also difficult to determine whether the opinions (indicated by the underlined words) belong to the student or the author.

> Throughout the majority of the Tokugawa period, Japan resided in virtual isolation … (Meyer, 2009, p. 109). For half a century preceding Tokugawa rule, Iberian traders and Jesuit missionaries had a profound effect on … (Janson, 2000, pp. 5–8) … the number of Catholic converts estimated at 130,000 by 1587 (Sansom, 1950, pp. 126–127). Ironically, this early European success … (Sansom, 1950, pp. 171, 175). Towards the end of the Tokugawa era, a small Dutch outpost … played a pivotal role in … (Meyer 2009, pp. 120–121).

Example 2 Effective use of reporting verbs

The following extracts from two student essays show some effective use of reporting verbs (highlighted here) to establish clearly the distinct position of the author and the contribution of each work:

Extract 1 (1st year Anthropology)
Lee (2005) argues that ... As Bryson and Henry (2001) explain ... Massey (1995) describes ... However, Bryson and Henry (2001) allude to the notion of a 'shrunken world' ...

Extract 2 (2nd year Education; note the tense changes)
In *Learning to Labour*, Willis (1977) examines the way in which individuals ... In an ethnographic study of ... conducted in 2014, Wills found that ... He suggests that ...

Criterion 2 Retains original meaning

Your paraphrase or summary must accurately represent the author's ideas or position and not your own. Practise effective reading strategies to increase your understanding.

Criterion 3 Changes organisation or text structure

Present ideas in a different order from the original text. This ensures that the structure of your paraphrase or summary does not look too similar to the source text. When you apply the techniques of the reading strategy described earlier in the unit, you focus on ideas and meaning relationships. When you construct your paraphrase or summary from notes, you are less likely to follow the organisation of the source text.

Criterion 4 Uses different sentence structures

A good knowledge of how meaning is constructed in English can help you express other people's ideas differently. You are also able to select appropriate logical connectors to express a range of relationships.

The following sentence, for example, expresses a cause and effect relationship:

The school was forced to close for a week due to the potential risk to students from the flooding.

You can use different sentence structures and words to express the cause and effect relationship:

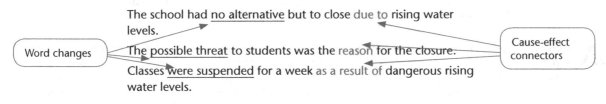

Word changes

The school had <u>no alternative</u> but to close due to rising water levels.

The <u>possible threat</u> to students was the reason for the closure.

Classes <u>were suspended</u> for a week as a result of dangerous rising water levels.

Cause-effect connectors

Criterion 5 Changes most of the words

When you use different sentence structures, you should also use different words or different forms of words. To be able to do this well, you need to expand your vocabulary base:

- think about **single word and phrase synonyms** (words with similar meaning) to replace words in the original text.

> Quotation:
> In his essay *On Liberty,* John Stuart Mill poses the question: 'what restrictions are legitimate, or morally justifiable, and what ones are unwarranted interference in the freedom of individuals to act as they wish to?'

For example, the word 'restriction' in the above quotation could be replaced by 'limitation', 'prevention', 'control', or 'prohibition'. The word 'freedom' could be replaced by a phrase ('to feel no restraint', 'not to be restrained/hindered/limited by'). 'Legitimate' could be replaced by 'according to the law' and so on.

- change the **word family** (part of speech). Knowing word families gives you more sentence structure options, as shown in the following examples:

> A person may be restricted (verb) from exercising his free will.
> This restriction (noun) goes against a person's right to act freely.
> The law is a restrictive (adjective) regulation which directly affects a person's freedom.

PRACTICE ACTIVITY 2.1

1. Paraphrase this sentence in three different ways, using the suggested sentence starters:
'And indeed Manet saw the Salon as the "true field of battle" where "one must measure oneself"'.

   a) To Manet, _____.
   b) Manet believed that, at the Salon, he _____.

2. In this extract, the same source is mentioned four times. Revise the in-text citation style. For example, use author tags and reporting verbs and reduce the repetition (see *Unit 2.2*).

> The transitional family structure changed with the industrial age, when men left the home daily to seek wage labour (Hook, 2006). Hook (2006) describes how this led to separation of men's and women's labour: men as breadwinners, women the caregivers. Today the familiar family model features both men and women, working outside the home but, as Hook (2006) says even though unpaid work time has increased for men, 'it has not compensated for women's decline nor reached parity with women's time' (Hook, 2006, p. 1).

3. Summarise the long quotation (indented) and integrate it into the sentence.

> In her study of Native North American perceptions of gender, Lang discovers that it is conflicting to say whether gender is biologically determined:
>
> > Even if a woman-man, for example, takes up the culturally defined woman's role more or less completely, he/she does not become a woman, he/she is classified as a winkte, a lhamana, heemaneh, an elxa, or whatever his/her tribe's gender term is for someone who was born male but chose to live a woman's life partially or completely. (Lang 1996: 191)

4. Below are three paraphrases of the following quotation:

> "The only purpose for which power can be rightfully exercised over any member of a civilized community, against his will, is to prevent harm to others. His own good, either physical or moral, is not sufficient warrant" (Mill, 1956, p. 13).

Measure each paraphrase against the 5 criteria to determine if it is an acceptable or unacceptable paraphrase. Mark with a × or a ✓ against each criterion in the checklist on the right.

Paraphrase 1
Mill's (1956) Harm Principle states that a person cannot be controlled unless he hurts other people.

[acceptable/unacceptable]

1. cites and refers to source

2. retains original meaning

3. changes text structure

4. uses different sentence structures

5. changes most words

Paraphrase 2
According to Mill's (1956) Harm Principle, the government or society cannot intervene to stop a person from acting in a certain way, even if he is injured by his own actions. The only condition for intervention is if his actions adversely affect others in the community.

[acceptable/unacceptable]

1. cites and refers to source

2. retains original meaning

3. changes text structure

4. uses different sentence structures

5. changes most words

Paraphrase 3
The Harm Principle states that exercising control to limit a person's freedom against his wishes is only right if the purpose is to prevent him harming other members of society. Intervening for his own physical or moral welfare is insufficient justification.

[acceptable/unacceptable]

1. cites and refers to source

2. retains original meaning

3. changes text structure

4. uses different sentence structures

5. changes most words

UNIT 3 **Clear structure and layout**

Key topics

3.1 Principles of structure, organisation and layout
3.2 Six steps to effective writing

When you receive feedback comments in your written assignment such as 'poor structure' or 'not well-organised in parts', do you know what they mean? This unit presents an overview of some general principles relating to structure, organisation and layout. From *Part III Developing your writing* to *Part V Putting it all together*, you will see examples of how these principles are applied by students writing longer essays.

3.1 **Principles of structure, organisation and layout**

STRUCTURE refers to the conventional structure of an essay or report. An academic essay or report is generally recognised as comprising three main elements: an introduction, the main body, and the conclusion. Each element has a particular function in the essay. The main body of an essay consists of several paragraphs, each discussing a main idea. The main body of a report consists of methods, results and discussion section (see also *Part II Types of University Written Assignments*).

Basic structure of an academic essay

The diagram below describes a useful strategy for apportioning length to the three elements of an essay:

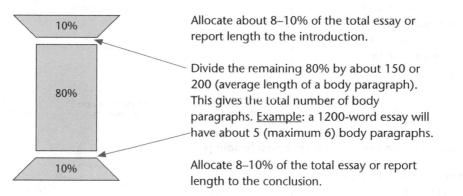

Allocate about 8–10% of the total essay or report length to the introduction.

Divide the remaining 80% by about 150 or 200 (average length of a body paragraph). This gives the total number of body paragraphs. <u>Example</u>: a 1200-word essay will have about 5 (maximum 6) body paragraphs.

Allocate 8–10% of the total essay or report length to the conclusion.

The strategy is a useful guide. It gives you control over the overall structure of your essay or report in relation to the assignment question. Too many body paragraphs gives your writing a fragmented look. The entire discussion may also lack coherence and connectivity.

ORGANISATION refers to the logical progression or flow of ideas in the body of the essay. It involves the ordering of ideas in a way that makes sense, enabling the reader to follow the discussion or reasoning easily. The organisational method you choose will depend on the assignment question (see *Part III, Unit 2 Methods of organisation*).

LAYOUT refers to the way your text *looks* on paper. It is just as important as presenting a logical structure. Here are some general principles to consider:

- **Divide your text into <u>visible</u> paragraphs**

  A whole-page of uninterrupted text can make reading difficult.

- **Use <u>consistent</u> paragraphing and spacing**

  Help the reader to follow the development of ideas clearly with paragraphs of consistent length and spacing.

- **Choose a clear layout: block or indented paragraphs**

  Some subject areas include specific presentation and formatting guidelines in their assignment instructions, including left and right margins.

  Block paragraphs with spacing

  Indented paragraphs with no spacing

  Indented paragraphs with no spacing

- **Decide between numbered or unnumbered headings**

  In long essays (3000 words), it is sometimes necessary to use headings. Be consistent in the way you distinguish between main headings and sub-headings.

  Most referencing style guides provide guidelines on the use of headings: the number of headings, different levels of sub-headings, and also the preferred typescript to distinguish between headings.

  Headings and sub-headings

  Numbered headings

3.2 Six steps to effective writing

Use this six-step approach to produce a well-structured and organised response that also answers the assignment question.

Step one Understand the assignment question

Assignment questions vary considerably across the disciplines. The assignment brief may be quite long, including additional requirements and conventions. Consider, for example, these types of questions from different disciplines:

1. Questions starting with a question word	*What* are the important attributes for the success of a political leader? *Discuss* in relation to the performance of two recent prime ministers. (Political Studies)
2. Questions starting with an instruction word	*Discuss* the legitimacy of raising taxes on tobacco with reference to the Mill's Harm Principle. (Philosophy)
3. Questions starting with a quotation or statement	International society has long recognised the economic disparity between North and South Hemispheres. However, it has not been reduced. Why? What are the implications? (Geography)
4. Questions with several parts	*Describe* … (250 words). *Write* a literature review on … *Discuss* and *compare* the different perspectives (600 words); *Reflect on* the discussion … (350–450 words); *Conclude with* … and *suggest* recommendations for (250 words) (Fine Arts)

In most cases, instruction words (mainly verbs) used in the assignment question can tell you <u>WHAT</u> skills are expected and <u>HOW</u> you are to structure and develop your response. In a question with several parts (Number 4 above), you are expected to deliver ideas differently for each part. Therefore, an understanding of the meaning of such instruction verbs can help you plan and write an appropriate response.

 See the classification of instruction verbs chart in Appendix B.

Step two Find the specific focus of the question

This step is critical for steps three and four. It ensures that your response is directly relevant to the question.

When you read the assignment instructions, you want to ask two questions:

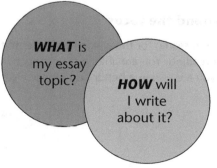

WHAT is my essay topic?

HOW will I write about it?

Some focus-finding strategies

Example question What are the important attributes for the success of a political leader? Discuss in relation to the performance of two recent prime ministers (from Political Studies).

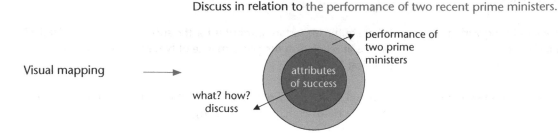

Underlining or circling ⟶ What are the important <u>attributes for the success of a political leader</u>? Discuss in relation to the <u>performance</u> of <u>two recent prime ministers.</u>

Highlighting ⟶ What are the important attributes for the success of a political leader? Discuss in relation to the performance of two recent prime ministers.

Visual mapping ⟶

Use a strategy that suits your learning style. Underlining, circling or highlighting (using different colours) are commonly used by students, but try visual mapping. It creates clearer distinction and emphasis. As you can see in the diagram above, the specific focus with key words are clearly identified in the centre; other words alluding to the relevant political context are written in the outer circle.

Step three **Draw a map of initial ideas around the focus**

Write down what you already know about the topic and other related concepts or theories gathered from lecture notes or your course textbook.

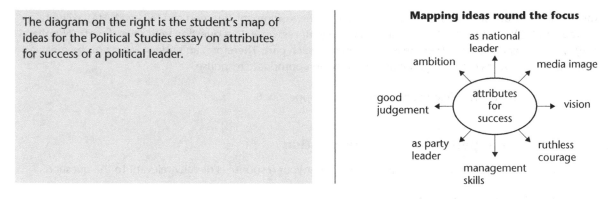

The diagram on the right is the student's map of ideas for the Political Studies essay on attributes for success of a political leader.

Mapping ideas round the focus

Step four **Read round the focus**

As you begin to gather research for the assignment, refer to the map of ideas from step three. The map provides a framework for your reading. You are able to see connections between ideas more clearly. With the focus to guide your reading, you are also in a better position to select relevant material for the assignment.

Step five Review your map of ideas

Once you have completed your research, review the map of ideas again. You might remove some ideas or you might group some ideas. In this step, you also think about the most logical order to present the ideas:

The arrows show that the student is considering combining some attributes because they may be related and could be discussed together. The numbers indicate that the student has also begun putting the attributes into a logical order.

Revised map of ideas

Step six Make a logical outline

This is the last step before writing begins. It represents a move from gathering ideas randomly round the focus to thinking about the <u>linear</u> progression of the ideas. You are now concerned with how to present your ideas in the most logical order in a conventional essay or report structure.

Example (same Political Studies question on the attributes of a political leader)

Look at the following outline for the Political Studies essay. What can the outline tell you about the organisational pattern used by the student? Read the comments to check your answer.

The outline shows that the student uses the standard essay structure.

The number of attributes to include is determined by the <u>essay length</u> and the technique described at the start of the unit.

The structure of the essay is guided by some basic principles:

- <u>Type of writing task</u>: comparison-contrast

- <u>Overall organisational method:</u> division/ classification

- <u>Comparison in body paragraphs:</u> uses a 'paired' approach – discusses both leaders' performance for each attribute

Logical order/essay outline

Introduction
Body points
1 party leader and national leader: 　　　　PM 1 – weak 　　　　PM 2 – strong
2 ambition: 　　　　PM 1 – weak 　　　　PM 2 – strong
3 ruthless courage & judgement: 　　　　PM 1 – weak 　　　　PM 2 – strong
4 vision: 　　　　PM 1 – weak 　　　　PM 2 – strong
5 management skill: 　　　　PM 1 – weak 　　　　PM 2 – strong
6 media image: 　　　　PM 1 – weak 　　　　PM 2 – strong
Conclusion

See *Part III Developing your writing* for more on organisational methods and techniques for developing ideas in body paragraphs.

UNIT 4 Coherent flow of ideas

Key topics

4.1 Four cohesive devices
4.2 Coherence within a paragraph
4.3 Coherence between paragraphs

What is coherence?

Coherence is the quality of ideas being logically related. A piece of writing is coherent when the flow of ideas from beginning to end is logical. Writing that is coherent is clear and can be easily understood. All the ideas are relevant to the central purpose of the writing task:

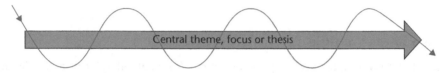

Central theme, focus or thesis

The logical flow or 'coherence' of ideas can be improved by the use of specific cohesive devices to provide meaningful links between ideas and to signal your intentions clearly to the reader. In written assignments, coherence occurs on two levels: [1] within a paragraph and [2] between paragraphs. We will look at some examples of how these two levels work later in the unit.

How can you achieve coherence in writing?

At university, you want to display a more mature writing style than has been required in high school or college writing. The four cohesive devices examined here will give you a wider range of techniques for connecting ideas than 'and', 'but', 'or' and 'so'.

4.1 Four cohesive devices

These are <u>reference pronouns</u>, <u>repetition</u>, <u>logical connectors</u> and <u>parallelism</u>.

➡ **Reference pronouns (*it, this, these, those*)**   These are useful cohesive devices because they allow you to <u>point or link back</u> to a previously mentioned idea or a key noun without unnecessary repetition.

Example:

pointing back to a single item in
the previous sentence

Screen printing is also known as serigraphy. It is a method of creating an image on
paper or fabric by pressing ink through a screen.

The Baltic Sea in northern Europe is only one fourth as salty as the Red Sea in the
Middle East. There are several reasons for this.

pointing back to the whole idea
in the previous sentence

➡️ **Repetition** A key noun may need to be repeated when the pronoun reference is unclear because there is more than one noun as shown in this example:

One difference between high school and university is that *it* offers more learning options.

Which noun does *it* refer to? You can achieve coherence by repeating the relevant noun:

One difference between university and high school is that university offers more learning options.

Repetition is important in writing because sometimes you need to provide more information on the same issue or idea. You can use the same word. To add interest, you can use a parallel word or synonym, which is a different word with the same meaning (e.g. motion, activity, movement). You can use a new form of the same word (e.g. act (verb), action (noun), activity (noun).

The following example shows the use of repetition in these three ways:

| repetition with a **parallel word** or synonym (for method) | Screen printing is a method of creating an image on paper or fabric by pressing ink through a screen. The technique is used both for making fine art prints and for commercial applications, such as printing company logos on coffee mugs and t-shirts. A significant characteristic of screen printing is that a greater thickness can be applied to the substrate than is possible with other printing techniques. Because of the simplicity of the application process, screen printing is a popular art form. | repetition with the **same word**

repetition with a **new form** of the same word (applied→ application) |

➡️ **Logical connectors** These are words or phrases used to signal a range of intentions and links between ideas.

The four sets of sentences below describe a logical progression of events. Different logical connectors are used to signal exactly what happens at each stage.

1) In 2006, a proposal to build a stadium near the city waterfront was seriously considered. In fact, several plans had already been drawn up. (EMPHASIS)
2) The plans were submitted to the City Council for consideration in April. However, objections to the plans came mainly from waterfront residents. (CONTRAST)
3) The main objection to the proposal was the possible destruction of the waterfront views. Furthermore, the resultant traffic congestion in the city centre would be phenomenal. (ADDITION)
4) In the end, the final total costs were considered too high. Consequently, the project was abandoned. (RESULT)

⚠️ When used appropriately, logical connectors help to guide the reader through your text. However, using too many connectors close together in the same text can have the opposite effect because they give too many signals to the reader:

If people stopped smoking, it might delay the onset of liver disease, as a result. In addition, the government could help by raising the tobacco sales tax. However, the government's resources are limited. Therefore, a new tax policy may thus be delayed.

Below is a list of some common logical connectors according to purpose.

Purpose	Example
Adding or reinforcing ideas	*in addition, ... moreover, ... another ... above all, ... furthermore, ...*
Clarifying or explaining further	*in particular, ... in other words, ... namely, ... that is, ... this means, more specifically, ...*
Emphasising	*As a matter of fact, ... in fact, ... indeed ... more importantly, ...*
Enumerating or listing (introducing ideas in logical sequence)	*first of all, ... to begin with, ... secondly, ... finally, ...*
Exemplifying/Illustrating	*for instance, ... for example, ... such as, ...*
Giving reasons	*for this reason ... due to ... because of ...*
Showing contrast or giving alternative perspective	*alternatively, ... although, ... by comparison, ... in contrast, ... despite, ... however, ... in spite of, ... instead, ... on the other hand, ... rather ...*
Showing result or logical consequence	*thus, ... therefore, ... consequently, ... as a result, ... subsequently*
Showing similarity	*both ... similarly, ... in the same way, ... equally, ... the same as ...*
Summarising	*to conclude, ... to sum up, ... overall ...*

Parallelism   This device involves the use of similar grammatical forms or sentence structures when listing or when comparing two or more items. It is sometimes referred to as balanced constructions or parallel structures.

Example:

This essay discusses three benefits of a university degree: better employment opportunities, secure future, and continued professional enhancement.

> Similar grammatical forms: adjective + noun

The success of the programme depends on the involvement of both the state and community. State involvement would secure some funding for the project; community involvement would ensure its continuity.

> Similar sentence structures

4.2 Coherence within a paragraph

Using the four cohesive devices can help you achieve a logical flow of ideas within a paragraph.

Example:

Three cohesive devices are used in this definition paragraph: reference pronouns, logical connectors and repetition:

	Action/Gesture Painting
[1] Repetition with different form of word	The process of creating an artwork in action painting is very important. 1. Action painters attempt to convey the boldness of lines and gestural movements within the expressive brushstrokes. 2. These 3. displays of physical 4. movements hint at the effort of the 5. painters to express personal emotions and their psychological inner self through art. 6. Unlike traditional artists, 7.action painters use formal elements such as line, colour and form to create artwork without any image in mind. 8. They 9. also employ a range of colours and tones, and 10. these 11. varying palettes create the illusion of 12. activity.
[2] Pronoun	
[3] Repetition with parallel word	
[4] Repetition with same word	
[5] Repetition with same word	
[6] Logical connector	
[7] Repetition with same word	
[8] Pronoun	
[9] Logical connector	
[10] Pronoun	
[11] Repetition with parallel word	
[12] Repetition with different form of word	

4.3 Coherence between paragraphs

In longer essays with several body paragraphs, it is also important to maintain a smooth transition from one paragraph to the next. Using these four cohesive devices gives you more effective and varied ways of moving ideas along, instead of using simple connectors such as *Firstly, Secondly, Another, Finally, Last but not least,* and *The last point.*

Read the following paragraph opening sentences from two student essays. Notice how cohesive devices are used to provide a smooth transition of ideas from one paragraph to the next.

Example 1 (1st year Philosophy) In this example, repetition is used to achieve coherence between paragraphs:

Repetition is used in three ways:	Under the harm principle, Mill would have believed the Government's decision to raise the tax on tobacco sales to be a legitimate restriction upon the liberty of those who purchase cigarettes.
with the same word (*government*)	
with a parallel term (*decision → main intention*)	Next paragraph: opening sentence:
with a different form of the word (*raise → raising*)	The Government's main intention in raising the tax on the sale of tobacco is clear:

Example 2 (1st year Political Studies, on a case study of defence diplomacy):

Cohesive devices	Defence diplomacy has contributed strongly to improving bilateral relations with the United States.
reference pronoun	Next paragraph
repetition using a parallel term	This successful defence diplomacy with the United States has laid the precursor for a possible Free Trade Agreement (FTA) with the world's largest economy.

repetition using the same word	Next paragraph

Next paragraph

Defence diplomacy complements New Zealand's standing as a responsible citizen in the international community by the provision of peace keeping ...

repetition using parallel terms	

Next paragraph

New Zealand's contribution to international security and a peaceful environment has a particular emphasis toward the Pacific region...

PRACTICE ACTIVITY 4.1

Read this introduction from a 1st year Geography essay, responding to this question 'Using sweatshops as an example, examine the associate geographies of production and consumption'.

What type of cohesive device is represented by each numbered boxed phrase: reference pronoun, repetition with same term, repetition with parallel term, or logical connector? The first one has been done as an example:

The geographies of production and consumption and 1. their associated nature, can be clearly examined through the example of sweatshops. In 2. geography, 3. consumption has traditionally been regarded as the end point of the 4. production cycle. 5. However, it is now widely acknowledged that both 6. processes operate in a system and cannot be separated from each other. Through 7. this lens and by using the example of 8. sweatshops, the complex interaction between the 9. making of the product and its final destination to shops and 10. consumers is discussed. This essay 11. also explores the different perspectives on how 12. production and consumption influence each other.

Identify the cohesive devices:

1. *reference pronoun*	7.
2.	8.
3.	9.
4.	10.
5.	11.
6.	12.

UNIT 5 **Accurate use of language**

Key topics

5.1 Common trouble spots

5.2 Grammar: problematic issues

5.3 Sentences: some key issues

5.4 Vocabulary: word use and spelling

Accuracy is the quality of being correct and precise by using the rules governing English grammar, sentences and word use. Accuracy is an important feature of written communication because if your writing contains a high error rate, the message you want to convey may be unclear. The reader's engagement with your writing may also be reduced.

We will look at some common areas of difficulty for students writing in English as an additional language.

5.1 **Common trouble spots**

Read the following extract from an essay from a student enrolled in a 1st year Academic Writing course, responding to the question 'What are the benefits of a university degree?' Can you spot some errors in language use?

> Firstly, have university degree improve a persons opportunity in life. Not only for employment but also for future studies and research. Finding a job can be difficult if the amount of people exceed the number of availiable jobs. Particularly the well-pay and high competing positions. In addition, there is often a close corelation between a level of education and poor in society which it reflects the difference in income between those with a university qualification and those without a university degree.

Check your answers with the error analysis below:

The analysis highlights errors in three categories, each of which is marked with a letter symbol in the text below: grammar [**G**], sentence structure [**S**] and word use [**W**]. (NOTE: Word use includes errors in word choice, spelling and word form, which concerns the correct use of nouns, adverbs and adjectives.)

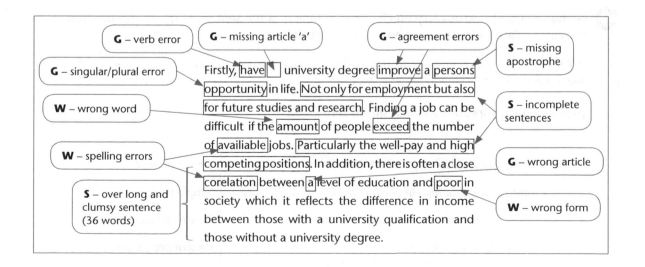

Corrected text:

Note the highlighted corrections in grammar (G), sentence structure (S) and word use (W).

Firstly, having a university degree improves a person's opportunities in life, not only for employment but also for future study and research. Finding a job can be difficult given that the number of people exceeds the number of available jobs, particularly highly paid and competitive positions. In addition, there is often a close correlation between the level of education and poverty in society. This is also reflected in the difference in income between those with a university qualification and those without.

Incomplete sentence is joined to the previous sentence

Long sentence is broken up into two sentences

5.2 Grammar: problematic issues

Agreement This relates to the concepts of singularity and plurality which are expressed differently in other languages. English has the following rules of agreement:

Rules of agreement	Example
1. Number-noun agreement	There are **two points** of view.
2. Noun-verb agreement	The **problem concerns** the lack of funds, The **problems concern** the lack of funds.
3. Pronoun-verb agreement	People should not ignore the factors that may affect **their lives** (NOT 'their life').
4. Extended subject-verb agreement	**One** of the main problems **concerns** the lack of funds. (NOTE: The principal noun is 'one' not 'problems')
5. Two joined nouns must agree	Both the **similarities** and **differences** are important.

Verbs In English, verbs carry much of the meaning of the sentence. The most common problems relate to <u>tense</u>, <u>voice</u> and <u>verb complements</u>.

Tense In English, tense is used to show the relationship between the verb and the time of the action described by the verb (see the chart of English tenses in *Appendix B*).

Examples of time expressions which signal tense

now, today, presently, at the present time	Simple present
last week, a year ago, In 2004, In the eighteenth century	Simple past
for ages, for years, since, recently, over the past two weeks	Present perfect
currently, at the moment	Present progressive
by the year 2020, next year	Future 'will'

Common areas of confusion

- between the present progressive and present perfect
  e.g. Youth crime is rising | has risen steadily for ten years.
  ANSWER: has risen
- between the present progressive and present simple
  e.g. This graph is showing | shows the trends in internet use from 2005 to 2015.
  ANSWER: shows
- irregular verbs and past forms

Three features which cause problems:

1. These verbs do not make their past forms by adding -ed, e.g.: *meet → met; take → took; speak → spoke; stand → stood.*
2. When used with 'has/have/had' or 'was', irregular verbs change their forms again, e.g.: *took → had taken; spoke → had spoken.* Some do not change, e.g.: *stood → had stood; met → had met.*
3. These verbs do not change for the past form: *cut, cost, hit, put, let, shut, broadcast.*

Voice In English, voice is concerned with emphasis. It is indicated by changing the form of the verb. Use the active voice to emphasise the <u>doer</u> or subject of the action. Use the passive voice (two-part verb) to emphasise the <u>action</u>. The following example shows how voice is used to change emphasis:

The government has promised | has been promised to monitor the housing market situation closely.
ANSWER: Active voice – has promised (emphasising the doer: the government)

Close monitoring of the housing market has promised | has been promised by the government.
ANSWER: Passive voice – has been promised (emphasising the action, close monitoring)

⚠ Look out for these errors:

a) when using modal verbs with main verbs in the active voice, e.g.

   can cause; will cause (NOT *can causes, can causing, will causes, will causing*)

b) when using verbs in the passive voice, e.g.

   is calculated, has been calculated (NOT *is calculate, has been calculate*)

Verb complements Some verbs need to be completed by other elements in order to have meaning. There are three patterns of completion:

<u>Pattern 1</u>: Verb + Object Some verbs need an OBJECT to complete their meaning.

   e.g. The people **enjoyed**. (The verb 'enjoyed' needs to be completed by an object. What did the people enjoy?)

   → The people **enjoyed the display** very much.

These verbs take this pattern:

admit	believe	feel	hear	like	notice	protect	search
attend	climb	fear	invite	love	operate	question	sell
admire	deny	guess	keep	miss	prepare	report	want

<u>Pattern 2</u>: Verb + Object + to + Verb

   e.g. Financial ruin **forced** him **to review** his plans. (NOT 'forced him review')

   e.g. He was **forced to review** his financial plans. (NOT 'forced review')

   e.g. He was **allowed to leave** early. (NOT 'allowed leave')

A smaller number of verbs take this pattern:

> advise ask convince enable encourage invite persuade request teach urge
>
> **Exceptions** Verbs following 'make', 'let', 'watch', 'see', 'hear' are not preceded by 'to':
>
> e.g. The radiation made the people suffer. (NOT 'to suffer')
>
> e.g. The lecturer let the students record the lecture. (NOT 'to record')
>
> e.g. Many people watched the building collapse. (NOT 'to collapse')

<u>Pattern 3</u>: Verb + -*ing* ending

The form of the verb ends with the -*ing* ending when it performs these functions:

- as the subject of a sentence to express an action, state, a general idea or concept:

    Swimming is good exercise.

    Watching too much television can be harmful to young children.

- as the object of a preposition:

    She thought about applying for the position of Project Manager.

- as the object of the verb:

    She particularly enjoyed teaching five-year olds. (NOT 'enjoyed to teach'; 'enjoyed teach')

    The workers spent hours repairing the leak. (NOT 'spent to repair'; 'spent repair')

These verbs take this pattern:

avoid	consider	contemplate	delay	prevent
risk	start	stop	succeed	suggest

Articles The articles (*a, an, the,* or *zero article*) are used before nouns to identify them in a specific way (see the chart of English articles in *Appendix B* for a summary of the use of articles).

Most common problems in student writing

- articles are omitted before nouns:

    e.g. Only small number of people are responsible for project.
    → Only **a** small number of people are responsible for **the** project.

- articles are incorrectly used. The main confusion is between 'a' and 'an', 'a' and 'the' and 'the' and 'no article'.

Four easy ways to use articles correctly

Articles identify nouns, so the logical place to start is to ask questions about the noun before selecting the article:

1. **ASK**: Is the noun a non-specific single unit? Does it begin with a consonant or vowel?

    YES → use Indefinite Articles 'a' or 'an':

    > Use 'a' before nouns beginning with a consonant sound

    This is a risk of critical importance

> Use 'an' before a noun
> beginning with a vowel sound

This is an issue of critical importance.

 When choosing between 'a' and 'an', consider how the first letter of the noun is pronounced. For example, although the word 'university' begins with the letter 'u', it is pronounced with a consonant 'y' sound and therefore 'a' is used before the noun 'university' NOT 'an'.

Test your understanding of this rule: Cover the answers below the table before you start. Place 'a' or 'an' before these nouns or noun phrases. Read each noun out loud if it helps you decide whether it begins with a vowel or consonant sound.

1. _____ university professor	5. _____ irregular pattern	9. _____ unemployed person
2. _____ social problem	6. _____ controversial topic	10. _____ honourable person
3. _____ economic growth	7. _____ argument	11. _____ typical situation
4. _____ practical solution	8. _____ global crisis	12. _____ hourly rate

ANSWERS: 1. a 2. a 3. an 4. a 5. an 6. a 7. an 8. a 9. an 10. an 11. a 12. an

2. **ASK**: Is the noun specific or uniquely identified? Am I saying 'this or that one exactly'?

   YES → use the Definite Article 'the':

   Read the chapter on the Battle of Britain (that chapter, that battle exactly)

   The role of a good leader is to inspire (the role specific to a good leader)

   The organisational culture of MARS Incorporated is management-driven (the culture that is specific to that company)

3. **ASK**: Is the noun an abstract concept or idea?

   YES → no article (Ø) is needed:

   Abstract concept: Ø Organisational culture is defined as

         Ø Global warming is causing Ø concern among the international community.

4. **ASK**: Is the noun used to make a general statement?

   YES → no article (Ø) is needed:

   Generalisation: Today, Ø computers are used in most areas of work (NOT A computer is used in most areas of work)

Prepositions   In English, prepositions are used to express relationships between words in a sentence (see the chart of prepositions in *Appendix B*).

One problem is with the common prepositions (e.g. *at, in, on, with, from, by, of*) because they can be used to express different relationships, e.g.

      at noon (expresses time)
      at school (expresses a state or condition)
      at the entrance (expresses a place)

Another difficulty is with prepositions that follow verbs, nouns and adjectives, e.g.

After a noun:	The majority of the people are against the proposal.
After an adjective:	The government is concerned about the housing problem.
After a verb:	These practices relate to the theory of scientific management.

5.3 Sentences: some key issues

Apart from writing a range of sentences, it is important to write with **good control** and **accuracy**.

Punctuation Many punctuation errors relate to the use of commas. Commas have a wide range of uses. Learn more about them in a good grammar book or a grammar website.

Here are two common errors:

- using a comma to separate two independent ideas (comma splice error)

  Insufficient financial assistance is a major problem, third world economies cannot survive without it.

- using no punctuation to separate two independent ideas (run-on/fused error)

  Insufficient financial assistance is a major problem third world countries cannot survive without it.

Correction

Insufficient financial assistance is a major problem. Third world countries cannot survive without it. ← Write 2 sentences

Insufficient financial assistance is a major problem because third world countries cannot survive without it. ← Join the sentences

Incomplete sentences

A basic formal English sentence has three key elements: a subject, a verb, and an object:

SUBJECT | VERB | OBJECT

e.g. The government | passed | a new law.

More elements (an ADVERBIAL or COMPLEMENT) can be added to this basic sentence to give details and other information:

SUBJECT | VERB | OBJECT | ADVERBIAL

e.g. The government | passed | a new law | in order to tighten security. ← Adverbial phrase to give reason or purpose

SUBJECT | VERB | OBJECT | COMPLEMENT

e.g. The new law | will make | the region | safe. ← 'Safe' complements the object 'region' (i.e. The region is safe.)

The following problems arise when one or more basic elements are missing:

The major problem insufficient financial assistance. ← Missing verb 'is'

→ The major problem is insufficient financial assistance.

For example, insufficient financial assistance. ← Missing subject and verb

→ For example, there is insufficient financial assistance.

Because there is insufficient medical assistance.

→ Because there is insufficient medical assistance, the death toll
continues to rise.

> Missing main clause

→ The death toll continues to rise because there is insufficient medical assistance.

People pursue wealth and status are unlikely to find happiness.

> Missing relative pronoun

→ People who pursue wealth and status are unlikely to
find lasting happiness.

Wrong word order

This problem occurs in long or complex sentences when elements are misplaced or are in the wrong order. The connection between the main idea and the subordinate idea becomes unclear as a result.

In the sentence below, the two subordinate clauses (underlined) are not placed next to the idea being described. The sentence is also too long.

The camera cover is equivalent of a man's weight, <u>which is made of strong plastic</u>, must be able to withstand a force of 750N, <u>so that the sharp camera parts cannot fall out.</u>

Correction Write two sentences and reposition the subordinate clauses.

The camera cover is made of strong plastic <u>so that the camera parts cannot fall out.</u>

It must also be able to withstand a force of 750N, <u>which is the equivalent of a man's weight.</u>

Overlong or 'rambling' sentences

The word 'rambling' means 'confused and lacking order'. Overlong or rambling sentences are caused by <u>lack of conciseness</u> (using unnecessary words), <u>repetition</u> and <u>insufficient</u> or <u>incorrect punctuation</u>.

Example 1 This sentence consists of 47 words (from a 1st year Japanese Studies essay).

Throughout both the Tokugawa and Meiji periods, Japan was impacted by the presence of the European powers and the United States who – from both within and outside the Japanese realms – influenced the education of the Japanese people and consequently brought social change to the entire Japanese realm.

Correction Remove repetition and unnecessary words:

During the Tokugawa and Meiji periods, the Japanese education system was influenced by the presence of European powers and the United States, which brought social change to the entire realm. (28 words)

Example 2 This sentence about two urban planning projects consists of 57 words:

Generally speaking, the committee prefers developing the One Tree Hill project over the Wilton Bush project but promoting the Wilton Bush redevelopment project will give the government an important role to play in quality control because ineffective regulation and implementation could exacerbate the negative impact and effective state legislation could mitigate the impact of land ownership and land contamination issues.

Correction Break up the long sentence. Use logical connectors to link sentences. Remove unnecessary words and repetition:

The committee prefers developing One Tree Hill. However, promoting the redevelopment of Wilton Bush will ensure effective state legislation and quality control of land ownership and contamination issues.

 There are no clear rules regarding length, but here is a useful guide. If your sentence is over 25 or 30 words and you have not finished the idea, stop and read it again to make sure that you are still in control of the idea. The solution to overlong sentences is not to write only simple or short sentences either. The aim in academic writing is to demonstrate the ability to write a range of sentences to communicate meaning accurately and clearly.

5.4 Vocabulary: word use and spelling

Apart from developing a good academic vocabulary, it is also important to use words correctly.

Be concise. Remove repetition and wordiness (using unnecessary words), e.g:

> (repetition) discuss ~~about~~ | check ~~up on~~ | circulated ~~round~~ | enter ~~into~~
> mention ~~about~~| revert ~~back~~ | emphasise ~~on~~ | counted ~~up~~
> ~~very~~ unique | ~~positive~~ benefits | five ~~in number~~ | red ~~in~~
> ~~colour~~ | very extreme | final ~~and conclusive~~ | ~~optional~~
> choice | first ~~and foremost~~ | basic ~~and fundamental~~
> ~~complete~~ stop | past ~~history~~ | now ~~at this point in time~~
> 10 a.m. ~~in the morning~~ | ~~true~~ facts | each ~~and every~~
> mandatory ~~requirement~~ | might ~~possibly~~ be | a final ~~and~~
> ~~last~~ point | various ~~and different~~ | more ~~and more~~

Replace nouns and noun phrases with concrete verbs, e.g:

> (Wordiness caused by over-use of nouns)
>
> The expansion of different metals depends on the degree of exposure to heat.
>
> → Metals expand at different rates when exposed to heat. OR →
>
> Metals expand differently when heated.
>
> There is a requirement for the attendance of all new academic staff at the initiation course.
>
> → All academic staff are required to attend the initiation course.

Use the right word. In English, some pairs of words are often confused because they are too similar in spelling and pronunciation. Here is a small sample, but always check in a good dictionary if you are unsure.

affect/effect compliment/complement cause/course	lose/loose number/amount its/it's	principle/principal past/passed whose/who's	weather/whether were/where

Use the correct form or part of speech. In English, the form of a word usually changes according to its function in the sentence. It could be a naming function (noun), a noun modifying function (adjective), an action function (verb), or a verb modifying function (adverb):

as a noun: The **analysis** of the findings took five days.
as an adjective: The problem needed a more **analytical** approach.
as a verb: A team of experts **analysed** the data.
as an adverb: The problem needs to be approached **analytically**.

Use correct spelling. When you learn a word, learn how it is spelt too. Consult a dictionary often. Here are some spelling points to look out for:

ie /ei ence/ance	br<u>ie</u>f	p<u>ie</u>ce	bel<u>ie</u>ve	rec<u>ei</u>ve	c<u>ei</u>ling	dec<u>ei</u>ve independ<u>ence</u>	attend<u>ance</u>	exist<u>ence</u>
double consonants	acco<u>mm</u>odation	co<u>mmitt</u>ee	co<u>mm</u>itment	co<u>nn</u>ection di<u>ff</u>erence	e<u>ff</u>ective	fi<u>tt</u>ed	i<u>mm</u>ediate	i<u>mm</u>igration	nece<u>ss</u>ary o<u>pp</u>ortunity	o<u>ccurr</u>ence	po<u>ss</u>ible	reco<u>mm</u>end	su<u>gg</u>est
silent letters (not pronounced)	s<u>c</u>issors	<u>p</u>sychology	recei<u>p</u>t	colum<u>n</u> <u>w</u>rong	s<u>c</u>ene	<u>h</u>our	<u>h</u>onest	de<u>b</u>t	sc<u>h</u>ool <u>k</u>night	ex<u>h</u>ibition	<u>g</u>uard

You can use British or American spelling but be consistent throughout the assignment. Do not switch randomly from one to the other in the same assignment.

PRACTICE ACTIVITY 5.1

<u>Grammar</u>   Correct any errors in article use, tense, voice and agreement:

1. Only a small number of people are responsible for the project.
2. The living wage contributes to the economic growth.
3. Firms will benefits as more products are consume.
4. Over the past few years, the minimum wage has generate much debate.
5. Recently, there are significant debate around world about paying wages as they affects consumptions and daily life directly.

<u>Sentences</u>   Improve these texts by breaking up in over-long sentences, introducing punctuation, and removing repetition and unnecessary words.

1. This design report describes in detail a design solution for the device that will solve the need for the device to perform all the necessary functions as specified in the project specifications. (Engineering)

2. The combination together of elements is evident and reflection of the artist's unique and special style in the way he uses different and various colours and hues for the addition of texture and emotion to the work. (Fine Arts)
3. Various research evidence throughout the 1990s looked at the teaching and learning of English and the conclusion was that pupils' knowledge and skills in the use of English could be substantially increased and improved to a more advanced and more proficient level. (Language Teaching)

REVIEW

Writing as you speak is not an appropriate style for academic written contexts.

Writing for university is a demonstration of scholarship and follows certain conventions that are universally recognised. Use these conventions correctly. Style guides are sometimes provided by your department. The commonly used referencing styles are also available in electronic format.

Writing that has a clear structure and organisation reflects logical thinking and careful planning. Even when writing in examination conditions, maintain good structure and organisation with logical and visible divisions.

Become a critical reader of your own writing:

- Read for **STYLE**: Have I used an academic writing style? Have I followed university writing conventions for quoting, citing sources and referencing? Have I presented my writing in a clear and readable way?

- Read for **FOCUS**: Have I answered the question? Is the content relevant?

- Read for **SENSE**: Do my ideas flow smoothly? Can the reader follow my thinking and reasoning? Have I provided adequate signals to guide the reader?

- Read for **ACCURACY**: Have I used basic grammar correctly? Are there instances of rambling, over-long or incomplete sentences? Is my vocabulary appropriate to university and academic contexts?

Grammar   Invest in a good grammar resource such as Harrison, M., Jakeman, V., and Paterson, K. (2016). *Improve your grammar: The essential guide to accurate writing.* 2nd ed. London: Palgrave.

Sentences range and control   Write a range of sentences to add interest and a mature quality to your writing.

Vocabulary   Develop a systematic way of learning vocabulary. Establish goals (e.g. learn five new words a day). Invest in a good dictionary which shows how a word is used in different contexts not just its meaning. Use a concordance. A concordance is an alphabetical list of words in a text with the context displayed on a computer screen. A concordance enables you to see how a word is used with other words. A very easy concordance to use can be found at www.just-the-word.com.

The table below presents some of the search results from this website for the noun 'impact' with its 'word partners' (these are other words that can be used before and after 'impact'.

Verbs before 'impact'	Words before 'impact'	Prepositions after 'impact'
assess (the) impact	Articles: *an/the* impact	*impact on*
consider (the) impact	Pronoun: *its* impact	*impact of*
evaluate (the) impact	Adverbs: *some* impact	

Part II

Types of University Written Assignments

Writing is an important feature of university study in all subject areas. The written assignments are much more varied than what you have experienced at high school or college. You are also expected to demonstrate a range of writing skills, which become increasingly more complex as you progress from the first to the final year of undergraduate study.

Part II presents different types of written assignments you may be asked to do during your university study. Extracts of student essays are used to illustrate features of structure and style, rather than how the different parts are developed. Techniques for writing introductions, conclusions and developing ideas are covered in *Part III Developing your writing*.

Extracts for reflective and visual analysis essays are much longer because they are not discussed elsewhere in the book.

Undergraduate written assignments vary in length between 500 and 3000 words. Most assignment questions set a word limit for the essay or report.

Main units

Unit 1 Essays
Unit 2 Case studies
Unit 3 Reports
Unit 4 Literature reviews
Unit 5 Research proposals

Key topics

1.1 Analytical essays
1.2 Visual analysis essays
1.3 Discursive essays

1.4 Reflective essays
1.5 Argumentative essays

Essays are the most common types of undergraduate written assignments, especially in the Arts, Humanities and Social Sciences. In academic contexts, essays usually require a point of view or some indication of your position or thesis on the issue. Depending on the assignment question and type of essay, the thesis may be explicitly stated at the beginning of the essay or implied and stated more clearly at the end of the essay.

This unit presents <u>five</u> types of essay you may write at university: analysis, visual analysis, discussion, reflection and argumentation. These labels may not be used in the assignment question itself, but you are often instructed to 'analyse', 'describe' or 'discuss' an issue (see a list of instruction words and their meaning in Appendix B).

Analytical, discursive and argumentative essays are particularly challenging. You will find some full-length examples in Part IV and Part V.

1.1 Analytical essays

Analysis involves breaking a subject down into smaller parts and examining each part systematically. Each part is then developed further with concrete examples, descriptive details and other evidence from research. The aim of the analysis is to increase the reader's understanding of the subject by providing the facts of <u>what</u>, <u>when</u>, <u>where</u>, <u>how</u>, and <u>why</u> something is or happens.

Analytical essays usually have a narrow focus, which allows you to examine an object, person or subject very closely and in detail. For example, you may be asked to compare and contrast two or more methods, policy documents or films, critique or review an art work or an artist, film or article, or explain causes and effects.

Another type of analytical essay – visual analysis – is unique to these disciplines: art, painting, sculpture, design and architecture. We will examine visual analysis essays in the next unit.

The following diagram summarises the main features of analysis essays:

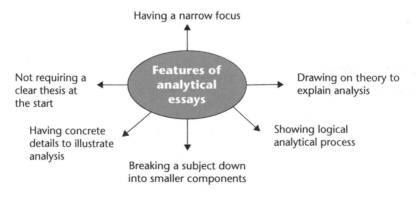

Sample questions

The expected skills and approach to constructing an appropriate response can be determined from certain words in the assignment question, highlighted in the following sample questions:

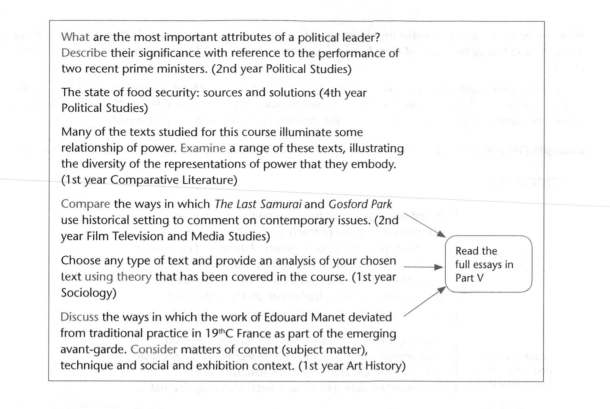

What are the most important attributes of a political leader? Describe their significance with reference to the performance of two recent prime ministers. (2nd year Political Studies)

The state of food security: sources and solutions (4th year Political Studies)

Many of the texts studied for this course illuminate some relationship of power. Examine a range of these texts, illustrating the diversity of the representations of power that they embody. (1st year Comparative Literature)

Compare the ways in which *The Last Samurai* and *Gosford Park* use historical setting to comment on contemporary issues. (2nd year Film Television and Media Studies)

Choose any type of text and provide an analysis of your chosen text using theory that has been covered in the course. (1st year Sociology)

Discuss the ways in which the work of Edouard Manet deviated from traditional practice in 19thC France as part of the emerging avant-garde. Consider matters of content (subject matter), technique and social and exhibition context. (1st year Art History)

Read the full essays in Part V

Structure and Style

As we saw in Part I, Unit 3, academic essays have three structural elements: an introduction, main body and a conclusion. Ideas proceed smoothly to the conclusion through logical organisation and development.

In longer essays, headings may be used to identify the different points of analysis more clearly:

Example (Postgraduate Political Studies on 'The state of food security: sources and solutions').

The following outline is derived from the headings and sub-headings used in the essay. You can see that the complex topic of food security is broken down into smaller components for the purpose of analysis:

logical progression of analysis

INTRODUCTION
BODY
    Defining food security
    Current state of food security
    Current food security efforts: role of international organisations
    Causes of food insecurity
        Natural
        Political
    Addressing food insecurity
        Realist approach
        Neo-liberal institutional approach
        A third way: research and development
CONCLUSION: future of food security

When no headings are used, coherence or flow is achieved by using connectors and other devices to create a smooth and logical transition of ideas from one paragraph to the next (see *Part I, Unit 4 Coherent flow of ideas*).

The following short article review is an example of an analytical essay. Instead of headings, each paragraph is clearly identified with a signalling word or cohesive device. These are highlighted in the example text. The boxed annotations in the left margin point to the structural elements of the article review.

Example (1st year Anthropology: article review of 'Powwow and Competitions' by Scales; 350–400 words)

STRUCTURE   **STYLE**

Summarises content and focus

Based on data derived from thorough fieldwork, as his methodological approach, Scales discusses Native American powwows, social events of intertribal celebration involving singing and dancing, in the Central Plains of Canada and the Northern Plains of the US. The article distinguishes between traditional' and 'competition' powwows and seeks to explain why ...

Examines first point, relates to theoretical issues

The major theoretical issues are the tension between 'modernity' and 'tradition' and the seemingly paradoxical nature of competition as identity-fostering and community-building in social events. Scales argues that ...

Examines second point, relates to article

Despite this suspicion, since competition can result in hostilities, the popularity of competition powwows has grown since the 1950s. Scales argues that ...

Supports with evidence from other texts

Another example of identity-building aspect of competitive performing arts can be found in the *Sokayeti,* an annual, government sponsored music and dance competition, in Burma (Myanmar). Douglas (2003) argues that ...

Notice the use of the present simple tense throughout

Concludes with comment on overall significance

In summary, the article shows that competition, ironically, can result in people feeling and imaging things together in similar ways. A mutual understanding of the shared ethical values and aesthetic codes can highlight a common identity in the context of competition.

1.2 Visual analyses

A visual analysis is more technical than the analytical essays presented in the previous unit, requiring visual language and specific techniques. The label 'visual analysis' is used here to refer to writing which describes the elements of static images (as in a painting) or moving images (as in a film clip) and other visuals related to sight. Visual analyses are particularly relevant for students of fine arts and architecture. This unit is not a definitive resource on writing about art or design. At university, you should be able to locate resources in these subject areas in the main library collections.

A visual analysis is more than just a recording of descriptive details. It involves analysing the composition of the art form using precise <u>language of description</u> and <u>visual vocabulary</u> unique to the art form, describing <u>visual elements</u> such as shape, colour, texture and mood, interpreting their meaning and evaluating their overall effect.

The following diagram summarises the main features of visual analysis essays:

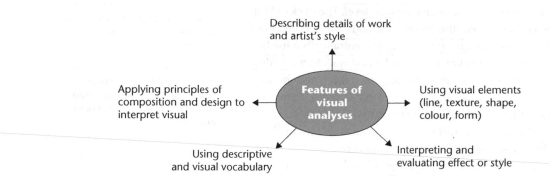

Sample questions

Visit an art gallery or museum and select FIVE art works that portray a contemporary theme. Compare the art works in terms of subject-matter and style. (1st year Fine Arts – Painting)

Locate an area on campus and discuss the use of space, function and flow. (1st year Fine Arts – Architecture)

Review a comic (visual narrative) and explore issues pertaining to page layout or design, panel construction, narrative, and image/ word relations, using theoretical tools and language from the course. (3rd year Film and Media Studies).

Analyse a scene from a film to show how the scene contributes to the overall theme of the film. (2nd year Film and Media Studies)

Write a response to a musical composition of your choice. (2nd year Music)

> Read the full essay in Part V

Structure and Style

Visual analyses use the standard essay format. However, unlike other types of essays, which organise information topically, visual analyses are often organised in order of <u>space</u> and <u>location</u>. They describe how individual objects fit into a physical space in a way that makes sense to the reader. Depending on the art form, you might consider the following organising principles:

horizontally	from left to right or right to left
vertically	from upper to lower or top to bottom
by distance	from foreground to middle ground to background
by size or proportion	from small to large, large to small, part to whole or whole to part
diagonally	from one corner to the opposite corner
in a circular line	clockwise or anti-clockwise
by compass points	to/in the north, south, east, west

Visual analyses are characterised by the use of prepositions, descriptive language and visual vocabulary. Read the following description of the interior of a bistro.

The Shamrock is a few steps below street level. The thick ceiling-to-floor curtains make the interior lighting dim and shadowy even during the day. To the left near the entrance is a full bar, which takes up the entire length of the east wall. In the middle of the room are four large rectangular tables and benches made of natural wood and painted a dark colour. Patronage seems low for this time of day, with only two elderly men sitting at one of the tables. Three lanterns of oriental design hang down from the ceiling. Two large artworks of some impressive modern architecture are displayed on the wall opposite the bar.

> The boxed prepositional phrases provide compositional details.

> The highlighted expressions consist of adjectives and nouns describing texture, size, colour and shape.

See the Language of description chart in *Appendix B*.

Example 1 Visual analysis of a painting (two-dimensional art form)

STRUCTURE

STYLE

Introduces work and artist (date, title, medium, size, style)	Painted in 2008, *Big Head,* measuring 400X300mm, is one of many oil paintings in self-portraiture by Mary McIntyre. In *Big Head,* the self-portrait is featured as part of a broader narrative rather than as the principal subject. McIntyre's style is derived from a combination of classicism, renaissance and surrealist features.

> Notice the use of the present progressive to describe activity

Presents visual details – figures, appearance, activity **Examines line, colour, texture, composition (how parts interact)** **Organises analysis spatially – moves from top to bottom**	The self-portrait takes the form of a classic sculpture, notably the marble white colour and unseeing eyes. The top half of the painting and slightly to the left is dominated by the monumental sculpture head of the artist set against a sky blue background. The entire bottom half of the painting is in a dark brown colour forming the wide sweep of her cloak from left to right. Standing half-way up the cloak – on her arm – and slightly to the right of the painting are two small male figures, with hands in their pockets. Their heads are tilted upwards looking at the towering sculpture head. Next to them on the left is their white dog. The well-defined outlines put the images into sharp focus, making them clearly visible despite their small size.

> Location words and prepositions (highlighted here) show how parts interact

Interprets the painting	The towering sculpture as a position of power and strength is enhanced by the low viewing angle of the male figures and the dog, mere mortals compared to the majestic form of the sculpture. The cloak stands in for the mountain, commonly used by the artist as a signifier of power and stability.
Evaluates overall style and effect	The composition is masterfully executed. The painting's visual accuracy is achieved through the artist's attention to line and symmetry, use of strong blocks of colour and contrast and a smooth painting style with well-defined outlines.

Example 2 Visual description of a sculpture (three-dimensional art form)

This Art History student's analysis of a free-standing sculpture reflects learnt knowledge about techniques and relevant visual vocabulary. The organisation of the visual analysis is unique to three-dimensional art forms, being focused on individual parts and how they make up the whole, overall shape and form.

Follow the structure and style of the analysis by reading the comments in the boxes to the left and right of the text.

STRUCTURE   **STYLE**

Introduces sculpture and key visual elements

Molly MacAlister, *Maori Warrior* (bronze, 3225 mm) 1964–1966, Queen Street. Molly MacAlister's statue is representative of a Maori warrior as suggested by the traditional cloak. However, the statue is stylized to be a modern rendition of a traditional Maori figure. This is clear in the treatment of texture, form, composition, line and space.

Uses simple present tense throughout

Uses the visual elements to organise the analysis

The statue is made out of bronze … It has been cast in separate parts, as can be seen by the lines across the sculpture. The surface has a weathered, natural texture, as if made from clay or representing a feathered cloak. The statue has a limited palette, its dark brown showing no bronze shine … but rather a play of light with dark shadows in the textured cloak and beneath the brows and chin. The only touches of colour are tints of green where the metal has worn. This makes the sculpture part of the surrounding environment, referencing both the dulled hues of the city behind and the earth beneath […]

Uses technical visual words

Interprets the visual elements and effects created

The form of the statue is bulky and solid, as if hewn from stone, rising from its distinct base like an obelisk … At almost 3 metres tall, the statue is almost double the height of an average human … The statue's composition is static, the only movement being suggested by the turn of head. All this gives the statue a formal, monumental quality … The vertical line of the statue pulls the viewer's gaze upwards … The arching edge of cloak also leads the viewer's eyes up to look at the statue's face …

Evaluates significance

The space in which the statue sits extends beyond its immediate surroundings […] It is the first thing arrivals see.

PRACTICE ACTIVITY 1.1

Test your understanding of visual analysis by trying these practice activities. You may wish to have a look at the *Language of description* chart in Appendix B before you begin.

1. Focus on organisation

   The sentences in the following description of the Statue of Liberty in New York are in scrambled order. This is a famous landmark but if you need to, view it on the internet first before trying this activity. Consider how you might begin to describe it. Then put the sentences in order to form a logical description.

[1] The Statue of Liberty is an internationally known symbol of freedom that was completed in 1886.

[2] The statue is of a woman wearing long, flowing robes.

[3] It is placed near the entrance to the New York City harbour.

[4] On her head, she has a crown of seven spikes that symbolise the seven oceans and the seven continents.

[5] The statue weighs 450,000 pounds and is 152 feet (46.5 m) high.

[6] In her left hand, she carries a tablet with the Declaration of Independence date 'July IV MDCCLXXVI' written on the cover.

[7] The statue is mounted on a 150-feet-high rectangular stonework pedestal with a foundation in the shape of an irregular eleven-pointed star.

[8] In her raised hand, the woman holds a torch, symbolising enlightenment.

[9] Together with the pedestal it reaches a height of 305 feet (93 m).

[10] The exception is the torch, which is coated in gold leaf originally made of copper.

[11] The statue is a hollow construction made of a covering of pure copper laid over a steel framework.

[12] At her feet lies a broken chain, which symbolises an escape to freedom.

2. Focus on <u>spatial composition</u> (Architecture)

   <u>Assignment brief</u>: Locate an area on campus and discuss the use of space, function and flow. The student is studying the use of space and flow in the University's English Language Centre, by applying learnt knowledge about spatial design and how people move and interact in different ways. Below is the plan of the Centre:

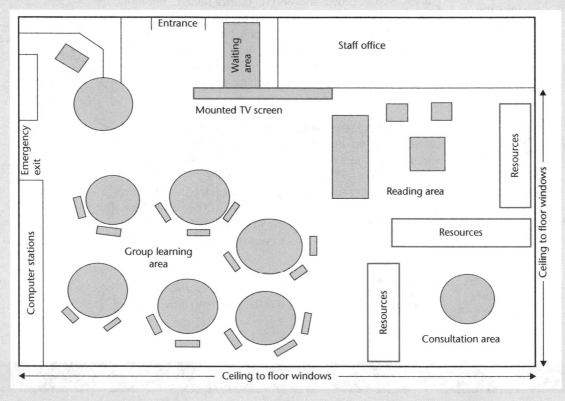

<u>Two suggested organising principles</u>

[1] Whole to part principle

   a) From the entrance, survey the entire <u>space</u>: give the overall structural framing of the room (e.g. wall and windows, open space. Impression – comfortable, airy, spacious, bright?).

   b) <u>Line</u>: move your eyes down and up (from carpeted floors to florescent lighting in the high ceilings).

c) <u>Function and flow</u>: consider the way fixtures and furniture are arranged; follow your own journey or walk through the space – left to right (computer stations on the right, tables in the centre, consulting corner, adjacent reading corner and back to the entrance).

[2] Part to whole/Most prominent (largest) to least (smallest) principle

   a) Start with the most prominent feature (the cluster of tables and chairs, for example).
   b) Describe features to the left and right.
   c) Survey the entire space from the entrance.

1.3 Discursive essays

Discussion is the action or process of writing about something by taking into account different perspectives on an issue before arriving at a conclusion. Discursive essays are generally more <u>exploratory</u>, requiring careful discussion of the connection between theory and practice.

An opinion or decision on the subject is usually required but it may not be stated explicitly in the introduction. It is usually stated in the conclusion but without the degree of persuasion of argumentative essays (see 1.4 and *Part IV Presenting a point of view*).

The following diagram summarises the main features of discursive essays:

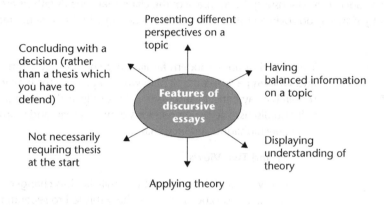

Sample questions

Notice in particular the highlighted parts of the question and the emphasis on application of knowledge and theory.

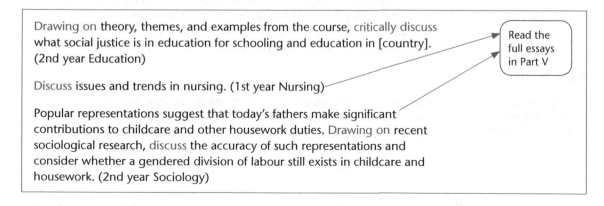

Drawing on theory, themes, and examples from the course, critically discuss what social justice is in education for schooling and education in [country]. (2nd year Education)

Discuss issues and trends in nursing. (1st year Nursing)

Popular representations suggest that today's fathers make significant contributions to childcare and other housework duties. Drawing on recent sociological research, discuss the accuracy of such representations and consider whether a gendered division of labour still exists in childcare and housework. (2nd year Sociology)

Read the full essays in Part V

The overall shape of discussion may be represented as follows:

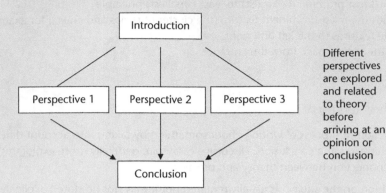

Different perspectives are explored and related to theory before arriving at an opinion or conclusion

The two examples below display the style of discussion especially in terms of drawing on theory and explaining different perspectives on the topic.

Example 1 (2nd year Sociology, discussing the accuracy of the claim that today's fathers are contributing more to housework by drawing on sociological research and considering whether a gendered division of labour still exists)

INTRODUCTION	The organisation of modern families has changed over time, with men and women participating in paid work to provide for family ... This research essay critically discusses ... Secondly, it draws on ... Thirdly, it will also discuss the power relations between men and women. Lastly, this essay highlights research that ...
Does not state a clear thesis	
BODY 1	**History and Two Views**
	The history of men's involvement in family life has changed significantly over time ... Hook (2006) describes how this led to separation of men's and women's labour ... The dominant role of breadwinner began to be challenged during the mid-twentieth century, where a
Draws on sociological theory →	'second transformation' within industrial societies took place – married women were leaving 'the home to pursue waged work' (Hook, 2006, p. 1). Today the familiar family model features both men and women, working outside the home but, as Hook (2006) says, even though unpaid work time has increased for men, 'it has not compensated for women's decline nor reached parity with women's time'.
CONCLUSION	
Ends with a comment rather than a clear thesis	This essay has pointed to research highlighting the view that male participation has increased over time with women's decreasing ... Research suggested that history, the media and women's inability to let men parent and participate in unpaid work could be barriers to men doing more at home.

Example 2 also displays the style of discussion. It presents the topic in the introduction. Like Example 1, it draws on knowledge and theories to support the discussion of different perspectives. Unlike Example 1, it does have a clear thesis in the conclusion, which gives a more satisfying end to the discussion.

Example 2 (2nd year Education, discussing if social justice can be achieved through education by drawing on themes, theories and examples from the course)

INTRODUCTION

Explains topic, gives scope, but does not give a clear thesis

Egalitarian ideals of a modern democratic society suggest that through education, social justice can be achieved. The struggle towards social justice is an attempt to challenge societal inequality and to improve society and the lives of individuals. This essay introduces Bailey's (2010) writings on liberal education ... It then looks at possible critiques ...

BODY

Discusses different perspectives, draws on research. Note the use of author tags and reporting verbs.

Improving the lives of individuals and society is a general theme in education. Dale and Robertson (2009) argue that education is a social contract in which individuals give up some rights in order to better their own lives and society. Meyer (2001) also emphasizes that the goals of a modern nation-state education are to achieve 'individual equality and collective progress'.

An important way of challenging this inequality and achieving social justice is education. Many educational theorists argue that education is a means of challenging inequality in society and achieving social justice. Freire (2000), a famous educational theorist, argues that ... Bailey (2010) argues that social justice can be achieved through a liberal education.

CONCLUSION

Ends discussion with a clear position/thesis on the issue

In conclusion, as inequality continues to rise in New Zealand, education is ever more important in challenging inequalities and achieving social justice. A liberal education equips individuals with the ability to think critically and challenge inequality in society. A liberal education is therefore emancipatory and can help to achieve social justice.

1.4 Reflective essays

Reflective essay assignments are common in the Arts and the Social Sciences. Reflective writing is an activity in which you provide a personal response to an event, experience or situation.

In academic contexts, when you evaluate the experience and explain how you have been changed or influenced by it, you need to provide support using academic theory and other people's ideas. Finally, you also need to consider what implications the experience might have for similar tasks in the future.

The following diagram summarises the features of reflective essays:

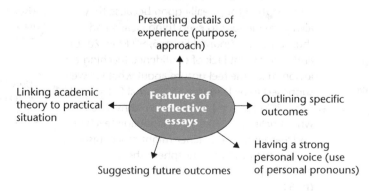

Sample questions

Reflect on teaching practice by referring to journal entries and peer feedback. (2nd year Language Teaching)

Select a reading or short story, reflect on the theme(s) and relate to personal experience. (1st year English)

Write a socio-autobiography. (1st year Sociology)

Structure and Style

Personal evidence and a personal voice are features of reflective writing. Therefore, the use of personal pronouns and reference such as 'I', 'I think' or 'my' is acceptable. However, as we saw in *Part 1, Unit 1 Appropriate writing style*, excessive use of personal pronouns is undesirable.

The following examples show different approaches to reflective writing.

Example 1 (2nd year Language Teaching, reflecting on language teaching practice).

This reflective writing is one of several tasks that the student has to complete. According to the assignment brief, the reflection must include references to journal entries and peer feedback.

You will notice that the extract below focuses on reflection and justification. It has the style of a journal entry. There is no formal introduction or description of the task. The personal voice is clearly evident (highlighted here), but the reflection is also grounded in considered analysis and connections to theory.

STRUCTURE

STYLE

Description: gives source of inspiration → The teachers [who] left a lasting impression on me throughout my school and university years were the ones who inspired me to want to be a teacher. These teachers listened to students' dreams and desires and encouraged them to achieve their true potential. I aspire to be such a teacher.

> Uses past tense here

> Uses first person pronouns

Reflection: quotes from journal entries → Good teaching and learning occur when teachers are … The importance of these qualities is often repeated in my journal entries and evaluation forms, with statements such as 'I found this group really good because they always made sure to everything clearly and thoroughly …' (Journal Entry 6, 9th May, 2016), and 'Their slight lack of confidence teaching the lesson made me feel unsure about what we were supposed to be learning …' (Journal Entry 1, 11th April, 2016) …

> Uses past tense

Justification: relates to theory/other research to support reflection → Tomlinson (2013) sums up exactly what I believe defines good language teaching and learning: 'The teacher might make mistakes …, but the positive atmosphere she creates might inspire and motivate her students …' (p. 51)

> Uses APA in-text citation style

Example 2 (1st year Sociology: a socio-autobiography; actual length: 1796 words)

The student is required to reflect on the relevance of THREE sociological concepts to her work experience and this affects the structure of the reflection. The emphasis is on relating theory to a practical situation. Unlike Example 1, this reflective essay uses the standard essay format. The three elements (introduction, main body, conclusion) are clearly visible.

STRUCTURE   **STYLE**

INTRODUCTION

Identifies three concepts

This socio-autobiography will discuss sociological concepts in relation to my personal experiences and those of my colleagues at ... The concepts I will cover are deskilling, McJobs, and Hochschild's concept of emotional labour.

> First person pronouns are used throughout the reflection.

BODY

1 Explains first concept

One of the central aspects of managerial control begins with the process of 'deskilling' identified by Braverman (1998) ... Deskilling involves ... (Curtis, 2013, p. 297). Through this process, workers no longer require the knowledge they once possessed ...

2 Explains second concept and relates to job

As part of my job as a sales assistant, I am required to ... we have special equipment to roll out and measure the fabric. ... The electronic till calculates all the information I require, ... The use of these specialised machines shows aspects of Fordism and McDonaldization ...

3 Explains third concept

As a result of a capitalist society, many people work in 'McJobs'. McJobs are considered to be low-paying jobs, which offer little opportunity for career advancement (Curtis, 2013, p. 298). These positions are often taken up by young people, who are more likely to be hired due to their ...

4 Relates third concept to job

Although I do not work at a fast-food restaurant, my job presents many of the criteria of a McJob. One of these criteria is the almost non-existent advancement of staff from the shop-floor to high or managerial positions; ... Additionally, the majority of the employees are students like me ...

> Shows understanding of the question

5 Justifies with evidence from research

Working in a position that requires interaction with customers involves dealing with emotional issues and conflict (Biron & van Veldhoven, 2012, p. 1261). In *The Managed Heart*, Hochschild (2012) argues that such jobs demand 'emotional labour'. She defines emotional labour as 'the management of feeling to create a publicly observable facial and bodily display' (p. 7) ...

		Uses a narrative style and past tense
6 Relates concept to experience with anecdotal accounts	Part of my job as a sales assistant entails that I perform emotional labour which can be difficult to implement. Once, I ... Many of the staff at my workplace have also been victims of abuse from irate customers. Although it has never happened to me, I have witnessed such abuse to my colleague's first-hand. On one occasion in particular, ...	
CONCLUSION **Evaluates with a brief comment**	This socio-autobiography has talked about three sociological concepts in relation to my personal experiences as a sales assistant. These concepts have helped me understand the many avenues surrounding managerial control of the labour process in the workplace.	

While personal pronouns are acceptable in reflective essays, excessive use can also give your writing a conversational and emotive style, which is inappropriate for reflective writing in university contexts. Here is a revision of the paragraph before the conclusion. Notice that the same message can be presented without using personal pronouns and personal reference, as shown in the the following revision of body paragraph 6:

> Part of a sales assistant's work entails performing emotional labour which can be difficult to implement. The staff at ... have also been victims of abuse from dissatisfied customers. There was an incident in which one of the staff members was ...

Review matters of academic style in *Part I, Unit 1*.

1.5 Argumentative essays

In the Arts, Humanities and Social Sciences, in particular, the written assignments are concerned with issues or topics that people have different opinions about. In other resources in books or on the internet, you may see them referred to as 'claim essays' or 'stance or position essays'. Your task is to respond to the claim or position presented in the question by indicating your position and defending it with concrete evidence, good judgement and logical reasoning.

Argumentative essay questions requiring a point of view, logical reasoning and argumentation supported by evidence are often written in a particular way which indicates the key elements of argumentation, as shown in the following example from Business.

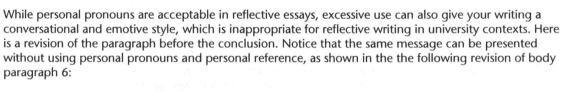

Point of view required

Do you think it is possible for entrepreneurship to be taught? Develop a clear argument that indicates your view and justify your choice using appropriate evidence and examples.

Logical reasoning

Evidence

The issue you have to respond to may also be presented as a statement which represents an extreme position, as in this example from 1st year Anthropology:

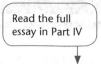

Read the full essay in Part IV

'Art is corrupted by technology'. Develop an argument that either agrees or disagrees with the statement.

In terms of writing style, argumentation makes more demands on language than analytical or discursive essays. The distinctive structure and style features of argumentation are examined in detail in *Part IV Presenting a point of view*.

UNIT 2 Case studies

A case study is a discussion of a specific organisation, person or situation in a real-life context to investigate a problem, arrive at a decision and propose solutions. Case study assignments are commonly used in Business, Law, Political Studies and Nursing.

There are some variations. In some case study assignments, you do not gather your own data using research methods such as observations, interviews or site visits. Instead, you use existing descriptions or published information on a case. You may be given a *scenario*, which is a fictional sequence of events or setting.

Most undergraduate case study assignments are concerned with the application of knowledge. You discuss the evidence from the case, relate it to relevant theory, generalise and predict future trends from the case analysis.

The following diagram summarises the main features of case studies:

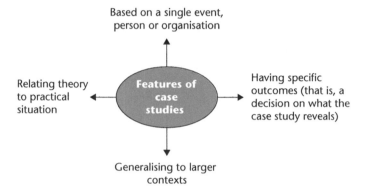

Sample case study assignments

Analyse the organisational culture of a firm of your choice, indicating whether the firm manufactures a culture or if it is generated naturally by employees. Discuss using relevant theories and analyse the firm's culture from a mainstream and critical perspective. (2nd year Management)

Contract law application: The case of Farm Hands 215 Ltd versus Flay and Groan Ltd. (1st year Law)

Use a case study to justify nursing intervention and develop a nursing care plan. (2nd year Nursing)

Use a case study to determine if famine is a security issue. (2nd year Political Studies)

Structure and Style

Undergraduate case studies typically use the standard essay structure and prose style, but headings may be used in long essays. The exception is Law, which follows a distinctive structure and style.

Example 1 (2nd year Management: Analyse the organisational culture at a firm of your choice, indicating whether the firm manufactures a culture or if it is generated naturally by employees. Discuss using relevant theories and analyse the firm's culture from a mainstream and critical perspective.)

Read the full essay in Part V

This student has chosen to study the organisational culture at Mars Incorporated to determine whether there is evidence of a culture and its contribution to the firm's success. Here are the last three sentences from the conclusion:

Mars' success was found to be associated with the culture that the original founders and subsequent owners implemented and managed throughout the years. This strong culture, rooted on the foundation of The Five Principles, unifies staff towards a common professional purpose. This strength in unity has consequently led to the large success of the organisation.

Example 2 (3rd year Nursing, using a case study to justify intervention and devise an individualised nursing care plan)

The student uses the case of a patient who presented with an episode of generalised seizure to describe clinical procedures, formulate a diagnosis, and recommend appropriate interventions for patients with a similar complaint.

In the first body heading after the introduction, the student presents the relevant patient details. As reported by the student, the most challenging aspect of this part of the essay was <u>managing the tense shifts</u>, because the patient's medical history covers different time periods (see the chart of English tenses in Appendix B).

Client details

Present
Mary is a 77-year-old European woman. She has presented with an episode of generalised seizure. During the session, Mary displayed altered levels of consciousness for 30 seconds.

Medical history
Mary's medical history shows that she has no problems with alcohol and has never been on any anti-epilepsy medication. Between 2004 and 2007, Mary had experienced only two episodes of syncope (loss of consciousness). Since August 2008, however, she and her husband have noticed ...

Incident summary
On the day of admission, Mary had just finished playing a round of golf when she suddenly felt dizzy and collapsed. Her husband reported that Mary hit her head on the concrete pavement and lost consciousness for about 30 seconds.

In the diagnostic assessment of the case, reference is made to specific details from the patient's record, as shown in the highlighted sentence here:

As part of nursing assessment for seizure patients, it is important to know about past health history relating to injuries, central nervous system trauma, alcoholism, tumours or stroke (Brown & Edwards, 2004). A neurological examination is necessary for such patients to detect any modifications in patients' neurological condition. Although Mary did not exhibit all these symptoms, she had altered levels of consciousness during the session, indicating abnormal electrical discharges from the brain.

While headings are used in the case study, there is no heading entitled 'Conclusion'. This may reflect subject area practice. The last heading 'Nursing interventions' consists of four paragraphs, each justifying the diagnosis and recommended care plan, as shown in the opening sentences:

Firstly, assessing patients' neurological status is the most significant form of nursing intervention.

Secondly, anti-epileptic drugs are very effective for preventing further seizures and avoiding hospitalisation.

In addition, nurses should be familiar with emergency procedures and management when patients are having seizures.

Finally, patient education should be included in the care plan.

Example 3 (3rd year Political Studies: using a case study to investigate a problem)

The student uses the case of Somalia to determine if famine is a major contemporary security risk. The student explains the rationale for choosing Somalia:

> The study of the events of 2011 in Somalia is of particular interest as it presents a contemporary and critical case of famine ... In rooting the actions of al-Shabaab in Somalia's colonial past and considering the past and present methods of Western intervention, post-colonialism provides an alternative perspective through which al-Shabaab's actions and the famine crisis can be understood.

This body paragraph gives an account of the <u>events</u> of 2011 which led to a state of famine in Somalia:

> **The case study of Somalia**
> The case study of Somalia presents a contemporary and critical case of famine [...]. Exacerbated in early 2011 by a combination of poor harvest and infectious disease, famine in Somalia was officially declared by the UN in July, at which point the famine had claimed tens of thousands of lives, with projected estimates of 750,000 deaths by December 2011. Usually a state's government declares famine, but in this case the UN had to intervene, due to the lack of central government in Somalia. It declared famine in various zones in the south, which is inhabited by 2.8 of the 3.7 million suffering from famine. Deaths have further spread to neighbouring countries, such as Kenya, where more than 400,000 Somali refugees have fled, bringing with them cholera, malaria and other diseases. Complicating the situation further is the role of the Islamist militant group al-Shabaab, which placed limitations on Western aid. However, the situation is more complex.

Time expressions and past tense

Statistical data/facts

The student's conclusion is that the famine concept is flawed and suggests an alternative perspective.

Example 4 (1st year Commercial Law: using a case study to apply the law). The student is given a setting or scenario and is asked to assume the role of legal adviser to a client.

The case/scenario

Reference: ABO and ABP v ZYP [2013] NZDT65 (2 April 2013). Retrieved from www.disputestribunal. govt.nz. Creative Commons Attribution (BY) 4.0 International Licence. (Names have been added for this assignment.)

> James and Susan bought a second-hand washing machine from Ben on the online auction site, Trade Me, for $150 and paid an extra $40 delivery fee. The machine stopped working one month after the purchase. James and Susan wanted Ben to replace the washing machine or have it repaired. This was declined. James and Susan are claiming compensation to the amount of $115.

The typical structure of law essays is ILAC, which stands for Issues, Law, Application, and Conclusion.

In this case, the <u>issues</u> to be decided are: (a) whether Ben has met the contractual obligations; and (b) whether James and Susan are entitled to compensation. The relevant <u>law</u> is the Sale of Goods Act 1908 ('SGA'). <u>Application</u> involves relating the law to specific aspects of the case. The <u>conclusion</u> in this case is that the claim cannot succeed because Ben has met his contractual obligations and James and Susan did have one month's use of the machine.

Example 5 (2nd year Law – contract law assignment)

The case

This extract from introductory sections shows the ILAC structure:

(ISSUE)	*Contractual obligations to Mr Flay*
(LAW)	**A Relevant Facts** In January 2013, Farm Hands entered into a long-term contract with Mr Flay. [...]. The primary legal issue is whether this price amendment is enforceable, given the apparent absence of consideration in the agreement.
(APPLICATION)	**B Legal Application** 1 Additional consideration 2 Issue of additional benefits as consideration
(CONCLUSION)	This case is dependent upon the willingness of the court to depart from historic legal precedent such as *Stilk v Myrick* and *Foakes v Beer*. To succeed against Mr Flay, Farm Hands must maintain that ... It must also argue that ... Finally, a relegation of Farm Hands' obligation to pay ... requires proof that no practical benefit existed to serve as consideration for the variation in contract.

UNIT 3 **Reports**

A report is a specific form of writing that gives a full account of what has been observed, done or investigated in a laboratory or experimental study. It has structural elements not found in essays and is visually distinguishable from essays by its use of headings and numbering systems.

Undergraduate reports are common in the Physical Sciences (e.g. Engineering, Chemistry and Physics), Social Sciences (e.g. Anthropology and Sociology) and Life Sciences (e.g. Psychology, Medical, Health and Biological Sciences).

Report writing gives you practice in preparing a professional document. It also tests your ability to describe, explain and analyse results of an experiment or study.

The following diagram summarises the main features of reports:

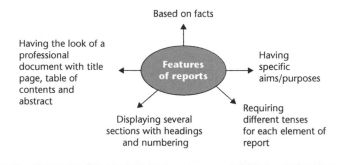

Structure and Style

Report formats may vary across subject areas, but the following elements are found in most formal reports. Undergraduate reports are more likely to have an **IMRDC** structure.

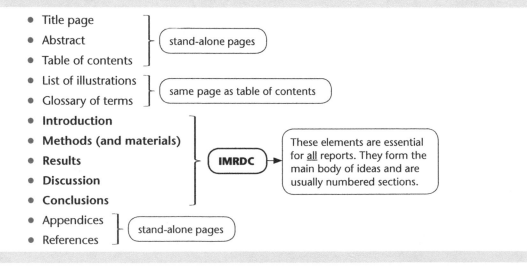

The inclusion or omission of some elements depends on the subject area and the type of report.

A **report conclusion** is different from an essay conclusion. Usually written with an 's', it is made up of a series of specific statements that are directly and logically drawn from the results. In some reports (especially technical reports), the conclusion may be written as a numbered list.

In the sample reports below, the total number of words used for each element is provided to indicate their relative significance. There are some variations, but in general, the Discussion element is the longest part of the report.

The use of <u>tense</u> is significant in reports. In the examples below, tense shifts are highlighted in the main text.

3.1 Laboratory reports

Example 1 (3nd year Medical Sciences) The report has a conventional IMRDC structure.

The number of words for each element of the report shows its relative size in relation to the whole report. In this report, you can see that the Results and Discussion sections take up almost one-third of the total length. The tense shifts are highlighted:

gives title and aim at top of the first page

EXPERIMENT: Comparison of body size and body composition between lean and obese mice.
AIMS: a) To dissect organs, weigh and measure body size and blood glucose levels. B) To learn how the agouti gene causes obesity in mice.

IMRDC explained

I explains what and why

INTRODUCTION (actual length: 682/3699 words)
Obesity is an increasingly prevalent issue that affects society ... the use of animal models can help us better understand ... The Agouti mouse model provides a way to study an aspect of the genetics of obesity ... Overall, ... (Miltenberger et al., 1997).

> Uses present simple tense

M describes how it was done

METHODS (actual length: 429/3699 words)
Two mice were dissected and measured in this experiment. One was a yellow mouse (Grade 1 on the range of coat colours) and the other was ... After euthanisation, blood from each of the mice was collected by cardiac puncture and ...

> Uses past tense and passive

R describes what was found

RESULTS (actual length: 1114/3699 words – includes 6 graphs)
Figure 1 shows that the average blood glucose level in male wild-type mice was ... The results of a Student T-test gave a ...

> Uses past tense

D comments on the results, explains their significance

DISCUSSION (actual length: 1331/3699 words)
As Agouti mice show symptoms of insulin resistance and diabetes, it was expected that ... Thus, the significant difference found only in females, as seen in Figure 1 does not seem to agree with findings published in previous studies (Bultman et al., 1992) ...

> Uses present simple tense

C establishes what can be drawn from findings

CONCLUSION (88/3699 words)
Overall, we were able to see the differences ...

> Uses past tense

⚠️ **Active and Passive Voice in METHODS section** (review active and passive forms of verbs in Part I, Unit 5)

In the above example, the passive form of the verb was used throughout (e.g. *were dissected, was measured, was collected*). However, sometimes the description of the method may shift from the active to the passive form of the verb, depending on whether the emphasis is on the doer or the action, as shown in this description from a 1st year Psychology laboratory report:

Procedure:	
The 20 participants initially [1] completed a brief questionnaire that provided them with seven statements relating to empathy. Each participant then [2] gave a rating of one to five to each statement … This was done so participants could acquire their first empathy score. Following this, the participants [3] were put into pairs … Each pair [4] was given two scenarios relating to the recent Christchurch earthquake. Each participant in the pair [5] was given a different scenario in which they [6] took turns being the victim and interviewer.	[1] Active [2] Active [3] Passive [4] Passive [5] Passive [6] Active

In short reports, the RESULTS and DISCUSSION elements are highlighted, as shown in the following example from Psychology. Students undertake short experiments every two weeks and all that is required in the report are the findings and the discussion of the findings.

Example 2 (1st year Psychology: short laboratory report, using a prescribed template, reproduced from the student's report)

This report template provides specific guidelines. It is also clear from the marks and space allocation that the Discussion is the more significant element of the report. In general, the Discussion is expected to be significantly longer than the Results section.

(Write neatly within the boxes provided)

Please provide all information requested in this box for every laboratory assignment submitted for marking.
Name:
Laboratory Session:8
Full Name of Instructor:
Aim of Experiment: Mental Rotation and Verbal Fluency

RESULTS

Write a brief description of the main findings of the experiment in the space below (2 MARKS). You should also construct a table that summarises the results (1 MARK).

(Two tables precede the description)

The data from the mental rotation and verbal fluency tasks was processed using SPSS. The experiment showed that … This was due to … The results from the verbal fluency task showed a significant difference between …

DISCUSSION

Write a brief discussion of the results from the experiment in the space below. Your discussion should be about one page long. You must NOT EXCEED the space provided. (7 MARKS)

For the verbal fluency task, females obtained a significantly higher score than males. This result is consistent with … In contrast, our findings for the mental rotation task differed from …

A possible reason for this could be …

The experiments could have been improved if …

In summary, females outperformed males in verbal fluency tasks … but our results were inconsistent with previous findings … Further research in this area could include …

3.2 Research reports

A research report is a formal report written in the style of published academic papers. A research report is likely to have all the formal elements.

Example (3rd year Biological Sciences, on the 'Effects of Temperature Increase on Heart Rate in *C. Japonica'*). The style used in this report is explained by this note from the student:

> The lab report didn't actually have a topic/question. It was based on our 3 hour lab and we were just told to use relevant literature and write in the style of a scientific report our findings. We were to view it as writing a paper for a scientific journal.

Here is the outline of the report. The length of each section is indicated.

Title page	None
Title	Effects of Temperature Increase on Heart Rate in *C. Japonica*
Abstract	178 words
Introduction	360 words
Materials and methods	331 words
Results (with 4 figures)	330 words
Discussion	903 words
Concluding remarks	138 words
Total length	2042 words

In accordance with the conventions of scientific journal articles, this report includes an abstract.

An <u>abstract</u> is a descriptive summary. Usually written as a single paragraph and on a new page, an abstract is a short version of the report or research paper. It provides an overview of the main contents of the entire paper. The length of an abstract is usually about two-thirds of a page (between 3 and 8 per cent of the total length of the report).

You would normally write the abstract after completing the report. By then, you will be much clearer about what you have done, how you have done it and what you found out. However, the abstract is the first part of the report to be read. Therefore, it has an important function. It has to be concise and yet complete enough for the reader to understand the main content of your report.

Structure and Style

An abstract has the three basic elements of a standard essay structure: introduction, main body and conclusion:

Introduction	states briefly the precise aim of your investigation or proposal; may also establish significance or relevance of your research topic
Body	a) outlines briefly the method(s) and materials used
	b) summarises the main findings
Conclusion	establishes what was concluded; may also point to implications for further study.

Here is the abstract preceding the report on the effect of temperature increase on the heart rate of *C. japonica*. As you read, focus on the progression of ideas. (178 words – 8 per cent of the total report length)

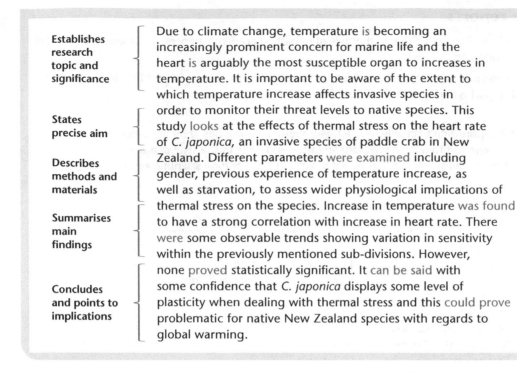

Establishes research topic and significance	Due to climate change, temperature is becoming an increasingly prominent concern for marine life and the heart is arguably the most susceptible organ to increases in temperature. It is important to be aware of the extent to which temperature increase affects invasive species in order to monitor their threat levels to native species. This
States precise aim	study looks at the effects of thermal stress on the heart rate of *C. japonica*, an invasive species of paddle crab in New
Describes methods and materials	Zealand. Different parameters were examined including gender, previous experience of temperature increase, as well as starvation, to assess wider physiological implications of thermal stress on the species. Increase in temperature was found
Summarises main findings	to have a strong correlation with increase in heart rate. There were some observable trends showing variation in sensitivity within the previously mentioned sub-divisions. However,
Concludes and points to implications	none proved statistically significant. It can be said with some confidence that *C. japonica* displays some level of plasticity when dealing with thermal stress and this could prove problematic for native New Zealand species with regards to global warming.

Note the highlighted tense changes

3.3 Technical reports

Technical reports are common in Engineering with different format requirements. Use the guidelines in the course handbook for the preferred report format. The example below is typical of engineering reports.

Example (2nd year Mechanical Engineering: a feasibility report)

This is a report on the viability of setting up a methanol plant. Figures and statistical information feature prominently, showing calculations of costs, production capacity, emissions levels and environmental impact.

Longer reports may also use a complex numbering system in the middle sections. This is an extract from the Table of contents page of the feasibility report:

2.0 Methods and materials
    2.1 Process line diagrams
    2.2 HAZOP study
3.0 Economic considerations
    3.1 Set-up costs
    3.2 Operational costs

Conclusions is written as a bulleted list and in the plural because it consists of a series of statements:

5.0 Conclusions
We think a methanol plant is commercially viable. It should break even after two years.
- There are large reserves of natural gas in the world. It can therefore be bought in bulk at low prices.
- Methanol is more expensive than natural gas, but with a production capacity of 200,000 tonnes, the annual revenue from selling methanol should be close to $87 million.

The report includes a <u>summary</u> on a separate page after the title page. A summary has the same purpose as an abstract. Structurally, there are some differences. The summary presented here seems to reflect disciplinary practice. It has to be of a specified length (about 300 words) with clear paragraphing.

Here is the full summary from the report. You can see that it has almost the same structural elements as an abstract, but there are some differences:

a) A summary is usually longer than an abstract.
b) It is organised into paragraphs like an essay.

SUMMARY

Establishes purpose

This report examines the issues involved in setting up a methanol plant with an output of 200,000 metric tonnes per year to determine its commercial viability including the environmental and operational impacts.

Uses present simple tense

Describes procedures, materials

A process line diagram for the system was first mapped using *Visio*. Technical drawings were made using *Autocard* of the main units: steam reformer, shift reactor, methanol reactor and distillation column. Qualitative calculations were made on the consumption, production and emission of some streams. Estimations of set-up costs were made using ... An environmental impact analysis and a HAZOP study were also conducted.

Uses past simple tense in the passive throughout

Weighs up findings and provides a decision

The environmental analysis shows that the main waste gases discharged from a methanol plant are hydrogen sulphide, carbon monoxide, carbon dioxide, methane and hydrogen. The calculations reveal the dangerous levels of each waste gas ... The HAZOP study reveals the effects of valve malfunction or rupture in the pipe inlets on liquid levels in the reactor ... In addition, thermal stress could also cause ruptures, so regular checking of the heat exchanger is recommended. The HAZOP study also reveals sources of contamination and corrosion ... Therefore, the study recommends the use of stainless steel to build the reactor.

Uses present simple tense and modal verbs

Provides a decision

Our estimates show that the cost of production is about $200 million. With a production capacity of 200,000 tonnes, the annual revenue from selling methanol should be about $87 million a year. Our conclusion is that the methanol plant is commercially viable. Revenue is expected to be quite high because there is a high demand for methanol, while the large yield of methanol in production also ensures less wastage and larger profits. (Total length: 309 words)

Uses present simple tense and modal verbs

UNIT 4 **Literature reviews**

A literature review brings together arguments from multiple sources to make a case for a research proposal or new investigation. It involves a thorough investigation and assessment of what has been written and researched on a topic. You may be asked to write literature reviews in your third or final year of study at university.

A literature review can be the assignment itself to establish a case for a research proposal or integrated into a research proposal assignment. In undergraduate writing, a literature review is more likely to be integrated into your research proposal. In this case, the review is guided by your research question or hypothesis (see Research proposals in Unit 5).

Literature review writing requires more than just summarising skills. It critically assesses arguments from various sources on the same subject. The key function is to establish if there is sufficient coverage of the subject you are investigating or if there is a gap in the literature that may be addressed by your research proposal or investigation.

The following diagram summarises the main features of literature reviews:

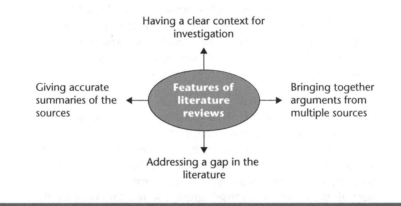

Structure and Style

A stand-alone literature review may be structured like a report (usually the IMRDC structure). A literature review in a research proposal may be structured like an essay with an introduction, the main body with several body paragraphs and a conclusion.

An important style feature is the tense of the verb which changes depending on whether the student is <u>reporting</u> the findings or <u>commenting</u> on them. Notice these changes in the examples below:

Example 1 (A stand-alone literature review from 2nd year Population Health)

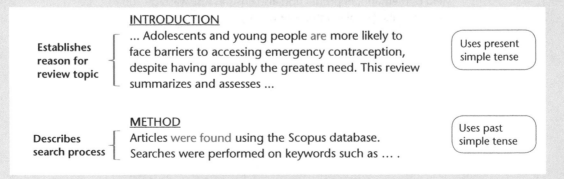

Presents findings under several headings	**RESULTS** There are two broad categories of barriers … . The first is … . The second is … .

Lack of knowledge about own risk of pregnancy
Some studies found that … . One study found that … (Johnson et al., 2010) … There was also a belief that … (Williamson et al., 2009).

> Uses the past simple tense

Comments on limitations and suggests areas for further research	**DISCUSSION** (includes conclusion) Studies in this review employed … Some used a quantitative approach … Although quantitative data … has limitations, … Some studies were biased. This is problematic because … More research is needed to …

> Uses past simple to report findings and the present simple to comment on them

Example 2 (A literature review as part of a research proposal assignment from 3rd year Psychology)

The literature review is the first section after the introduction. It is written to provide the rationale for a proposed study of the effects of background music on working memory in musicians and non-musicians. The student relates the review findings to her proposal.

Establishes the aim of the proposal future 'will'	… This study will use functional magnetic resonance imaging (fMRI) to test the hypotheses that background music has a greater negative effect on working memory in musicians than non-musicians, and that musicians display different patterns of neural activation when completing a working memory task compared to non-musicians.

> Uses future 'will'

Reviews findings of specific studies	British office workers in one recent sample were found to … (Haake, 2011). … Similarly, a large study of school and university students in several countries found that … (Kotsopoulou & Hallam, 2010). Research studies into the quantitative effect of background music on task performance and memory have also yielded mixed results. A study conducted in 1945 by … reported that … Hallam, Price and Katsarou (2002) found that playing 'calming' music …, while 'aggressive' music … decreased their scores.

> Uses past simple tense throughout

Points to significance of proposal	The use of fMRI in this proposed study will allow a far more in-depth comparison of … than a simple behavioural study … Schmithorst and Holland (2003) used fMRI to show that musicians and non-musicians employ different cognitive processes when attending to music. Several differences were observed, but the most relevant to this study is that … This study aims to determine whether … .

> Uses future' will and present simple tense

We finish this unit with a brief explanation of annotated bibliographies. Like a literature review, an annotated bibliography investigates what has been written on a specific subject area but it is usually a stand-alone assignment and there are differences in its overall presentation.

What is an annotated bibliography?

An annotated bibliography is an alphabetical list of academic sources with full bibliographic details like a reference list. The difference is it includes a short descriptive and evaluative paragraph (referred to as the 'annotation') which summarises the purpose and content of the source. The annotation is usually between 150 and 200 words.

What is expected?

The key function of an annotated bibliography is to provide a list of what is available in a given subject area and evaluate each source separately. The annotation shows evidence that you have read the source and examined it carefully.

It includes an evaluation of the quality and usefulness of the source. You may also point out similarities and differences between sources.

Whether the source is a journal article, a chapter from a book or the whole book, an annotation has the following elements:

1. Full citation details of source
2. Brief summary of source content
3. Description of general structure, methodology or approach and special features (e.g. glossary, appendices)
4. Evaluation of coverage, quality of arguments, approach and limitations
5. Significance or overall usefulness in relation to the topic

Sample entry (2nd year Anthropology; actual length: 190 words) The student is required to compile an annotated bibliography consisting of five sources investigating methods for determining the origin of various artefacts.

Gives full citation details (Harvard style)	Neves, W.A., Gonzalez-Jose, R., Hubbe, M., Kipnis, R., Araujo, A., and Blasi, O., 2004. Early Holocene human skeletal remains from Cerca Grande, Lagoa Santa, Central Brazil, and the origins of the first Americans. *World archaeology*, 36(4) pp. 479–501.
Summarises content	This article looks at the crania morphology of some of the earliest settlers of the South America found in ...
Describes method or approach	They do this by comparing the skeletons of human ...
Describes findings or arguments	They found that the skeletons showed a relation to Africans, Asians, Australians and Easter Islanders. This showed that they are not like Native Americans and probably did not ..., thus supporting the multiple crossings model for settlement of the Americas.
Evaluates quality and usefulness	A minor problem with this research is that they used ... It does not account for environmental impacts that may have affected the gene pools of these earlier populations upon entry into the America's.
Compares with another entry	Like the study by ..., this study focuses on similar morphological characteristics not genetic DNA lineage or ecological impacts.

Notice the highlighted tense changes

Variation: In some annotated bibliography assignments, you may be specifically asked to identify a number of concepts for each source and extract a sentence or quotation from the source text that illustrates each concept. The annotation will include a brief discussion of how the text relates to the concept and/or quotation.

UNIT 5 **Research proposals**

In your third or final year of undergraduate study, you may be asked to submit a research proposal on a topic related to your course. You will need to establish a clear purpose for your proposal. This involves stating at least one research question, which is a statement of what you expect to find.

A research proposal assignment includes detailed planning and methodology and persuasive argumentation. More specifically, it tests your ability to

- undertake and design a complete piece of research
- formulate specific research questions to focus your research
- relate your topic to theory and other similar research
- justify your proposed study
- suggest your study's contribution to the generation of new knowledge and understanding
- design a clear methodology.

The following diagram summarises features of research proposals:

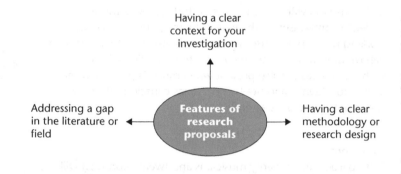

Structure and Style

A research proposal has structural elements found in reports, but there is some variation in terms of emphasis and tense use. A research proposal is approached differently from a research or laboratory report, particularly in the Methods, Results and Discussion sections. In particular, you will notice the use of the future 'will' to establish aim and 'could', 'may', 'likely to', 'expected to', or 'hope to' to explain proposed procedures and expected results and conclusions.

<u>Basic structural elements:</u>

Title page	may not be required
Abstract	usually not required in undergraduate research proposals
Introduction	provides relevant background information and theoretical framework and explains research question or hypothesis
Literature review	establishes a gap in the area to be addressed by your proposal
Research design	describes procedures for data gathering and analysis
Discussion	discusses expected findings
Conclusion	establishes the contribution of proposed research

Example (3rd year Psychology; Length: 2775 words).

This research proposal uses headings for the Method and Discussion sections. The conclusion is included in Discussion. The length of each section is provided to indicate how the student has constructed the research report. Notice the highlighted tense shifts, particularly the use of the future aspect ('will') and modal verbs ('would', 'could') to express an opinion or make a suggestion.

Introduction

States the hypotheses (157 words)

… This study will use functional magnetic resonance imaging (fMRI) to test the hypotheses that background music has a greater negative effect on working memory in musicians than non-musicians, and that musicians display different patterns of neural activation when completing a working memory task compared to non-musicians.

> Uses future 'will'

Literature review

Summarises findings of past studies (511 words)

British office workers in one recent sample were found to … (Haake, 2011) … Similarly, a large study of school and university students in several countries found …

> Uses past simple tense

Identifies a gap

… The use of fMRI in this proposed study allows a more in-depth comparison of the effect of background music on working memory in musicians and non-musicians than a simple behavioural study … The study aims to determine whether such differences are also present when music is playing in the background while another task occupies conscious attention, and is not deliberately attended to.

> Uses present simple tense

Methods

Provides details of the research design, parameters, and how the data will be analysed (1424 words)

Participants
Forty participants (twenty musicians and twenty controls) will participate in this research.

Stimuli
The three background auditory stimuli will be …

Experimental design
A change-detection task consisting of four components will be used to test working memory in this study. An example of this change-detection task is shown in Figure 1 below (not included here) In each trial, participants will first view a display featuring nine shapes arranged in a 3 x 3 invisible grid. The display will be viewed for one second then erased. In the Fixation sequence, the participant will fixate on a cross … After three seconds, a test display featuring two shapes, labelled 1 and 2, will be shown for one second … When the test display disappears, the participant will respond by pressing a buzzer … There will be a five-second rest period before the next trial …

> Uses future 'will' throughout to describe or proposed method (see options on the next page)

Pre-processing
Image pre-processing will be performed using …

Data analysis
Behavioural data will consist of …

Discussion

Suggests value of proposed study

This study will make a valuable contribution to … As yet, no published research has used fMRI to show … Given the mixed results of behavioural studies in this area, and the poor spatial resolution of EEG, this fMRI study could be instrumental in determining … Furthermore, no published studies have explicitly compared …

Uses modal verbs and language of possiiblity

Discusses expected findings against hypothesis

If the hypothesis that musicians are more negatively affected by background music than non-musicians is correct, then we can expect to see significant differences between musicians and non-musicians in the music condition, but not necessarily in the white noise and silence conditions. It is also possible that …, which would suggest that they are more affected by background sound in general than non-musicians. A significantly lower mean accuracy in the musician group … would support this hypothesis.

Conclusion

Summarises contributions and implications of proposed study (147 words)

Overall, it is hoped that this study will help to clarify current knowledge about the effects of background music on memory. Specifically, the use of fMRI will allow … This new information could lead to … The comparison of musicians and non-musicians aims firstly to …, but also to determine whether musical training should be taken into account in future studies into auditory distraction and memory. Practically, if significant behavioural differences are noted, this study could encourage …

Uses future 'will' and modal verbs

⚠ **Tense use variation:** In this proposal, use of the future 'will' (in both active and passive forms) is predominant. However, the present simple tense (in both active and passive forms) can be used in the Methods section to describe how the design works, e.g. 'In each trial, participants first **view** … The display **is viewed** for one second … Image pre-processing **is performed** using …'

REVIEW

Understanding different types of writing for university enables you to employ structure and style that is appropriate for the type of assignment.

Writing is a thinking process. Review the six steps to effective writing explained in Part I, Unit 3 to help you read an assignment question and plan a correct and relevant response.

The annotations that accompany all the examples explain the purpose of the different structural elements that are unique to a particular type of assignment.

The highlighted words in the main text point to the explicit use of cohesive devices and other expressions that ensure coherence and clarity of development.

Part III

Developing Your Writing

Developing your writing is the <u>composing</u> or <u>building</u> stage of the writing process. Structuring, organising and extending ideas are key aspects. Here, you think about the most effective way to

- introduce the topic of the assignment question,
- expand the topic further in the main body, and
- end the discussion with a logical conclusion.

Part III examines techniques for building ideas in different parts of your writing. Most of the examples relate to essays. In academic contexts, developing your writing also involves supporting your ideas with evidence from research, course knowledge and theory. The practice of citing evidence gives your writing an academic quality and credibility. Review the conventions for using sources in your writing in Part I, Unit 2.

Main topics

Unit 1 Aspects of development

Unit 2 Methods of organisation

Unit 3 Introductions and conclusions

Unit 4 Paragraph structure and construction

Unit 5 Techniques for developing your writing

Most of the extracts of student writing are presented in their original form. Omissions or changes in the original texts are indicated by three dots.

UNIT 1 Aspects of development

A well-developed piece of writing has

- **logical organisation.** This means the progression of ideas <u>makes sense</u> to the reader. It is achieved by using an organisational method which fits the assignment question. Some organisational methods are described in the next unit.
- **effective development of ideas.** This involves building support for the topic in several body paragraphs by applying some principles of paragraph construction and using appropriate development techniques. Each technique advances the topic in a specific way and increases the reader's understanding.

Considering these two aspects of development gives you control over the writing process, because you will have a clearer idea of how you are going to construct an effective response to the assignment question.

How do these two aspects work together?

In the two examples below, the outlines are created from the headings used in the essays. Each outline shows clearly the method used for the overall <u>organisation</u> of the main topics and the technique used for the <u>development</u> of the body paragraphs.

Example 1 (1st year Film and Media Studies, discussing the effect of digital technologies on the form and style of film-making)

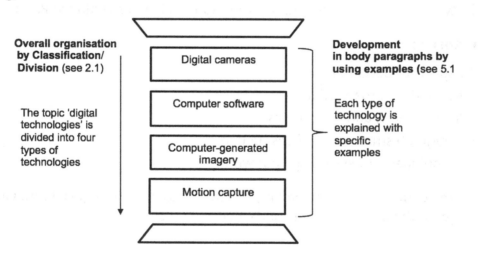

Example 2 (3rd year Sociology essay, reflecting on how <u>similar or different</u> the Expert Advisory Group's (EAG) view on child poverty is compared to those of National Governments (NG) in the 1990s)

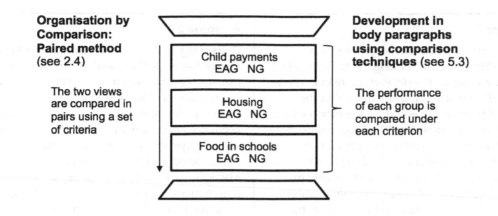

Organisation by Comparison: Paired method (see 2.4)

The two views are compared in pairs using a set of criteria

Child payments
EAG   NG

Housing
EAG   NG

Food in schools
EAG   NG

Development in body paragraphs using comparison techniques (see 5.3)

The performance of each group is compared under each criterion

Selecting the organisational method: why does it matter?

Selecting an organisational method that suits the assignment question is important because it shows that you have understood the purpose of the writing task. In some assignment questions, the main topics and the logical order are already given in the question.

Example In the assignment question below, the three questions following the first sentence explain what is expected in the instruction word 'discuss'. Topic divisions are suggested including the order they could be discussed in. You do not have to break down the subject-matter yourself. Your main concern will be setting out the topics clearly and developing the content for the question:

> Discuss the operation of the 'Propaganda Model' (Herman & Chomsky, 2002) in New Zealand. What are the main features of the propaganda model, generated through the five filters, for New Zealand audiences? How effective is the propaganda model in serving vested interests? How effective are efforts to 'decode' this propaganda? (Sociology)

However, some assignment questions are not as explicitly written. You have to decide WHAT to include and HOW to approach the assignment, as these questions show:

> Is gender equality simply a matter of treating women the same as men? (1st year Political Studies)
>
> Is caffeine a drug of abuse? (2nd year Health Sciences)
>
> Drawing on theory, themes, and examples from the course, critically discuss what social justice in education might mean for schooling and education in [your country] today? (2nd year Education)

In short answer questions, it is even more important to use a suitable organisational method to develop your answer. It could be the difference between a pass and a fail mark. Read the two responses to this short-answer Management assignment question: 'What is the connection between leadership and management?' In your view, which response answers the question? Why?

Response 1	Response 2
Drucker argues that the emergence of the 'knowledge worker' has made the task of leading and not managing people even more important. First of all, leadership may be defined as the potential to influence and drive the group efforts towards the accomplishment of goals by building an environment in which every employee can excel and develop. It involves establishing a clear vision for the company. Effective leaders are able to … Leaders facilitate … Strong leadership requires … Secondly, management is the function that coordinates the efforts of people to accomplish organisational goals by … More specifically, management is concerned with … Thus, organisations need both managers and leaders.	Drucker argues that the emergence of the 'knowledge worker' has made the task of leading and not managing people even more important. Leadership and management are distinct concepts but they are necessarily linked. A healthy organisational culture needs both managers and leaders. Both leadership and management are essential for individual and organisational success … Leaders facilitate … Managers work with leaders … In poorly performing organisations, the relationship between leaders and managers breaks down when leaders fail to articulate a clear vision. Organisations which are over-managed and under-led do not perform up to the benchmark. Therefore, organisations need both leaders and managers to be successful.

How did you do? Compare your thoughts with these comments:

In short-answer assignments, a concise response that directly addresses the theme or central idea of the question is more likely to receive a higher or pass mark. Choosing an appropriate organisational method is critical to producing a relevant answer.

Response 1 uses a separate method of organisation (see Unit 2.4). This means it discusses one item completely before turning to the next, as indicated by the use logical connectors of sequence (e.g. *first of all, secondly*). Its focus is on defining WHAT each one is and does. It fails to address the theme or central idea of the question, which is the connection between them.

Response 2 uses a paired method, examining both together to show HOW the two concepts are connected. The key terms are mentioned together (e.g. 'Leadership and management … Managers work with leaders'). Response 2 adequately addresses the central idea of the question.

UNIT 2   Methods of organisation

Key methods

2.1 Classification or division

2.2 Logical enquiry

2.3 Chronology

2.4 Separate and paired methods

In Part II, Unit 3, we looked at spatial organisation in relation to visual analysis essays. This unit examines four organisational methods used in other types of writing. These methods organise information topically rather than in order of space and location.

2.1 Classification or division

This method involves breaking a subject down into workable units by classifying or dividing it into types or categories and discussing each one in a systematic manner. It is often used in analytical essays, which involve close examination of a topic by breaking it down into smaller components. In terms of language and style, the progression from one category or type to the next may be signalled explicitly by using sequence markers (such as *the first, secondly, finally, a final point, another, also, the latest, the most recent*).

How does the method work?

Some assignment questions lend themselves easily to classification or division.

Example (1st year Film and Media Studies, discussing the effect of digital technologies on the form and style of film-making)

This sentence from the introduction tells the reader that the student is using classification to discuss the topic: 'Digital technologies such as cameras, computer generated image (CGI) and motion capture are transforming many aspects of film production as we move deeper into the twenty-first century.' Here are the opening sentences of the four body paragraphs, each of which introduces a type of digital technology:

Logical connectors show the progression from one technology to the next.

With the proliferation of digital cameras and software from the mid-1990s, distinctive changes within film form and style have taken place (Willis 3). The portability of digital cameras has revolutionised film-making.

Another digital technology that has significant impact is computer editing software. The most visible advantage is the reduction in production costs.

The proliferation of digital software has also led to many innovations such as computer generated imagery (CGI). [...] CGI has allowed for the transcendence from reality into hyper-reality.

One of the newest digital technologies successfully used is Motion Capture. It is the acquirement of a live actor's performance by digitally filming the actor's body.

1. (Text from 1st year Comparative Literature, examining different representations of power and power relationships in reading texts covered in the course)

Read the opening sentences (topic sentences) of four body paragraphs and complete the following tasks:

- In two or three words, identify the type of power relationship for each sentence.
- Underline any sequence markers used to move from one type to the next.

Types of power relationships

The belief that men are superior to women and therefore more powerful is clearly evident in a number of texts studied.

Political and institutional power is also represented in texts we have studied in a number of ways.

Ethnic groups are often oppressed and stigmatized in societies in the same ways that women are.

Another power relationship of interest represented in the texts is that between humans and nature.

2. (2nd year Education, arguing that socio-economic factors have an impact on educational attainment)

Read these topic sentences of the four body paragraphs. Complete the diagram on the right to show the classification of socio-economic factors:

Parsons (1959) sees school as a place of socialization, where children are trained to fulfil certain roles and structures of society.

Bowles and Gintis (1976) were seen as far more radical than Parsons. They believed that education was directly correlated to the way a capitalist society is organised.

Gramsci (1971) and Bourdieu (1986) looked at the way in which culture can impact educational attainment.

Apple (1982) looked at the political power teachers can have in a classroom.

Complete the diagram below:

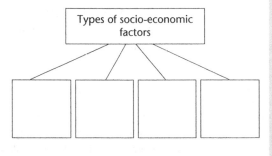

Types of socio-economic factors

Starting the topic sentence of each paragraph with the names of the researchers may remove the need for sequence connectors, as is the case here. However, if you wish to focus on the socio-economic factors, you may need to use sequence connectors to provide a smooth progression. In the revised text below, three sequence markers are highlighted:

A significant influence on educational attainment is the institution of learning itself. According to Parsons (1959), the school is a place of socialisation where children are socialised into fulfilling certain roles and structures of society. Another radical idea is that education is directly related to the way a society is organised. Bowles and Gintis (1976) believed that ... Culture can also have an impact on educational attainment. Finally, the teachers can have a powerful influence on children's perceptions of and belief in their ability to achieve educational success.

2.2 Logical enquiry

Logical enquiry uses a questioning approach. This method is useful for essays that require discussion, exploration and examination of complex subject matter, and in which you have to generate your content focus.

The method involves asking questions about a topic logically and with increasing complexity, progressing

- from **knowledge** questions (WHAT, WHO, WHERE and WHEN) in the early paragraphs
- to more **analytical** questions (HOW and WHY) in the middle paragraphs to explain how ideas relate to each other and to the thesis and essay question.

Each level of enquiry adds to the reader's understanding of the topic.

How does the method work?

Example (2nd year Political Studies, responding to this question: 'Is gender equality simply a matter of treating women the same as men?')

By applying logical enquiry, the student is able to identify the main issues of the topic in a systematic manner. The process below shows how the method is used to generate ideas and questions around the focus topic. Before writing begins, the questions are arranged in a logical order from knowledge to analytical questions:

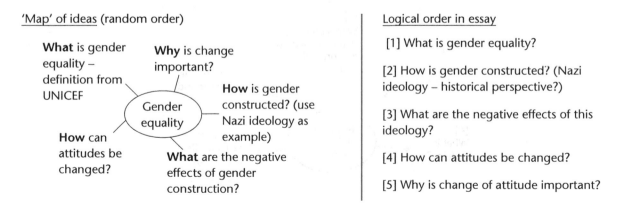

'Map' of ideas (random order)

What is gender equality – definition from UNICEF

Why is change important?

How is gender constructed? (use Nazi ideology as example)

Gender equality

How can attitudes be changed?

What are the negative effects of gender construction?

Logical order in essay

[1] What is gender equality?

[2] How is gender constructed? (Nazi ideology – historical perspective?)

[3] What are the negative effects of this ideology?

[4] How can attitudes be changed?

[5] Why is change of attitude important?

1. (3rd year Political Studies essay, examining this topic: 'The State of Food Security: Sources and Solutions'). It illustrates the use of the questioning approach of logical enquiry to generate a comprehensive description of the state of food security.

Write an appropriate question word against each main heading: WHO, WHAT, WHY, HOW. You may need to repeat one of the question words

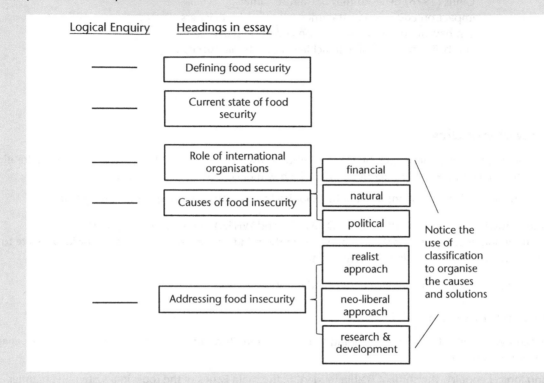

2. (2nd year Health Science, exploring if caffeine is a drug of abuse)

This 'map' of questions shows the application of logical enquiry in the initial stages of writing:

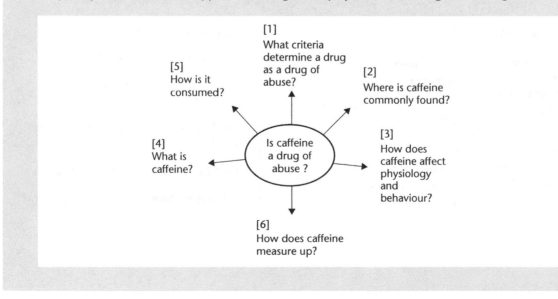

Below is an outline of the main headings used in the essay. Match the headings in the main body of the essay to the 6 questions in the map above:

Introduction

Source and consumption   Questions [ ][ ]

Properties of caffeine   Question [ ]

Physiological and behavioural effects   Question [ ]

Criteria for drug abuse classification   Question [ ]

Is caffeine a drug of abuse?   Question [ ]

Conclusion

2.3 Chronology

This method organises information in order of time and sequence. A chronological organisation would be relevant for assignment questions asking you to trace and assess changes in events, opinion or trends over a period of time. The method is therefore characterised by the use of verb tenses (notably past and present simple tenses and the present perfect – see the chart of English tenses in *Appendix B*), time expressions (*5 minutes later, after, in the 1990s*) and sequence markers (*the first step, finally*).

In the following questions, for example, the present perfect 'has changed' and words such as 'trends' suggest that a chronological method would be suitable.

> How <u>has</u> immigration <u>changed</u> attitudes towards an understanding of race? (History)
>
> Consider how the focus of healthcare workers <u>has changed</u> over time from treating and curing infectious diseases to managing chronic conditions. (Population Health)
>
> Discuss issues and trends in Nursing. (Nursing)

How does the method work?

Example 1 (2nd year Population Health Studies)

The first question of a two-part assignment asks the student to consider how the focus of healthcare <u>has changed</u> over time from treating and curing infectious diseases to managing chronic conditions.

Read this extract from the first two body paragraphs of the essay which address the first question.

The present perfect (has/have + *ed* verb) is used throughout to track changes from the past to the present.

For many years, the focus of healthcare has centred on diagnosing and curing communicable diseases, but in recent years this has moved to focus more on managing chronic conditions due to a rapid increase in the prevalence of chronic illnesses ... This change has come about due to ... (Yach et al., 2004).

New medical knowledge and technology has dramatically increased life expectancy and has contributed to an ageing population ... The frequency and severity of chronic conditions increase with age and this has caused a significant increase in ... This medical knowledge has also allowed people with chronic illnesses to live longer.

Example 2 (1st year History, discussing how immigration has changed attitudes towards understandings of race)

The question suggests a cause and effect relationship between immigration and changes in understandings of race. However, the student uses a chronological organisational method to track the changes in attitudes over time. The following opening sentences of each body paragraph link an attitude change to a particular time or event in history:

Time expressions (highlighted) and the past tense (underlined) track the changes in each period of history.

Racial tensions undoubtedly <u>increased</u> with the coming of immigrants to both New Zealand and American shores throughout the nineteenth and twentieth centuries in search of employment opportunities.

Throughout the nineteenth century America <u>experienced</u> great waves of immigrants from many various nations. This brought people that were similar, and often even visually indistinguishable from the long-settled Americans ... The need to create difference ... <u>gave</u> rise to 'scientific racism' in the 1900s.

Understandings of race <u>changed</u> as immigration <u>intersected</u> with the World Wars of the twentieth century. During the First World War, from 1914 to 1918, and the Second World War, from 1939 to 1945, suspicions and fears surrounding immigrants <u>were</u> greatly <u>intensified</u>.

In the post-war years, the most noticeable change in understandings of race, as a result of immigration, <u>was</u> the rise of nativism.

PRACTICE ACTIVITY 2.3

(2nd year Nursing discussing issues and trends).

A chronological method is used to organise the discussion of issues and trends in nursing and to argue that the current stereotypical image is perpetuated by the media. Follow the progression of ideas by completing these activities:

a) Identify some time expressions in the introduction that support the use of the chronological method.

b) Follow the chronological organisation by matching a heading from the options below to a body paragraph, numbered 1–4.

| 'Mother' era | Current status | Media image | 'Sex object' era |

Introduction	Over the last sixty years, the image of nursing has changed dramatically depending on the social, economic and political influences of the time period ...
Body 1	Although it is quite contrary to the nurses' professional role, the nursing profession has often been sexualised and this perception is consistently presented by the media. A modern cartoon illustrates this clearly.

Body 2

According to Warren et al. (1998), two major historical periods, the 'Mother' era and the 'Sex Object' era, ... have largely impacted the public perception of the role and image of the nurse. In 1820, Florence Nightingale ...

Body 3

The sexualised image of the nurse has historical origins from the mid to the late 1900s.

Body 4

There are many current factors that also create perceptions such as those shown in the cartoon. To many members of the general public, nurses are still seen as subordinate to doctors.

Conclusion

Although these stereotypical perceptions are still present, the nursing role is increasingly valued as a worthy career ...

2.4 Separate and paired methods

These methods are relevant for assignments which analyse differences and similarities, explain causes and effects and present for and against arguments. The <u>separate</u> method (referred to in some books as the 'block' method) involves discussing one item or aspect completely – in a block of paragraphs – and then turning to the next item.

The <u>paired</u> method (referred to in some books as the 'point-by-point' method) involves discussing the items together in the same paragraph, using a list of common criteria or standards to judge their performance or significance.

Sample assignment questions

Comparison-contrast assignments:

Using close reading and research, compare the ways in which *The Last Samurai* and *Gosford Park* use historical setting to comment on contemporary issues. (2nd year Film, Television and Media Studies)

Compare and contrast these two documents, noting how they frame the 'problem' in different ways and how this leads to different policy 'solutions'. (3rd year Sociology)

Regarding the still-tense situation in Georgia, how do US and European aims on the one hand differ from those of Russia on the other? (2nd year Political Studies)

Compare the opening paragraphs of two texts in terms of the speaker/writer's voice, language and stance or attitude toward the scene, topic, or subject'. (1st year English)

Cause-effect assignments:

How has capitalism led to mass surveillance of the work force? (1st year Sociology)

Discuss the effect of climate change on the marine eco-systems of Antarctica. (1st year Biological Sciences)

How do the methods work?

Separate and paired methods may be represented in the following diagram:

Separate (block)		**Paired (point-by-point)**	
Item 1	**Item 2**	**Criteria**	**Item 1 and Item 2**
Point 1	Point 1	Point 1	⟶
Point 2	Point 2	Point 2	⟶
Point 3	Point 3	Point 3	⟶

The method you choose will affect the overall structure and style of the essay as shown in the following example:

Example (1st year English short assignment: '<u>Compare</u> the opening paragraphs of two texts in terms of the speaker/writer's voice, language and stance or attitude toward the scene, topic, or subject')

Separate method: The texts are discussed in <u>separate</u> paragraphs.

Text 1: voice and style — In terms of voice, Bohannon uses first-person singular pronouns to suggest she is retelling a personal experience. Bohannon's narrative style stresses the ways in which language affects cultural understanding. She gives dialogue privilege within her text, allowing her to better convey the importance language has in relation to various cultures.

Text 2: voice and style — Park, however, primarily uses first-person plural pronouns to show he is reporting a shared perspective. Park's use of plural pronouns encourages the reader to engage with the text's issues as they are reported. Park's text details the effects British colonisation had on Maori life and culture. Park's text primarily reports events and can be read as a monologue.

> A single contrast marker introduces the comparison

Paired method: <u>Both</u> texts are compared in the <u>same</u> paragraph on one point of comparison. More contrast markers are required to make the comparison clearer.

<u>First point of comparison:</u> Voice Texts 1 and 2 compared — Bohannon uses first-person singular pronouns to suggest she is retelling a personal experience. Park, however, primarily uses first-person plural pronouns to show he is reporting a shared perspective. Bohannon's choice of singular pronouns and narrative allows the reader to follow the narrative as she experienced it. By contrast, Park's use of plural pronouns encourages the reader to engage with the text's issues from a cultural perspective, as they are reported.

<u>Second point of comparison:</u> Style Texts 1 and 2 compared — The two texts also differ in the way the writers' narrative style, which reflects the writer's attitude on the issues. Bohannon employs a narrative style and dialogue to stress the ways in which language affects cultural understanding while Park's text details the effects British colonisation had on Maori life and culture. Park's text primarily reports events and can be read as a monologue.

> Contrast markers show how the discussion turns first to one text and then to the other on the same point

Which method works better: separate or paired?

In short assignments which deal with less complex or fewer points of comparison or causes, discussing the information separately is acceptable. In longer essays, however, a separate organisational method is less effective because the writing can be <u>too descriptive</u> and the comparisons can become less clear to the reader as the writing progresses.

Related considerations:

1. <u>Order</u>: You may also consider arranging the comparison points or causes and effects according to their significance or severity.
2. <u>Emphasis</u>: In comparison-contrast assignments, for example, if there are more differences than similarities, you might discuss the similarities first followed by the differences. Most academic essays requiring causal analysis emphasise both causes and effects. However, in some assignments you may investigates single cause and its effects. For example, in a report of a case-control study from a 3rd year Population Health report, the student focuses on the risk factors or causes of coronary heart disease. In a Biological Science study, the student investigates the effects of temperature on the heart rate of a crab species in different settings. In these studies, the causes or effects could be organised by order of significance or severity.

PRACTICE ACTIVITY 2.4

1. (3rd year Political Studies essay, discussing the attributes of a political leader in relation to the performance of two recent prime ministers)

Study the <u>topic outline</u> below, which is derived from the body paragraphs.

Attribute 1:	Party leadership and national leadership. PM 1 and PM 2 compared in the same paragraph (*PM 1 is/has ... On the other hand, PM 2 ...*)
Attribute 2:	Ambition, political acumen and stamina PM 1 and PM 2 compared in the same paragraph (*PM 1 is/has ... PM 2, however, showed ...*)
Attribute 3:	Ruthless courage and judgement PM 1 and PM 2 compared in the same paragraph
Attribute 4:	Vision PM 1 and PM 2 compared in the same paragraph
Attribute 5:	Management skills PM 1 and PM 2 compared in the same paragraph
Attribute 6:	Media image PM 1 and PM 2 compared in the same paragraph

Which method is used to organise the comparison? ☐ Separate ☐ Paired

2. (From 1st year Asian Studies, comparing and contrasting the Western influence on education in Tokugawa and Meiji Japan and the effects this had on the society as a whole)

Read the opening sentences of the first five body paragraphs which compare the Western influence on the education system of the two regimes:

---

[1] Throughout the majority of the Tokugawa period, Japan resided in virtual isolation from the outside world (Meyer, 2009, p. 109). [2] After Tokugawa Japan withdrew into seclusion from the outside world, the artificial island of *Dejima* remained Japan's only regular contact with Europe for over two centuries. [3] During the later Tokugawa years, many educational institutions turned to European ideas. [4] In 1868 the Tokugawa Shogunate was overthrown, and the emperor, known as Meiji, was restored to power. [5] In 1871, with the formation of the Ministry of Education in Japan, the Meiji oligarchy instigated a program of educational reform (Meyer, 2009, p. 159), adopting a western-influenced education system.

a) Which method is used to organise the comparison of the two regimes?
   □ Separate □ Paired
b) Which sentence begins the contrast section of the comparison? _____

3. (Post-graduate Political Studies on 'The State of Food Security: Problems and Solutions')

This is a long essay (close to 3000 words). Read the cause-effect development under the heading 'Causes of food security'. Are the causes and effects discussed together (paired method) under the same heading or separately? _____

Causes of food insecurity
Financial

The financial cause of food insecurity has two dimensions; poverty, and the price of food. ... Poverty causes an inability to purchase food, and limits a country's ability to invest in enhanced food production, creating a self-reinforcing cycle. Even small increases can have significant effects on poverty levels.

Natural

Natural disasters and extreme weather events are often direct causes of food insecurity. Drought is the underlying cause of the ongoing famine in East Africa; ... Other natural disasters also impact food security; in 2010 fires ... Climate change will play an increasingly important role in food security as world temperatures continue to rise ... Climate change is also likely to increase the number of extreme weather events, which will destroy crop harvests and fertile land.

Political

Military conflict, political instability, and economic embargos can create food insecurity .... Armed conflict in the Horn of Africa has physically disrupted farming activities ... The civil war in Somalia caused its food production to drop by a third ... In Libya, the civil war of 2011 disrupted local farming activities and restricted imports of food through its ports.

UNIT 3 **Introductions and conclusions**

Key topics

3.1 The role of introductions and conclusions
3.2 Some common problems

3.3 A model for constructing introductions
3.4 A model for constructing conclusions

One of the challenges of writing is beginning the essay or report because you think you are constructing something from nothing. Ending the essay or report can also be challenging because you feel you are just repeating the same information. This unit describes models for constructing effective introductions and conclusions that reflect their respective functions in a piece of extended writing.

In terms of length, the general guideline is to allocate about 8–10 per cent of the total essay or report length each to the introduction and the conclusion. You will notice that some of the conclusions included in this unit are well below this guideline. Some conclusions are shorter than the introduction. This could be due to practices in the subject area. Nevertheless, the percentage is a useful guideline. A very short introduction or conclusion (under 4 or 5 per cent of the total length, for example) could indicate that it has not adequately fulfilled its purpose at the beginning or end of the essay.

3.1 Role of introductions and conclusions

What does the introduction do?

- A good introduction provides the reader with an entry into the essay.
- It makes clear to the reader <u>why</u> you are exploring a topic and tells the reader <u>what</u> specific aspects to expect.
- An effective introduction has the key function of aiding understanding by establishing a relevant <u>context</u> or setting for discussion in the body of the essay.

What does the conclusion do?

- The conclusion is just as important as the introduction because the reader needs to experience a <u>logical ending</u> and <u>a sense of completeness</u> to the discussion.
- The conclusion is your last chance to show the reader that you have answered the assignment question. It could make a difference to the final assignment grade.
- The content of the conclusion is derived from the ideas discussed in the main body of the essay or report.
- It DOES NOT add new ideas. Its function is to remind the reader of the main arguments raised by summarising and critically reviewing them.

Example (1st year Music, writing a response to a musical composition)

The introduction and conclusion paragraphs in this critique of the third movement of Webern's String Quartet op.5 are short but they are concise and appropriate to the narrow focus of the assignment and type of essay. More significantly, the way they are written clearly shows the student's understanding of their respective functions.

The third movement of Webern's *String Quartet op.5* explores the notion of musical time and defies the classical presumption that music must have harmonic progression to define a clear trajectory. Webern instead creates this trajectory through the use of counterpoint in structure, pitch organisation, timbre and rhythm.

Provides immediate entry into musical piece

Explains composer's style

Identifies specific aspects or techniques (gives scope)

Conclusion

In just 23 bars, Webern defines an atonal harmonic language and uses it as a springboard from which to explore ideas of musical time and create forward motion without traditional harmonic or melodic progressions. It is the counterpoint between intervallic cells, rhythmic motifs, timbres and sections that gives this movement its drive and clear trajectory. Atonality provided new dimensions of musical expression in the twentieth century, characterised by expanded use of new tone colours and extended techniques.

Reviews style and techniques with evaluative language

Reminds reader of the key aspects

The end sentence places the composition in a larger context (points to the influence of atonality on musical expression)

3.2 Some common problems

Essay introductions: two problems

Problem 1 The introduction is <u>too short</u>. A short introduction may not provide sufficient background information to help the reader understand the topic and issues involved completely.

Problem 2 The introduction focuses on <u>telling the reader what the essay is about</u> (scope element).

Example (2nd year Education, on the ideas of Paulo Freire; about 4 per cent of total length)

> Paulo Freire was a Brazilian educator who was most well-known for his idea that education was never neutral and always political. I will introduce and critically evaluate three of Freire's main ideas, which are the 'banking concept' of education, praxis and conscientisation. I will then explain how he believed education had the power to transform society because Freire believed education could serve as an instrument of either oppression or liberation.

More background information is needed to understand the words 'never neutral and always political' in the opening sentence. For example, some explanation about Paulo Freire and the times he lived in would help the reader understand why he saw a link between education and politics.

Essay conclusions: three problems

Problem 1 The conclusion is <u>too similar</u> to the introduction. This is problematic because their respective roles in a piece of writing are not defined clearly.

Example (1st year Geography, examining the associated processes of production and consumption, using the example of sweatshops)

You can see that the same expression and statements (highlighted here) appear in both the conclusion and the introduction.

Conclusion	Introduction
It is clear that the geographies of production and consumption are associated. These processes can be clearly examined using the example of sweatshops, as well as examining the corporations which use sweatshops. Throughout the course of this essay, the geographies of production and consumption, individually, have been examined using sweatshops to illustrate these processes. Because of the interlinked nature of both production and consumption, the influences these two processes have on each other have also been examined and numerous arguments have been presented. The associated nature of production and consumption as well as the relation of these processes to sweatshops is clear.	The geographies of production and consumption, as well as their associated nature, can be clearly examined through the example of sweatshops. Although consumption has long been regarded in geography as the endpoint of the production cycle, it is now widely acknowledged that both processes operate in a system and cannot be separated from each other. Through this lens and by using the example of sweatshops, the processes of production and consumption will be discussed. This essay will then examine several different perspectives on how production and consumption influence each other.

Problem 2 The conclusion consists of <u>general</u> and <u>vague</u> statements that do not remind the reader of the key issues.

Example 1 (1st year Geography)

These sentences from the conclusion are too vague:

    a) It is clear that the geographies of production and consumption are associated.
    b) The associated nature of production and consumption as well as the relation to sweatshops is clear.

Instead, it would be more useful to state exactly what is clear about the associated nature of consumption and production:

    Production and consumption are essential economic activities. The primary function of production is to ... The primary function of consumption is to ...

Example 2 (1st year History, examining to what extent Japan's modernisation following the Meiji restoration was an imitation of Western developments; about 5 per cent of the total length)

Following the Meiji restoration, the Japanese did appear to imitate Western developments to some extent. Closer examination, however, reveals that for the most part, these developments were carefully selected and adopted to suit the purposes of the Japanese government. Periods of indiscriminate imitation were limited both in time and scope and were followed by a return to emphasis on Japanese values and identity. As a result, Japan successfully used Western developments to become a modernised nation and avoid colonisation by the West while retaining its own identity and values.

> Which specific developments? What limits exactly?

Problem 3 The conclusion is too short

Example (1st year Comparative Literature, examining diverse power relationships in texts studied; about 3 per cent of the total length)

As mentioned earlier, one of the functions of the conclusion is to remind the reader of the main points or arguments raised. The conclusion below is too short to fulfil this function successfully.

The relationships of power within the text studied for this course are extensive and various. They are usually represented in terms of the power of one over the other, or in terms of resistance to that power.

In addition, the words 'extensive' and 'various' are too general and vague. Instead, remind the reader what the power relationships are.

3.3 A model for constructing introductions

So how do you construct effective introductions and conclusion? The model below displays the key elements that make up a good introduction. It helps you to construct an effective introduction of adequate length:

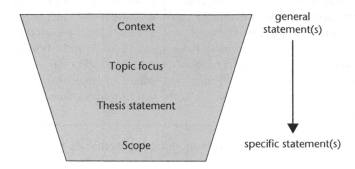

Explanation of the model

The shape of the introduction model (an inverted trapezium) shows visually the movement of ideas from a broad or general point to a narrower and more specific focus. In terms of <u>proportion</u>, the context and topic focus elements make up about two-thirds of the introduction. The thesis and scope elements make up about one-third or slightly less.

Context gives the relevant background or circumstances surrounding the topic or issue. Contextual information could include historical or statistical facts, relevant theories, or a definition (as a quotation or paraphrase).

 DO NOT start with a question or a series of questions or a story. These techniques are more appropriate for public speaking and debates than academic writing contexts. Keep the background information <u>closely related</u> to the topic. The relevant context can be derived from key words in the assignment question. For example, a closely related context for a Business essay arguing whether entrepreneurship can be taught would be modern business practice and the role of entrepreneurship in it. On the other hand, beginning with an analysis of social problems caused by drug addiction in a Law essay arguing whether marijuana should be legalised, would be too broad a context. It could also mislead the reader or cause the reader to question its relevance to the question.

Topic focus is what the essay is specifically about. It explains the main reason for writing the essay and identifies the central issues related to the key words in the assignment question.

Thesis statement is your point of view or position on the topic or issue. Most university writing concerns issues and a point of view is usually expected. In argumentative writing, an explicit thesis is required. In essays discussing or exploring a range of issues, the thesis may be stated only in the conclusion. In reports of experimental studies, the thesis is not usually present in the early stages of the report (see *Part IV Presenting a point of view* for more on thesis statement writing).

Scope identifies specifically the main points of discussion to be covered, ideally in the order they will be presented. The purpose of the scope element is to let the reader know what to expect in the main body of the essay or report.

How does the model work?

The following introduction is constructed with all four elements of the model.

(2nd year Management case study essay, analysing the organisational culture of a firm from a mainstream and critical perspective; about 10 per cent of total length)

Culture is an important organisational facet and plays a vital role in influencing employee behaviour. Organisational culture is defined as 'the shared values and beliefs that provide the norms of expected behaviour in an organisation' (Hogan & Coote, 2014, p. 1). It outlines what is important to that business and what its overall objective is. It provides a blueprint for employees on how to perform certain tasks and how to relate to other colleagues. Organisational culture can be manufactured by the firm according to its business philosophy and practice or allowed to emerge naturally. Kermally (2005) explains that in a firm with a strong manufactured culture, it is relatively easier to know what behaviour is expected as opposed to a business culture in which the behaviours and attitudes emerge naturally. Mars Incorporated has a manufactured culture which has led to its overall success. This essay focuses on seven principles of business practice at Mars Incorporated and relates them to Schien's and Handy's theories on culture and management. It also compares ...

CONTEXT
☑ facts
☐ theory
☑ definition
☑ quotation

TOPIC FOCUS

THESIS

SCOPE

Applying the model: essay introductions

Complete the practice activities below to examine how students writing in different subject areas use the model to construct introductions to their essays.

In most introductions, there is a movement of ideas from general to specific. However, you will notice that in some of the example introductions, the model elements are in a different order and some elements are not present. In each case, the percentage length of the introduction is provided. When you check your answers in the Answer Key in Appendix A, read the comments on each introduction.

PRACTICE ACTIVITY 3.1

1. (1st year Academic English, on the living wage debate; about 10 per cent of total length)

All four elements of the model are used in the same order to construct this introduction.
Write the sentence number(s) under each element

[1] The wage debate is an economic and social issue to fight poverty and ensure income equality. [2] The amount of wages paid is significant because it affects consumption and the standard of living directly. [3] In 2012, New Zealand launched The Living Wage campaign to support the wage debates (Brown et al., 2014). [4] Those who advocate paying a living wage subscribe to the view that a living wage is 'income necessary to provide workers and their families with the basic necessities of life' (King & Waldegrave, 2012, p. 24). [5] However, support varies. [6] Those against the living wage argue that it would slow down economic growth. [7] This essay will argue that a living wage benefits individuals and the economy in three ways: a) it provides consumption efficiency; b) it increases productivity; and c) it creates better financial outcomes for society.

CONTEXT
Sentence(s) _____

TOPIC FOCUS
Sentence(s) _____

THESIS
Sentence(s) _____

SCOPE
Sentence(s) _____

2. (2nd year Film, Television and Media Studies, comparing the ways two films use historical settings to comment on contemporary issues; about 10 per cent of total length)

This introduction is also constructed using the four elements of the model, but with some variation in the order of the elements. Write the elements in the space provided in the right margin.

[1] The genre label 'historical film' is one of several used to describe films with narratives set wholly or partly in the past (Chapman 2). [2] Other labels include costume, period or heritage film. [3] These films put fictional characters in historical settings and provide glimpses of a past era and its social concerns. [4] The accuracy of their representation of the past may be debatable. [5] However, the visual accuracy of the setting achieved through mise-en-scene of authentic period objects and costume enable these films to reflect on social attitudes of the period in a specific and vivid manner. [6] The following is an exploration of how two historical films, *The Last Samurai* and *Gosford Park*, construct images of the past that demand audience reflection on issues of class and East-West intercultural and transnational relations, which still have relevance today.

a)_____

b)_____

c)_____

d)_____

3. (2nd year Law, on whether marijuana should be legalised; just over 10 per cent of total length)

[1] The legalisation of marijuana is currently a contentious issue. [2] The legal position of marijuana varies throughout the world, ranging from 'blanket suppression' to allowing minor amounts for personal use. [3] In New Zealand, marijuana is governed by the Misuse of Drugs Act 1975. [4] Despite this, 42% of adults in New Zealand over the age of 15 reported trying it. [5] This raises the question of whether it is beneficial to regulate or criminalise marijuana. [6] This essay will discuss the main strengths and weaknesses for the legalisation of marijuana. [7] Following from the introduction, Part II will examine the advantages of legalising marijuana. [8] Part III will analyse the disadvantages of marijuana legalisation. [9] Finally, Part IV will conclude that marijuana should not be legalised.

Answer these questions:

a) Which <u>one</u> of the following options is used to provide the context from sentences 1 to 4?   □ DEFINITION   □ FACTS   □ THEORY

b) Which sentences provide the topic focus?   Sentence numbers [   ]

c) Which sentence states the thesis?   Sentence number [   ]

Applying the model: report introductions

As we saw in *Part II Types of university written assignments,* reports have a different structure from essays. Introductions in reports reflect subject area practices, so always check with your department. In some disciplines, short paragraphs are preferred. As the following examples show, the introduction model is still applicable, but with some variations.

PRACTICE ACTIVITY 3.2

1. (2nd year Biological Sciences laboratory report; about 13 per cent of total length)

The introduction is in two paragraphs, but the model elements are still visible.
Fill in each space with the correct element from these options:

TOPIC FOCUS | THESIS | CONTEXT | SCOPE

Introduction

Temperature is a major abiotic factor, which affects almost all aspects of physiology. This is especially pertinent in ectothermal animals as their body temperature is determined by the temperature of their environment (Guderley & St-Pierre, 2002). The heart in particular is very sensitive to increases in temperature and is generally the first to fail under thermal stress. Thus, heart rate provides a good indicator of the effects of thermal variation on the stress levels of an animal (Iftikar et. al., 2010).

a) _____

☑ facts
☐ theory
☐ definition
☐ quotation

b) _____

Charybdis japonica is a eurythermal, invasive species of paddle crab inhabiting the waters of New Zealand. The ultimate temperature limits for this species are 4°C–34°C (Fowler et al., 2011). Thermal limits are an important environmental constraint on marine species. They are even more important in relation to an invasive species such as *C. japonica*, as temperature can restrict how far the invasive species can spread and expand (Fowler, 2011). This study aims to determine how heart function varies with temperature and what this might mean for the animal both physiologically and ecologically.

c) _____

d) _____

2. (2nd year Medical Science laboratory report; about 10 per cent of total length)

You will notice that the presentation is different from the previous example. Can you still identify the model elements?
Write these elements in the space provided: CONTEXT | TOPIC FOCUS | SCOPE

AIMS
To measure the rate of metabolic energy consumption.
To observe the differences in energy consumption

a) _____

INTRODUCTION
Metabolism in the human body involves … Metabolic rate is defined as … (Tortora & Derrickson, 2014). The resting metabolic rate (RMR) is defined as … This rate will increase with activity …

Energy is derived from three main forms … Energy derived from these fuels is stored and used in different ways … The chemical reactions converting stored energy into energy available for work is not fully efficient. This leads to …

b) _____

Stored energy is converted into mechanical energy in the human body through aerobic and anaerobic respiration. Anaerobic respiration is …

In this experiment, mechanical energy expenditure is measured through the use of a mechanical 'ergometer' – a stationary bike. Energy produced through metabolic reactions in the subject's body is converted into mechanical energy, allowing the subject to cycle at various speeds.

c) _____

3.4 A model for constructing conclusions

The conclusion model works in the opposite direction to the introduction. It moves the reader from the narrower and more specific content focus of the discussion to a more general and broader context which is related to the subject-matter.

The model below displays the key elements that make up a good conclusion. Using the model helps you to write a strong ending and gives the reader a sense of completeness to the discussion.

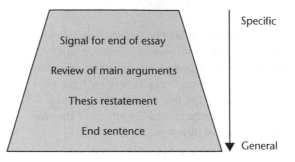

Explanation of the model

Signal for end of essay. Common practices among students include using a heading 'Conclusion' (common in reports) or signalling with words such as 'In conclusion', 'To sum up', 'Overall' or 'Finally'. Signalling the end of the essay in this explicit manner is not always necessary but it is commonly done. An explicit signal word may not be needed if a heading is used for the conclusion.

Review of main arguments. A review is more than a summary of the main points. It uses evaluative words (active verbs, adverbs and adjectives) to show how and why the points discussed are significant in relation to the assignment question and thesis. A summary restates the main points. DO NOT ADD NEW INFORMATION.

Thesis restatement. This restates your position on the topic or issue with more authority because you have established evidence to back it up. In essays of a more exploratory nature, and in reports, the thesis may be absent or only suggested in the introduction but stated more explicitly in the conclusion.

End sentence. This is a final comment that reinforces the overall argument and ends the conclusion – and the discussion of the topic – in a satisfactory manner. Here are some ways of ending the conclusion:

- Point to a wider but related context by referring to implications or the need for further investigation of the issues you have raised.
- Link the entire discussion to the essay question and thesis. By doing this, you also remind the reader about the significance of the topic.
- End with a quotation. Do not use this strategy unless the quotation is relevant and particularly meaningful (see *Part I, Unit 2 Using quotations: DOs and DON'Ts*).

How does the model work?

Example (3rd year Political Studies on The State of Food Security: Problems and Solutions; about 7 per cent of essay length)

Although slightly below the percentage guideline, the following conclusion illustrates effective use of all elements of the model. The main headings used in the body of the essay are presented in a box in the right margin to give you an idea of the main topics. You can see that there is a conscious effort to match the review statements to the main topics.

Conclusion: The future of food security

Food insecurity is indeed one of the most pressing issues which modern policymakers must deal with. Although the Green Revolution vastly improved food security worldwide, it lulled many into a false sense of security. Spikes in the price of basic foodstuffs in recent years have also reignited Malthusian concerns over the availability of food. Demand for food is growing rapidly in emerging economies. Current efforts to improve food security are well-intentioned but poorly coordinated, creating wasteful overlap between UN agencies and research programmes. A realistic response would be to view food insecurity as a conventional security threat. This perspective would place greater pressure on the world's major powers to intervene. A neo-liberal institutional approach would see greater potential to provide greater focus on global food security efforts. I argue that the most effective policy is a second green revolution, or a 'gene revolution' through greater use of GE crops. States must place greater emphasis on cooperating to address food insecurity through coordinated research and development programmes. The issue risks fuelling conflict and damaging economic growth, to say nothing of the humanitarian imperatives.

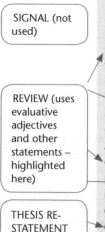

SIGNAL (not used)

REVIEW (uses evaluative adjectives and other statements – highlighted here)

THESIS RE-STATEMENT

END SENTENCE point to wider contexts

Main headings from body:

Current state of food security

Role of international organisations

Causes – financial, natural, political

Addressing food insecurity

- realist approach
- neo-liberal
- second 'Green Revolution'

REVIEW and END SENTENCE elements: some problems

REVIEW element: Two problems

Problem 1: Review is like a summary.
An easy way to distinguish between them is to associate a review with HOW and WHY aspects and a summary with WHAT aspects or description.

Example (2nd year Education, on the ideas of Brazilian educator, Paulo Freire; about 8 per cent of total length)

The conclusion has an adequate length but it is a descriptive summary rather than a review. Sentences [1]–[6] define WHAT the concepts are. This is unnecessary in the conclusion because the concepts would already have been defined in the main body of the essay.

---

[1] Freire's banking concept of education describes a classroom where the teacher has all the knowledge and the student knows nothing. [2] Students passively accept what they are being taught without learning to be critical and questioning of what they learn. [3] Freire introduces a problem-posing education as an alternative where the students are encouraged to ... [4] In a problem-posing classroom, both the teacher and student are learners. [5] Praxis is a term used to describe people becoming active critics of society by ... [6] Conscientisation, a process that arises out of praxis, refers to people becoming active participants ... [7] Freire believed education had the potential to transform society.

Focuses on WHAT (defines, describes)

Here is a revision of the conclusion which includes review statements. The review focuses on HOW and WHY Freire's educational philosophy matters, using verbs which describe activity or action specifically, referred to here as 'active verbs':

> Freire's educational philosophy and pedagogy promote a student-centred system of learning that challenges how knowledge is constructed and delivered in formal education systems, which have a banking concept of education. Freire's problem-posing method of education transforms classrooms to opportunities for critical thinking and questioning. It is a teaching and learning pedagogy that highlights the impact of active learning and critical thinking. A critical and active education empowers people with the capacity to decide their own destinies.

active verbs

Problem 2 Review includes <u>new information</u>. What is considered new information? The following is an extract from the conclusion of a 1st year Sociology essay on how capitalism led to mass surveillance in the workplace. The new citation and facts (highlighted here) constitute new information:

> In 'What is capitalism?' Fulcher (2004) identifies the need for employers to discipline workers and keep costs to a minimum. There is also evidence to suggest that in some cases, productivity could increase by as much as 25 per cent. In looking at how capitalism has led to mass surveillance, I have discussed surveillance of the workplace. However, there are other forms of surveillance that could be discussed in relation to capitalism, such as the use of mass surveillance in politics or consumer surveillance. Overall, capitalist-driven surveillance benefits employers but the cost of the loss of workers' rights and freedom could be counter-productive in the long run.

New information

Irrelevant information (these are not in the essay)

END SENTENCE element: This element is often missing in conclusions in student writing or it is confused with thesis restatement.

Example (1st year Music, writing a response to a musical composition)

This extract was presented at the start of this unit as an example of a concise conclusion, despite its short length. It does not have an end statement.

> In just 23 bars, Webern defines an atonal harmonic language and uses this as a springboard from which to explore ideas of musical time and create forward motion without traditional harmonic or melodic progressions. It is the counterpoint between intervallic cells, rhythmic motifs, timbres and sections that gives this movement its drive and clear trajectory.

Suggested improvement

Adding an <u>end statement</u> that points to the significance of atonality promoted by Webern would move the conclusion from the specific to a more general but related context, as shown in the following end sentence:

> An influential figure of musical modernism, Webern embraced atonality as a new aesthetic, which provided new dimensions of musical expression in the twentieth century in the form of expanded use of new tones, colours and extended techniques.

A model is a guide and not all elements are used by students to construct their conclusions. Let us examine how students writing in different subject areas conclude their essays.

The main purpose of these practice activities is to enable you to test your understanding of the conclusion model, which reflects the role of conclusions as distinct from introductions.

Determining the full effectiveness of the conclusions presented here may be difficult since the main content in the body of the essay is not provided. However, a statement of the scope from the introduction (and thesis, if present) are included to give you an idea of the body content.

Read each conclusion and determine if there is evidence of the use of the conclusion model by ticking the boxes in the right margin. Mark each box with a ✓ if the element is present and an × if it is absent or unclear. The approximate length of the conclusion is indicated as a percentage of the total essay length. It shows whether it is closer to the percentage guideline of 10 per cent or well below. The first one has been done as an example:

Example (2nd year Education, on the ideas of Brazilian educator, Paulo Freire; about 8 per cent of total length)

Scope: 'I will introduce and critically evaluate three of Freire's main ideas, which are the 'banking concept' of education, praxis and conscientisation. I will then explain how he believed education had the power to transform society because Freire believed education could serve as an instrument of either oppression or liberation.'

Freire's banking concept of education describes a classroom where the teacher has all the knowledge and the student knows nothing. Students passively accept what they are being taught without learning to be critical and questioning of what they learn. Freire introduces a problem-posing education as an alternative where the students are encouraged to actively engage with what they are being taught and be critical of things in society. In a problem-posing classroom, both the teacher and student are learners. Praxis is used to describe the term of people becoming active critics of society by understanding theory and combining it with practice and conscientisation as a process that arises out of praxis which refers to people becoming active participants who challenge and transform society rather than passive citizens who just accept what they are taught and never learn to question ideas. Freire saw education as an instrument of oppression or liberation. His educational philosophy and pedagogy is founded on his belief that education had the potential to transform society.	☒ Signal
	☒ Review
	☒ Thesis restatement
	☑ End sentence
	  ☐ uses quotation
	  ☑ points to larger context
	  ☐ links back to thesis/ essay question

Comment: The thesis restatement is implied rather than stated explicitly. The conclusion sums up Freire's ideas but does not state clearly or critically evaluate if they had a real impact.

NOW YOU TRY

1. (3rd year Political Studies, on the attributes of a political leader with reference to the performance of two recent prime ministers; 4 per cent of total length)

Thesis: that 'while there are many factors that aid a political leader to gain and retain power, it is the personal attributes that leaders utilize and exploit to their advantage that mark a successful leader'

Successful leadership attributes differ with the times. Lange's vision, nationalism, intellect, and charisma were not enough to secure his leadership in the face of party fracture and unpopular reform. Lange's success, by the ultimate measure of longevity in office, is less than Clark's, who utilised her integrity, stamina, strategic and managerial abilities to control her caucus, tend the nation, and retain power for three consecutive terms. Comparatively Clark was clearly an exceptionally successful leader.	☐ Signal
	☐ Review
	☐ Thesis restatement
	☐ End sentence
	  ☐ uses quotation
	  ☐ points to larger context
	  ☐ links back to thesis/ essay question

2. (1st year Business on entrepreneurship; 5 per cent of total length)

<u>Scope</u>: 'This essay will describe the competing theories about entrepreneurship and the most common argument used to justify the idea that entrepreneurs must have a specific set of inherent personality traits. Then this essay will explain the reasons why, contrary to the widely-accepted myth, it is possible for entrepreneurship to be taught to aspiring entrepreneurs.'

In conclusion, there is sufficient evidence to suggest that a person can learn to become an entrepreneur through education. Despite the enduring belief that entrepreneurs must possess a specific set of innate personality traits, real life observations suggest that a person can become an entrepreneur without being born with the ideal entrepreneurial personality traits. Additionally, even though it is difficult to teach entrepreneurial soft skills such as the ability to think creatively and take calculated risks, there is evidence to suggest that students can acquire and improve those skills by participating in activities that simulate real-life entrepreneurial experience. Therefore, it is possible for an individual to learn to become an entrepreneur through education. Entrepreneurship is a discipline and to quote Drucker (1985), it is 'capable of being learned, it is capable of being practised'. (p. viii).	□ Signal
	□ Review
	□ Thesis restatement
	□ End sentence
	    □ uses quotation
	    □ points to larger context
	    □ links back to thesis/ essay question

3. (1st year Academic English, on the living wage debate; about 8 per cent of total length)

<u>SCOPE:</u> 'This essay will argue that a living wage benefits individuals and the economy in three ways: a) it provides consumption efficiency; b) it increases productivity; and c) it creates better financial outcomes.'

In conclusion, every worker in New Zealand should be paid a living wage because it increases motivation and productivity of employees which in turn will contribute to economic growth significantly. A living wage has notable benefits that employers should consider. Economists David Neumark and Scott Adams argue that a mandate for the living wage will have advantages for both employees and employers (McCrate, 2003). It is more than just about raising wages, but about achieving better outcomes by enhancing the welfare of employees, improving the work environment and conditions. In the long run, there will be better financial outcomes for society because reduced spending on social costs will benefit all other areas of society.	□ Signal
	□ Review
	□ Thesis restatement
	□ End sentence
	    □ uses quotation
	    □ points to larger context
	    □ links back to thesis/ essay question

4. (2nd year Law, on whether marijuana should be legalised; about 7 per cent of total length)

The campaign towards the legalisation of marijuana is a reality in many countries. However, without concrete evidence supporting the benefits of medicinal marijuana, potentiality of revenue boosts and improvements in the justice system, the weaknesses of legalisation seem to outweigh the strengths. The health effects of marijuana, the gateway theory and increased use of marijuana in children are far more significant concerns. Without public discussion and thorough research into the advantages, legalisation of marijuana in New Zealand is not a wise decision.	□ Signal
	□ Review
	□ Thesis restatement
	□ End sentence
	    □ uses quotation
	    □ points to larger context
	    □ links back to thesis/ essay question

Applying the model: Report conclusions

Conclusions in reports tend to be concise because they are drawn from results and discussion and are directly related to the aims of the study. They do not display all the elements of the conclusion model. The format and presentation may be determined by the type of report. In some subject areas:

- The conclusion is a summary of the main findings from the Discussion section of the report.
- The conclusions are written as a numbered list of precise statements.
- The plural form 'Conclusions' is used.
- The tense may vary depending on the type of report (e.g. the past simple tense for reporting actual findings or the future 'will' for reporting expected results).

The two report conclusions follow subject-area conventions. However, the overall purpose of the conclusion is clear: to remind the reader of the main findings, as shown in the following examples:

Example 1 (2nd year Medical Sciences laboratory report; about 4 per cent of total length)

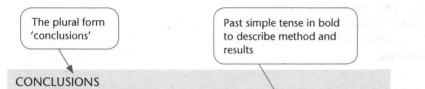

The plural form 'conclusions'

Past simple tense in bold to describe method and results

CONCLUSIONS

The rate of metabolic energy consumption was measured indirectly by observing the heart rate, respiration rate and proportions of inspired and expired O_2 and CO_2. These factors directly affected the rate of respiration and change according to the amount of mechanical energy expended. Metabolic energy consumption was lowest at rest and increase in energy consumption depended directly on the rate of mechanical energy expenditure.

A summary of what was found – corresponds to the two aims of the experiment stated in the introduction

Example 2 (2nd year Mechanical Engineering report, on the viability of establishing a methanol plant; about 5 per cent of total length)

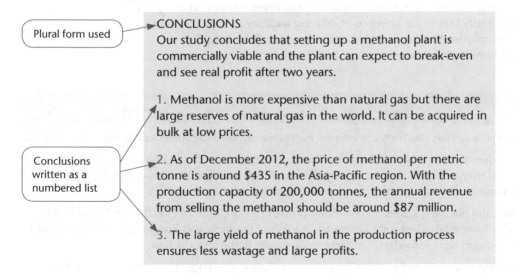

Plural form used

CONCLUSIONS
Our study concludes that setting up a methanol plant is commercially viable and the plant can expect to break-even and see real profit after two years.

Conclusions written as a numbered list

1. Methanol is more expensive than natural gas but there are large reserves of natural gas in the world. It can be acquired in bulk at low prices.

2. As of December 2012, the price of methanol per metric tonne is around $435 in the Asia-Pacific region. With the production capacity of 200,000 tonnes, the annual revenue from selling the methanol should be around $87 million.

3. The large yield of methanol in the production process ensures less wastage and large profits.

Identify the element from the Conclusion Model in the a) and b) boxes in the following report conclusions.

1. (1st year Psychology laboratory report, investigating the impact of role-play on empathy; about 6 per cent of total length)

> a) _____
>
> In conclusion, this study looked at the differences between empathy scores calculated prior to participants taking part in a role-playing activity, and those calculated after participating in the activity. Our findings suggest that there were statistically significant differences. The original hypothesis of the study (that empathy scores would be significantly higher following the role-play exercises) was upheld, while the null hypothesis was rejected. Hence, the results indicate that role-play exercises can be drawn upon to increase empathy in those who participate in the exercises.
>
> b) _____

2. (3rd year Psychology research proposal report on the use of functional magnetic resonance imaging (fMRI); about 5 per cent of total length)

> a) _____
>
> Overall, it is hoped that this study will help to clarify current knowledge about the effects of background music on memory. The comparison of musicians and non-musicians aims firstly to further understanding of the complex effects that musical training has on the brain, but also to determine whether musical training should be taken into account in future studies into auditory distraction and memory. Specifically, the use of fMRI will allow visualisation of the anatomical areas used when attempting a working memory task in the presence of differing auditory stimuli. This new information may lead to improved understanding of ... Practically, if significant behavioural differences are noted, this study could encourage ...
>
> b) _____

REVIEW

Starting and ending your writing effectively are essential to create a unified and coherent discussion or argument.

A commonly asked question is whether the introduction or the conclusion should be written first or last. Advice regarding this may differ, but a good strategy is to write the introduction first – even if it is just a draft. The introduction gives you a focus to develop the main discussion.

During the thinking and planning stages of the writing process (see Six steps to effective writing in Part I, Unit 2), you will also have established sufficient understanding of the topic and how far you want to go with it. This means that you do have something concrete to work with in the introduction.

Use the models to help you construct effective beginnings and strong endings. The introduction prepares the reader for the main content of the writing. The conclusion reminds the reader of the key points raised and the importance of what you have written. More importantly, it draws the discussion to a satisfactory ending, giving the reader a sense of completeness.

Use the 10 per cent length allocation as a guide. If your introduction or conclusion is well below this percentage guideline (under 5 per cent of the total length, for example), test it against the model.

UNIT 4 **Paragraph structure and construction**

Key topics

4.1 Basic principles of paragraphing
4.2 The TEC model for paragraph construction
4.3 Effective topic sentences

The brief discussion of paragraphing in Part I, Unit 4 emphasises the importance of clear presentation and layout. This unit discusses the principles that govern paragraphing in more detail and describes a model for constructing a coherent paragraph. Understanding these principles will give you a framework for developing ideas in logical paragraphs in the main body of the essay.

4.1 Basic principles of paragraphing

Why does paragraphing matter?

Paragraphing is useful for splitting discussion points. Readers generally associate a paragraph break with the start of a new point or a different aspect of the same point. Effective paragraphing also increases readability.

This is an image of a page from a 2nd year Medical Sciences laboratory report, which discusses the function of the kidney in regulating fluid volumes in the body. This section is over two pages long and written without any paragraph breaks. The reader comments that the discussion is difficult to follow.

Discussion

The urine flow rate described the amount of urine the body produced in one minute. The sodium excretion rate measured the amount in mmols of sodium ions excreted by the body in one minute. The free water clearance rate outlined the amount of water in mLs discharged in one minute. The GFR measured the quantity of blood filtrate through glomerula in the kidney in mLs per minute. The kidneys control urine concentration by varying the amount of water and sodium reabsorbed in the distal regions of the nephron The general trend of subject 1 in sodium excretion vs time was decreasing. Because subject 1 did not drink anything throughout the whole experiment, he was the first one to conserve the amount of of Na⁺ in the body in order to maintain osmolarity ... At first the sodium excretion rate of all were n early the same, however, that of subject 1 increased. The rate of subject 2, 3 and 4 dropped a little 20 minutes after the beginning of the experiment and then started to go up. Because subjects 2 and 3 drank a relatively large amount of water, the osmolarity of their bodies was lower than that of subject 1. In this case, it was sensed by the osmoreceptor in the anterior hypothalamus, and their bodies would have to reserve the sodium balance The reabsorption of Na⁺ in the kidney is regulated by the steroid hormone aldosterone. The more aldosterone is secreted, the more Na⁺ is absorbed. One target of aldosterone was to increase the activity of Na⁺/K⁺ ATPase. Aldostrerone is syntheisized in the adrenal cortex and its primary target is the last third of the distal tubule and the portion of the collecting duct that runs through the kidney cortex. The major cell of aldoterone acts on its principal Cekks. From here, it can be said that the response time of aldosterone is relatively fast. At the time of 20 minutes after starting the experiment the sodium excretion rate of subject 4 also dropped and then increased. This was probably due to the sympathetic and parasympathetic reflexes. As he was lying down at time zero, his sympathetic activity was suppressed and hisd parasympathetic activity was elevated. More blood flowed from the skeletal muscle to the gut and kidney. In order to maintain water and sodium levels, the sodium excretion dropped. There was a big decrease between the third and fourth samples in subject 1. After that the rate dropped gradually due to the reservation of sodium. Because the body lost more sodium, more aldosterone was released at each given time to reserve Na⁺ concentration Although all the four subjects did different jobs in the lab, the overall trends of them were similar, especially at time 120 minutes. At first the trend of subject 3 was similar to subject 2. However, it went up significantly at time 60. Subject 3 had done some extensive exercise for 15 minutes after his diuresis was firmly established, then a urine sample was collected immediately. After the exercise, subject 3 sweated a lot. Through sweating he lost not only water but also salt. After exercise, a small quantity of sodium but not water could be reabsorbed by the skin and probably thqt was why at about 80 minutes his sodium elimination nrate was the highest. Owing ot the small amount of sodium absorption, his body had to increase the sodium excretion rate and reserve water to maintainnormal osmolarity. This could also be observed in the urine flow rate graph On account of the loss of water from sweating the blood pressure of the body must drop to a relative extent. JG cells in the kidney produce renin and change the angiotensingogen produced by the liver to ANG 1 if a drop in blood pressure is sensed by it. ANG II is produced from ANG 1. ANG II does a lot of impressive jobs in the body. Activation of ANG II receptor in the brain increases ...

The reader indicates possible paragraph breaks in the student's text with the symbol 'Z'.

There are four paragraph breaks on this page.

The breaks appear to correspond to the five functions of the kidney.

What principles govern paragraphing?

Effective paragraphing is not a random activity. It is guided by two basic principles:

- Paragraph length
- Paragraph structure

Paragraph length

The length of a paragraph should be sufficient for a satisfactory discussion of the central idea. In academic writing, an average length for a paragraph of substance is between 100 and 150 words (about 10 per cent of the total length). The following examples show two common problems related to length: many short paragraphs and paragraphs with variable lengths.

- <u>Short paragraphs</u>   A sequence of short paragraphs can give your essay a fragmented look. The reader may find that the discussion lacks substance or that the discussion of the topic is too simplistic or incomplete.

  Example (3rd year Political Studies, discussing the attributes of a political leader with reference to the performance of two recent prime ministers)

Too many short paragraphs break up the flow of the essay. It may be difficult for the reader to see the connection between ideas.	A successful political leader needs to excel on two fronts: party leadership and national leadership. Party leadership requires ... (50 words) ... ultimately failed in his party leadership ability: left-wing ideologies were disregarded ... ; ministers defected ... (59 words) By contrast, ... successfully ... . In fact, ... (60 words)

- <u>Variable lengths</u>   **Example** (2nd year Art History, examining Manet's avant-garde style of painting)

Inconsistent paragraph sizes can give confusing signals to the reader.	Another element that upset traditional viewers was Manet's scandalous technique. Traditionally, painting involved ... Manet did away with transitions between tones ... (122 words) Form has also been outlined in thick dark lines, [showing] the influence [of] Courbet's work and Japanese prints. These styles had been embraced by the painters of Manet's generation as being free from the traditions of the academy. (40 words) Traditionally, artists would start their paintings with a dark undercoat to give the illusion of depth. Manet abandoned this in favour of off-white undercoat, making his paintings luminous. (77 words) Such painterly qualities are exemplified by Manet's application of paint, for as Gardener mentions, he used 'art to call attention to art'. (199 words)

This is not to say that all the body paragraphs must be of the same length. Some variation is acceptable. In the above example, the second paragraph is quite short. The third paragraph lacks a clear topic sentence for the paragraph. The reason could be that the content is linked to the previous paragraph. When you have many short paragraphs or inconsistent paragraph sizes, check each paragraph's content and the connectivity between paragraphs. Consider if some of the short paragraphs could be joined to create better content coherence or flow.

Paragraph structure

Developing your writing is about building the body of your essay or report with several paragraphs, each dealing with a <u>single</u> topic or main point. A body paragraph has a clear structure:

- a <u>beginning</u>, which presents the specific theme or central idea of the topic;
- a <u>middle</u> section, which develops the idea with relevant supporting details presented in a logical and coherent manner (see also *Part I, Unit 4 Coherent flow of ideas*);
- an <u>ending</u>, which signals completion of the topic.

4.2 The TEC model for paragraph construction

The TEC model provides a workable framework for developing ideas in a paragraph in a way that reflects the basic principles of adequate length and structure. Using the model also ensures that your paragraph has <u>unity</u> (contains relevant supporting details) and <u>coherence</u> (shows good connectivity and flow from one sentence to the next).

T= **TOPIC SENTENCE**. This tells the reader specifically what the paragraph is about. It contains a word or phrase which identifies the <u>central idea</u> or <u>theme</u> of the topic. The topic sentence is usually stated at the beginning of the paragraph.

E= **ELABORATION/EXPANSION**. This develops the main content of the paragraph. It consists of several sentences which advance the theme or central idea presented in the topic sentence. The purpose of elaboration and expansion is to enable the reader to understand the topic completely by providing relevant examples and other details and to produce a convincing discussion or argument by referring to evidence from research and course knowledge (see *Unit 4 Techniques for developing ideas*).

C= **COMMENT**. This is the last sentence of the paragraph. It signals the end of the discussion of the topic. It is a statement on its significance in relation to the essay question and your thesis or position.

 This last element may not always be present, but it is a useful way to end the discussion of a main point. <u>DO NOT</u> use this element to tell the reader what the next paragraph will be about.

How does the TEC paragraph model work?

Example (1st year Film and Media Studies essay, discussing the effect of digital technologies on the form, style and narrative of film)

This is the first paragraph in the main body of the essay, discussing the effect of one type of digital technology – digital cameras – on film-making. Its structure reflects effective use of the TEC model.

TEC structure		Development (S2-S5)

Logical connectors to improve flow of ideas

T [1] The appearance of digital cameras from the mid-1990s has changed the form and style of film-making. [2] The portability of digital cameras, as opposed to the burdensome nature of their 35mm counterparts, has given more freedom to filmmakers, allowing shooting to be spontaneous, flexible and more emotive (Reid 256–257). [3] In Danny Boyle's 2008 film, 'Slumdog Millionaire', for example, portable digital cameras were used to capture the urgency of Mumbai's slums. [4] Without the burden of organizing sizeable equipment, cinematographer Anthony Mantle was thus able to rapidly shoot without disturbing the ambience of the slum to create a realism that is virtually impossible with a 35mm camera. [5] As Boyle explains, 'I wanted to be thrown right into the chaos as much as possible' *(Slumdog Millionaire Shot with Innovative SI-2K Digital Cinema Camera)*. [6] Digital technology has therefore allowed for spontaneity and realism to develop in contemporary cinema. This is a significant change within film form and style.

E {

C

1 Opens with a general statement

2 Identifies a specific theme

3,4 Illustrate with specific example

5 Supports with a quotation

6 Relates to theme or controlling idea

Key strengths of the paragraph:

- The topic sentence (T) contains a <u>central idea</u> or <u>theme</u> ('freedom to filmmakers' stated in sentence 2).
- The supporting sentences (C) (sentences 3–5) elaborate on and expand the theme in specific ways and are <u>relevant</u> to the theme.
- The use of logical connectors creates <u>coherence</u> and flow of ideas.
- The comment (C) on the specific effects of 'freedom' on film-making in the last sentence links back to the theme, signalling the <u>end</u> of the discussion of the topic.

4.3 Effective topic sentences

Writing a topic sentence can be challenging because you have to generate it yourself. Usually positioned at the start of a paragraph, a topic sentence serves two purposes: a) it prepares your reader for the content to follow and b) it gives you a clear focus to build the main content of the paragraph.

There are two common problems:

- confusing topic with purpose by telling the reader what you are going to do;
- writing a general rather than specific sentence.

Problem 1 Purpose versus topic

These opening sentences **state <u>purpose</u>** (what you will do):	**Revision: states topic** (what the paragraph is about):
Let me briefly explain about the cause of the war.	Two main events led to the outbreak of war between ... and ..., namely ... and ...
Next, we will look at how Hiroshima and Nagasaki were changed by the atomic bomb.	The atomic bombing of Hiroshima and Nagasaki brought lasting environmental problems which still affect people's lives today.
I will now give reasons why I think the Smithsonian Institute's view is wrong.	The Smithsonian Institute's decision to focus on the technological magnificence of the Enola-Gay is flawed because it does not acknowledge the historical context.

Problem 2 General versus specific sentence

In both sets of sentences, S1 is too general. S2 contains a central idea or theme, which identifies the paragraph topic specifically:

SET A   S1:   The theme of friendship in the story appeals to young readers. (What kind of friendship appeals exactly?)

S2:   The theme of friendship between a pet and its owner appeals to young readers.

SET B   S1:   The responsibility of health professionals in maintaining patient confidentiality is of great importance. (What is important exactly?)

S2:   In maintaining patient confidentiality, it is important for health professionals to establish trust between themselves and their patients.

> Theme or central idea

PRACTICE ACTIVITY 4.1

1.   Applying the TEC paragraph model

The text is from a 1st year History essay explaining how immigration has led changes in attitudes and understandings of race. The eight sentences expand one change in attitude and understanding of race as a result of immigration – the rise of nativism. They are in scrambled order. Using the underlined expressions to guide you, put the sentences in order to form a unified and coherent TEC paragraph:

[1] In an attempt to preserve nativist ideals, New Zealand and America began to introduce new policies to limit the influx of undesirable immigrants.
[2] The 1924 quota laws meant that each nation was allowed to let 2% of its American population to immigrate to America.
[3] These immigration restriction policies were viewed to be a direct response to the attitude that immigration had ultimately become a danger to the preservation of racially pure, national identities.
[4] The most noticeable change in understandings of race, as a result of immigration, is the rise of nativism.
[5] From 1920 onwards, New Zealand introduced immigration permits that made it more difficult for non-British and non-Europeans to enter the country.
[6] With new immigrants arriving in America and New Zealand, citizens sought to distinguish themselves from immigrants.
[7] This law also meant that races with older roots in America were favoured above more recent and undesirable immigrants, such as Asians and Southern and Eastern Europeans.
[8] America too introduced quotas to restrict immigration in order to preserve their national identity.

2.   Identifying the central idea or theme

The following topic sentences are from four body paragraphs of a 1st year English essay, reviewing a book by a well-known children's author, Dr. Seuss. Underline the words which express the theme or central idea in each topic sentence.

a. Dr. Seuss' books are targeted at beginner readers, so it is essential that the composition of images communicates emotion and ideas to support the text.

b. As well as using composition to communicate important ideas visually, Dr. Seuss allows his readers to relate to the characters.

c. Clarity of layout and text design for greater readability have always been important for Dr. Seuss, and this is exemplified beautifully in this spread.

d. Dr. Seuss' humorous touch is famous for rewarding exploration and imagination.

3. Selecting an effective topic sentence

Text 1 (A body paragraph from 1st year Business Management, arguing against Friedman's claim that the purpose of corporate social responsibility is to maximise profit)

_____
_____. Therefore, they have no right to just pursue profit maximisation for investors without considering the consequences. One example is the case of the Ford Pinto, which was put on the market only after a two-year production period. The company appeared to have followed government standards but there were some safety issues that were overlooked. This oversight for the sake of profit could cause the loss of lives because the vehicle could potentially burst into flames from over-heating because the fan belt was constructed from low grade material.

Which of the following sentences is the most effective topic sentence for the paragraph?

a) The first argument against Friedman's perspective is that managers' decisions can affect society in many ways.

b) The first argument against Friedman's perspective is that managers' decisions have a significant impact on the safety of the wider society.

c) The first argument against Friedman's perspective is that managers' decisions should not be just about profit maximisation.

Text 2 (A body paragraph from 2nd year Management, a case study of organisational culture)

_____
_____. However, Hogan and Coote (2014) maintains that it is still an imperative force that governs organisational behaviour, effectiveness and performance. Schein attempts to define culture according to three aspects/levels, the first being artefacts, which are the tangible features accessible to the senses (Knights & Wilmott, 2012). At Mars these are suits and lab coats that employees wear, the posters of the Five Principles displayed on the walls, the computer screens dispersed throughout the offices that constantly update staff on current financials and even the employment of staff who share similar morals and attitudes (Cubiks, 2010). These artefacts infuse a shared purpose and mission in employees and reiterate the team aspect of a business.

Which of the following sentences is the most effective sentence for the paragraph?

    a)   Assessing an organisation's culture is difficult because there is no consensus on what it means.

    b)   Assessing an organisation's culture is difficult because it refers to a range of different things.

    c)   Assessing an organisation's culture is difficult because it is determined by beliefs, values and customs which are not easily visible.

4.   Writing a topic sentence

(A body paragraph from 1st year History, on the 'Good War' myth, arguing why the Second World War was a 'good war' for America)

Read the argument in the following paragraph. Write an appropriate topic sentence that identifies clearly the main point of the argument.

_____

_____. The 1930s had seen America plunged into a deep depression that sent the U.S. economy into dormancy, leading to large-scale unemployment and social unhappiness. However, with the onset of the Second World War, the U.S. economy became fully mobilized. The Gross National Product increased from $91 billion to $161 billion during the war years. Unemployment was at its lowest by 1943, with the creation of 15 million jobs. There were significant increases in food production manufacturing output and production of important metals and substances. The country's economic superiority during the post-war years is clear evidence that the Second World War was indeed good for the American home front. The war ended the Great Depression and inaugurated the United States into a prosperous era of economic stability, in which it could command the manufacturing of a vast quantity of resources.

REVIEW

When developing your writing, apply the basic principles of paragraphing to present your ideas clearly and to increase reader engagement with your writing.

Use the TEC model to give you a workable framework to shape and build ideas with confidence. Test the effectiveness of the topic sentence [T] by identifying two or three key words in it that identify exactly the central idea or theme.

Read the expanded content [E] to make sure that each sentence advances the topic in a specific way so that the reader's understanding of the topic is complete. End the paragraph with a suitable comment [C] to complete development of the central idea.

Check that you have used appropriate connectors and other cohesive devices to help the reader follow the development of ideas (see *Part I, Unit 4 Coherent flow of ideas*).

UNIT 5 Techniques for developing your writing

Key techniques

5.1 Using examples
5.2 Writing extended definitions
5.3 Analysing differences and similarities

5.4 Explaining causes and effects
5.5 Describing data presented in figures and tables

This unit looks at some ways of elaborating on and expanding ideas in individual paragraphs in the body of the essay or report. Each technique is examined separately, although in practice, you may use more than one technique to build a whole essay (see these techniques in practice in the full-length essays in *Part V Putting it all together*).

In the extracts of student writing illustrating each technique, your attention will also be drawn to the following features:

- The TEC paragraph structure (review the model in Unit 4).
- Coherence in the development – that is, the use of cohesive devices to make connections between sentences clear (review devices in Part I, Unit 4).
- In-text citations to acknowledge external sources used as evidence. **Note:** Footnotes for citations using a footnote referencing style are not included (review conventions in Part I, Unit 2).

Developing your writing in the middle sections of the essay or report is effective if you fully understand what the task is. When reading the assignment question, check your understanding of what is required by asking questions, as shown below:

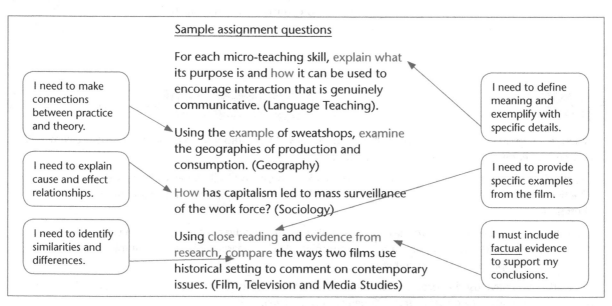

Choosing the right technique: why does it matter?

Choosing the right technique matters because it ensures that the development of ideas in the paragraph fits the purpose of the assignment. The development of ideas in the following paragraph does not answer the question.

Example (1st year Language Teaching, explaining the purpose of three micro-teaching skills in Communicative Language Teaching and how they can be used to encourage interaction and genuine communication)

The student is writing about error correction. The first paragraph defines what error correction is and does. Below is the second paragraph, which aims to address the second part of the question: 'explain how [error correction] is used to encourage interaction that is genuinely communicative'.

Read the reader's response to the second paragraph in the right margin. Do you agree with the reader?

> Error correction can be used to foster genuine interaction in the classroom by addressing any information gaps the student may have, as it provides information or clarification about the language that students will use in future communication. Error correcting gives students a chance to learn from their mistakes. Research about student attitudes towards error correction reveals that students like to have some independence and be given the opportunity to self-correct (Cole, as cited in Nunan & Lamb, 2006, p. 70), as it gives students the opportunity to find out the answer for themselves by testing out the language. As Scrivener explains, facilitating self-correction is also more effective in developing future communication skills.
>
> > There is some good evidence from research about the importance of the skill, but HOW exactly does it work?

The paragraph defines error correction. It does not explain with specific examples <u>how</u> error correction can be used to encourage genuine communication (see 5.1).

5.1 Using examples

This development technique uses specific instances to clarify and explain general statements made in the paragraph.

The word 'example' appears frequently in assignment questions, as shown below:

> Using the example of sweatshops, examine the geographies of production and consumption. (Geography)
>
> Discuss the role played by fear in the effectiveness of Cold War propaganda with examples from Eastern and Western Blocs. (Political Studies)
>
> Do you think it is possible for entrepreneurship to be taught? Develop a clear argument that indicates your view on the question, and justify your choice using appropriate evidence and examples. (Business)

In the first question, you are asked to use <u>a single example</u> to illustrate theoretical principles. In the second question, you are asked to provide <u>different examples</u> to explain a central idea. In the third question, you are asked to use <u>evidence</u> and <u>examples</u>.

What is the difference between <u>evidence</u> and <u>example</u>?

Evidence refers to theoretical and factual information resulting from research or investigation. An example is a general instance of typical behaviour. You use evidence to support your explanation of what the example illustrates or proves.

What types of examples can you use?

Depending on the assignment question, you may give an account of an incident or an activity. You may use a visual image to illustrate a particular style of painting or opinion. Your example may be the title of a film or book or poem.

How does the technique work?

There are three considerations when using examples:

- Use a relevant example.
- Introduce the example.
- Explain with specific details.

Example (1st year Language Teaching, describing how error correction is used to encourage interaction and genuine communication)

The following paragraph is a revision of the student's answer presented earlier. It gives examples of <u>specific learning activities</u> that support the theme or central idea stated in the second and third sentences – that error correction encourages interaction and communication. The paragraph also has all elements of the TEC model:

Paragraph structure   **Development**

Logical connectors

T One of the controversies about error correction is that it does not focus on language production and communication. However, it is possible to incorporate attention to language structures and make errors a natural process of L2 learning. Error correction can be turned into something meaningful and communicative through activities that require students to interact and negotiate with others. Pair and group-work are especially effective for this purpose. Students work in teams or pairs to complete tasks. For example, to practise correct question forms, an Interviewing task can be set in which students interview each other and then present a written profile of the person they interviewed. The pairs work together to correct errors in their respective profiles before presenting them to the class. A team error correction activity using a game format taps into the natural instinct to compete and test knowledge. Information gap or split information tasks also encourage interaction, requiring students to ask questions or request clarification from their partner or team member. According to Thompson (1996), pair and group work allow students to produce a large amount of output.

E

C

Four examples of specific learning activities (highlighted)

Justifies with evidence from research

PRACTICE ACTIVITY 5.1

1. (A paragraph from a 1st year Business Management essay responding to Friedman's definition of Corporate Social Responsibility (CSR))

Two examples are presented in the paragraph to support the first argument against Friedman's definition of the concept.

> [1] The first argument against Friedman's perspective is that managers' decisions have a significant impact on the safety of the wider society. [2] Therefore, they have no right to just pursue profit maximisation for investors without considering other people. [3] A taxi driver, for instance, has an obligation to take passengers to their destination in the shortest time possible, but this does not mean that the driver can break the traffic laws and put other people at risk. [4] Another example is the case of the Ford Pinto, which was put on the market only after a two-year production period. [5] The company appeared to have followed government standards but there were some safety issues

114   PART III

that were overlooked. [6] This oversight for the sake of profit could cause the loss of lives because the vehicle could potentially burst into flames from over-heating because the fan belt was constructed from low grade material. [7] Therefore, managers' decisions have impact on the safety of society.

Which example is not relevant to the subject or topic? Why? _____

2.   (A paragraph from 1st year Nursing, discussing issues and trends)

> The nursing profession has often been sexualised and this perception is consistently presented by the media. One example is a piece of artwork (DepositPhotos, 2012) used in advertising. It is a modern cartoon depicting four doctors in the top row of the picture and five nurses in the second row of the picture. The positioning of the doctors and nurses implies a hierarchy of the medical team as being superior to the nursing team. Furthermore, the physicians are all portrayed as male and the nurses as female, and associated with children. This is a reinforcement of the long-standing stereotype that nursing is synonymous with nurturing and mothering and is an inherently feminine profession (Fagin & Diers, 1983). Further to this, the cartoon is placed on a blue background. This could be seen to imply a perceived dominance of males as doctors in the healthcare setting, as blue is predominantly a male colour. Importantly, the nursing staff in the image are all seen to be holding non-technical equipment such as blankets and towels. In contrast, the medical staff are all pictured with stethoscopes and diagnostic tools, reinforcing the commonly held belief that nurses are merely doctors 'handmaidens' and their clinical role is purely to assist the physician in what he or she has ordered (Jind Bradley, 2003). This aspect of the image also suggests that nurses do not have a role to play in the assessment of patients. Finally, the nurses are all portrayed wearing short dresses. This very much depicts the widely held perception of nursing as a sexualised profession, in contrast to the actual role of the nurse in the healthcare setting.

   a)   What words in the topic sentence [T] identify the theme of the paragraph?
   b)   The example used in the paragraph is a visual image. The writer identifies specific details in the image and explains their significance in relation to the topic sentence. Can you give TWO examples of this technique?

3.   (A paragraph from 2nd year Political Studies, discussing the role played by fear in the effectiveness of Cold War propaganda, with examples from Eastern and Western Blocs)

> [1] The Soviet Union was successful in its black propaganda, and was able to create the 'optimum level of anxiety through fear in order to achieve its aims'. [2] In 1956, Radio Free Hungary announced that the U.S. would send support in the event of a popular uprising against Communist rule. [3] When the inevitable uprising occurred, no U.S. troops arrived, despite the radio's pleas for aid. As a result, Soviet tanks were able to enter Budapest to stop the revolution. [4] The station was, in fact, operated by the KGB who knew that intervention by the U.S. was unlikely. [5] Their black propaganda deliberately set up expectations that when not met made the U.S. appear unreliable and heightened fears of isolation in East Europe. [6] The strategy was useful to the Soviets as it created an environment in East Europe that was more susceptible to Communism. [7] This tactic of 'hostile isolationism' was started by Stalin and continued for some time after his death. [8] It pursued the Lenin-Marxist goal of spreading Communism throughout the world.

c) Which ONE of the following options describe the type of example used to show how black propaganda caused fear: ACTIVITY | VISUAL IMAGE | INCIDENT

d) Which sentences relate to the example specifically? _____

4. (A paragraph from 1st year Comparative Literature essay, examining representations of power in reading texts studied on the course)

As indicated by the topic sentence [T], the paragraph examines the superiority of men over women. The student uses different reading texts as examples to illustrate one central idea. Each text is followed by a specific detail that relates the text to the topic.

Paragraph Structure   **Development**

[1] The belief that men are superior to women and therefore more powerful is clearly evident in several texts. [2] [In 'Ruth's Song', Gloria Steinem explores her mother's lack of power as a woman in a patriarchal society ... [3] Not only does her father have power over his wife as the sole provider, but the male doctors that treat her mother also exercise power over her health ... [4] In 'Zahra Remembers', the physical power of men over women is also explored ... [5] Zahra's mother's betrayal of her husband is punished severely with both mother and daughter being beaten ... [6] The lack of power of these women ultimately leads to their destruction.

2.

3.

4.

5.

a) Identify two texts and their respective detail by filling in each box with one of these options: TEXT | SPECIFIC DETAIL

b) What is the purpose of sentence [6]? _____

5. (A paragraph from 1st year Music, arguing against the claim by Wagner that 'the symphony would be dead by the end of the nineteenth century')

[1] Another argument against Wagner's statement is to examine innovations in the arrangement of movement. [2] Traditional symphony consists of three or four movements but the works of composers such as Mahler, Stravinsky, Shostakovich and Schoenberg who were famous at the end of the nineteenth and beginning of the twentieth century perfectly exemplify the innovative and mature style of post nineteenth century symphonic form. [3] For example, Mahler's symphony No. 5, which was written between 1901 and 1902 consists of five movements ... [4] Shostakovich's symphony No. 8 is cast in five movements. [5] The last three movements are played without a break, which is a very good illustration of the diversification and innovation in the symphonic arrangements of the twentieth century. [6] Another notable example of innovation in symphonic movement is Stravinsky's well-known 1913 composition 'The Rite of Spring'.

a) Which word(s) in sentence [1] identify the <u>theme</u> or <u>central idea</u> of the paragraph?

b) How many examples are given to illustrate the theme? _____

c) Find two other expressions used to introduce examples besides '*For example*'.

_____

_____

5.2 Writing extended definitions

University written assignments often deal with complex concepts which need more than a one-sentence definition to be understood clearly. Extended definitions of concepts are commonly used by students in the first body paragraph after the introduction. Extension techniques vary depending on the subject area and the concept being defined.

The following diagram summarises some ways to develop an extended definition paragraph:

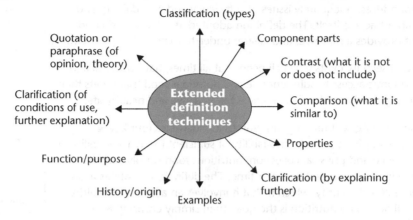

Study how some of these techniques are used to write extended definitions in the following examples:

Example 1 (1st year Business, debating whether entrepreneurship can be taught)

The paragraph has all the elements of the TEC model. Notice also the use of the logical connectors and other signals to help the reader follow the development of the definition:

Paragraph Structure   **Development**

Logical connectors

T   There are two competing theories about the definition of   Classification
entrepreneurship. Traditionally, entrepreneurship is defined in terms of
the personal characteristics. Proponents of this theory believe that
entrepreneurs are individuals who are more creative (Fisher & Koch,
2008, p. 1). In other words, those who are not born with these
entrepreneurial traits cannot become an entrepreneur, even if they are
trained to think and behave like an entrepreneur (Thompson, 2004,
p. 246). On the other hand, scholars who reject the traditional   Contrast
approach of defining entrepreneurship believe that entrepreneurship
E   is a behaviour as opposed to a set of innate personality traits. For
example, Spinelli and Adams (2012) defined entrepreneurship as 'a
way of thinking, reasoning, and acting that is opportunity obsessed,
holistic in approach, and leadership balanced for the purposes of   Quotation
value creation and capture' (p. 87). They believe that it is possible
to teach individuals to act and think entrepreneurially (Drucker,
1985, p. 23; Spinelli & Adams, 2012, p. 42). To this day, there is no
consensus on the definition of entrepreneurship. However, the theory
C   that entrepreneurs owe their success to a set of innate personality
traits and not all aspects of entrepreneurship can be taught through
education remains widely accepted.

Example 2 (4th year Political Studies on 'The state of food security: sources and solutions')

Paragraph Structure   **Development**

T   **Defining food security**

Defined in its most general sense, food security represents someone
having access to enough food to lead a healthy lifestyle. This definition
does not address adequately issues of sufficiency and affordability and
clarity about access itself. The definition adopted at 1996 World Food
Summit provides a narrower and clearer understanding of the problem:

> 'Food security exists when all people, at all times, have physical and
> economic access to sufficient safe and nutritious food that meets their
> dietary needs and food preferences for an active and healthy life.'[1]

Quotation
(footnote
referencing style –
footnote not
included)

E

The Food and Agriculture Organisation (FAO) identifies four key
components of food security: availability of sufficient food; accessibility in
terms of price and physical collection; nutritious food supply sufficient for
a healthy lifestyle; and stability over time. The definition identifies a key
problem in food security, which is that it involves an active and healthy
lifestyle. If adequate nutrition is the goal, then simply ensuring access
to food is insufficient. Access to clean water, sanitary conditions, and

 Components

Clarification

C   health care are necessary to transform food into a healthy lifestyle. Food
*in*security exists in the absence of one or more of the above components.

 Contrast

PRACTICE ACTIVITY 5.2

1.   (1st year Political Studies essay, debating whether force should be used to protect and/or improve the
     lives of others)

The student begins his argument with an extended definition of the key concept 'force'. How does the
student develop the definition paragraph? In each box, write the appropriate technique for each selected
sentence from these options:

CLASSIFICATION | EXAMPLE | CLARIFICATION | CONTRAST | PURPOSE

Paragraph Structure   **Development**

[1] To begin with, it is important to define the keyword in the question.
[2] In political contexts, force basically implies two meanings: armed
force and non-armed force. [3] Non-armed force is an economic
sanction. [4] Its basic purpose is to restrict foreign trade and finance or
withhold economic benefits such as state aid from targeted or other
targeted non-state actors to accomplish broader security or foreign
policy objectives. [5] For example, as part of the six-party talks in 2007
over North Korean nuclear disarmament, an important incentive for
North Korea to comply was the promise of aid. [6] By contrast, armed
force is the deployment of military power and weapons to protect the
interests of the state and its citizens. [7] The problem arises in the

S2

S4

S5

S6

case of using armed force since it is basically illegal for a single actor to use force in the international community unless it is for self-defence. [8] Only the UN and the UNSC can use armed force or authorise a single actor to use armed force if there is a real threat to peace. [9] This makes justifying intervention by armed force a controversial issue.

S7&8

2. (4th year Computer Engineering report about student's intelligent tutoring system (ITS))

This definition is the first paragraph in the introduction section. Write the appropriate technique in each box from these options: COMPARISON | COMPONENTS | FUNCTION

Paragraph Structure	Development
[1] Intelligent Tutoring System (ITS) is an intelligent computer programme used to aid learning using the latest technologies. [2] It plays a vital role in engineering education because it has the advantage of being able to provide a range of learning options, which include individualised tutoring, feedback and performance monitoring that is not bound by time. [3] This intelligent tutoring system consists of four components: the expert module, the student diagnosis module, the tutoring module, and the human computer interface. [4] These four components collectively test, instruct, guide and monitor independent learning. [5] Other ITS systems may have different components. [6]The Summary Sheet, for example, has an interface which engages students in a sequence of writing, obtaining feedback and rewriting. [7] However, they all share the common aim to engage students in innovative independent learning.	S2 S3 S5

3. (2nd year Education essay, explaining one of the views of controversial Brazilian educator, Paolo Freire – the 'banking concept')

Analyse the development of the extended definition by answering the questions below it:

[1] Freire (1972) used the term 'banking concept' to describe a one-sided concept of education in which the teachers have all the knowledge and the students have none. [2] In the classroom, this means the teacher deposits knowledge to the students who listen passively, follow instructions and learn what they are taught without being able to question or challenge it. [3] For example, students may be taught how to write or do mathematics in a certain way but they are not told why that is important or what the purpose of learning it is. [4] In other words, students are not encouraged to be active agents in the learning process or be critical about the ideas they learn. [5] Freire argues that the banking concept of education is oppressive [because] the oppressors can perpetuate information that allows them to stay powerful. [6] Therefore, not encouraging students to actively engage with the learning material can be seen as a political act of oppression.

a) Which words in sentence [1] identify the theme of the paragraph? _____
b) What extension technique is used in sentences [2] and [4]? _____
c) What specific words are used to achieve the purpose of this technique in each sentence?
    Sentence 2: _____   Sentence 4: _____
d) What extended definition technique is used in sentence 5? _____

5.3 Analysing differences and similarities

In Unit 2.4, we looked at comparison and contrast from an organisational perspective, and in particular, whether to compare the items separately or together, in pairs. This unit examines comparison and contrast as a development technique with a specific focus on style.

A feature of comparative analysis is the use of explicit markers to signal differences or similarities. Some contrast markers include *however, on the other hand, by contrast, unlike*. Some comparison markers include *both, similar, like, in the same way, also, neither ... nor*. Another feature is the use of concrete examples and evidence.

Focus on style: two aspects

➡ Use of comparison-contrast markers

- Minimal use of comparison-contrast markers

The following example is typical of the way students develop comparison-contrast ideas in their essays. It is a manageable approach and relatively easy to construct.

Example (3rd year Sociology essay, in which the student is asked to critically reflect on how similar or different the Expert Advisory Group's view on the issue of child poverty is compared to those of National governments in the 1990s)

First point of comparison	Development of first point of comparison
Child payments – EAG **Child payments – NG**	**Food In Schools – beyond the neoliberal appetite?** In addition to housing, the Advisory Group's report identifies the education system as a vehicle which can be utilised to address child poverty. One recommendation made in this regard is the provision of food to children in low-decile schools (EAG, 2012, p. 60). Feeding children in this direct manner can ensure that they have an adequate and nutritious diet (EAG, 2012, p. 60). The state's role is seen as vital in safeguarding the consistency of food distribution (Johnston 2013, n.p.). The Advisory Group (2012, p. 60) therefore recommends that the central government undertakes a leadership role in the food programme. By contrast, the National Governments of the 1990s regarded the direct provision of food to children as a responsibility outside of its mandate. In a system that emphasises self-reliance, the provision of food in schools is regarded as the responsibility of parents (Cheyne, 2005, p. 40). Furthermore, neoliberal policies dictate that parents who struggle to feed their children should make themselves more competitive on the job market ... (Kelsey, 1995, p. 279). To encourage this focus on paid work, the monetary value of most benefits were cut by as much as 24 percent (Kelsey, 1995, p. 277). These reforms saw drastic social implications as child poverty and food insecurity rates soared (St John, 2008, p. 80) ... National Government's policy in the 1990s therefore reflected the neoliberal values of individual responsibility and autonomy.

Uses one contrast marker

Uses other logical connectors to explain the difference

- Moderate use of comparison-contrast markers

Example (2nd year Film, Television and Media Studies, comparing how two films use historical settings to comment on contemporary issues)

This is the first body paragraph, which compares the historical settings of *The Last Samurai* and *Gosford Park*. A notable difference is that reference is made to the first film when the second film is discussed. This makes the comparison less descriptive. Notice also the use of other phrases of comparison (adjectives, negative statements, and prepositions) besides the standard comparison-contrast markers.

<u>Comparison point</u>: setting

[1] Both films are set in important periods of history. [2] *The Last Samurai* is set in 1870s Japan during the Meiji Restoration period. [3] It was an important period in Japanese history, one marked by strides towards modernisation. [4] This period also signalled the decline of the Samurai class and way of life. [5] The film uses many dramatic and varied settings to introduce the main themes of contrasting cultures. [6] By contrast, *Gosford Park* does not have such epic settings, but the setting of 1930s Britain is just as significant, particularly in relation to the crumbling of its rigid class system with the outbreak of the Second World War in 1939. [7] Unlike *The Last Samurai*, the entire action of *Gosford Park* takes place in a wealthy English country house, in which exist two social worlds: the downstairs world of the domestic servants and the upstairs world of their employers. [8] The single location provides greater opportunities for close observations of the two classes, without the need for dramatic and varied settings.

Emphasises difference

Comparison phrase

Mentions the first film

Adjectives of comparison

Contrastive adjectives

Preposition

- Over-use of comparison-contrast markers

Example (1st year English: Compare and contrast the portraits of the Squire (ll. 79–100) and the Clerk (ll. 287–310) in the General Prologue. What, if anything, do these two pilgrims have in common?)

The writer makes a good attempt to draw out the contrasts using mainly comparison-contrast markers. Many of the sentences begin in the same way.

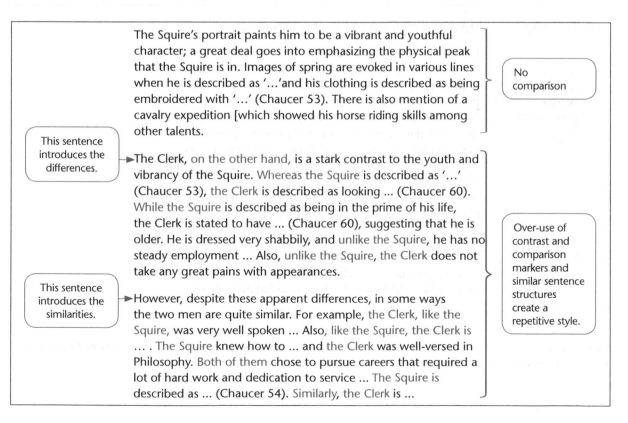

The Squire's portrait paints him to be a vibrant and youthful character; a great deal goes into emphasizing the physical peak that the Squire is in. Images of spring are evoked in various lines when he is described as '…'and his clothing is described as being embroidered with '…' (Chaucer 53). There is also mention of a cavalry expedition [which showed his horse riding skills among other talents.

No comparison

This sentence introduces the differences.

The Clerk, on the other hand, is a stark contrast to the youth and vibrancy of the Squire. Whereas the Squire is described as '…' (Chaucer 53), the Clerk is described as looking … (Chaucer 60). While the Squire is described as being in the prime of his life, the Clerk is stated to have … (Chaucer 60), suggesting that he is older. He is dressed very shabbily, and unlike the Squire, he has no steady employment … Also, unlike the Squire, the Clerk does not take any great pains with appearances.

This sentence introduces the similarities.

However, despite these apparent differences, in some ways the two men are quite similar. For example, the Clerk, like the Squire, was very well spoken … Also, like the Squire, the Clerk is … . The Squire knew how to … and the Clerk was well-versed in Philosophy. Both of them chose to pursue careers that required a lot of hard work and dedication to service … The Squire is described as … (Chaucer 54). Similarly, the Clerk is …

Over-use of contrast and comparison markers and similar sentence structures create a repetitive style.

Revision: Consider using other comparison vocabulary, combining sentences and varying sentence openings, as shown below:

> The Clerk, on the other hand, is in stark contrast to the youth and vibrancy of the Squire. The clerk lacks vitality, being described as looking '...' (Chaucer 60). He is stated to have '...' (Chaucer 60), suggesting that he is older than the Squire and without steady employment. Physical appearance is not as important to the Clerk. Instead of fine clothing, he wears ... .

Use verbs adjectives of comparison, prepositions.

> Despite these apparent differences, in some ways, the characters are quite similar. For example, both men were portrayed as well-spoken and well-mannered. Another similarity is in their pursuit of careers that required a lot of hard work and dedication to service and teaching. In terms of knowledge, they both exhibit ...

Vary sentence openings and combine sentences to avoid beginning with 'the Squire' or 'the Clerk'.

Biased comparison

This means the comparison is unfair because it favours or is against one party more than the other. In academic comparison-contrast analyses, it would normally be expected that some strengths are mentioned along with weaknesses. In the example below, although the evidence may be true, the comparison is unrealistic in that one prime minister is so negatively rated.

Example (3rd year Political Studies, discussing the attributes of a political leader in relation to the performance of two recent prime ministers)

First attribute	Development by comparison in two paragraphs
Extreme language – negative point of view	[1] A successful political leader needs to excel on two fronts: party leadership and national leadership. [2] Party leadership requires ... [3] National leadership identifies the changing mood of the nation and inspires nationalism. [4] ... ultimately failed in his party leadership ability: left-wing ideologies were disregarded in ...; ministers defected forming alternative political parties such as ... . [5] Traditional Labour voters suspended their support, as evidenced by the 1990 election results. [6] The unpopularity of his government's economic reforms even undermined the positive nationalistic efforts with his anti-nuclear and anti-apartheid stances.
Extreme language – positive point of view	By contrast, ... successfully garnered the support of her party, controlled her cabinet and caucus, and coalesced the party ... and inspired nationalism by her recognition of wars, collective grief and the debt owed to those who fought in them.

Revision: Use qualification or hedging strategies to present a fairer and more reasonable argument (see *Part IV Presenting a point of view: argumentation* for more explanation and examples).

Read the revision of sentences [4] to [6] in the first paragraph:

[4] ...'s party leadership style probably contributed to problems faced by his party during critical periods. [5] His left-wing ideologies were viewed to promote ... which could have been seen to contradict the ... [6] This could have explained why ... [7] To some extent, the 1990 election results reflected the growing lack of confidence of voters [...] [8] There was general approval of his anti-nuclear and anti-apartheid stances which did gain him a degree of national and international recognition and respect. However, these positive nationalistic efforts were regarded by some economists to have been undermined ...

These are 'hedging' words used to reduce the force of the verb. (See *Part IV Presenting a point of view* for more on this technique.)

PRACTICE ACTIVITY 5.3

Using the techniques illustrated in the examples, write a paragraph from the notes in the table, which compares two views on child poverty. The notes are adapted from a 3rd year Political Studies essay, which compares a 2010 report from an independent advisory group against the government's policies in the 1990s.

View of the Expert Advisory Group for Child Poverty Solutions (2010 report)	View of the government in the 1990s
– favours a return to universal welfare ideologies	– took a neo-liberal view: minimal state intervention
– universal child payments to be made available to all parents with children under the age of six	– removed family benefit payments (which lasted from 1945 to 1991)
– viable method of providing government assistance to families with young children	– promoted the ideals of personal individuality and self – reliance
– government – an important role in ensuring equal opportunities and sense of well-being	– believed that citizenship – not gateway to universal entitlement of rights
– evidence of success of universal payment schemes in other countries	– universal payments system – unsustainable
	– targeting low-income groups – fiscally more viable

5.4 Explaining causes and effects

This technique of development involves explaining the reasons for or results of an action, event or decision. The purpose is to show clearly the relationship between the cause and the effect by using appropriate language.

The technique is relevant in assignments in many subject areas. In each of the following assignments, you are required to show the relationship of factors (causes) that lead to a given situation (the effects):

A study of anorexia and its effects on human growth and development (Anthropology)

The relationship between socio-economic class and educational attainment (Education)

An examination of how immigration led to changed attitudes and understandings of race (History)

An examination of how capitalism has led to mass surveillance of the work force (Sociology)

Consideration of the environmental impact of setting up a methanol plant (Chemical Engineering feasibility study)

A case study examining famine as a security risk (Political Studies)

How does it work?

The following three examples show different ways of explaining causes and effects:

- explicit use of conventional cause-effect words (*causes, leads, is due to; has an effect on; affects, results in, contributes to, is linked to, has an impact on*).
- modal verbs (*can, may, could*) to indicate that the cause and effect relationship is less certain.
- other verbs and sentence structures.

As you study the following examples, notice in particular how the above language features are used to explain cause-effect relationships.

Example 1 (3rd year Anthropology essay, examining the effects of anorexia on human growth and development)

The following diagram shows the relationship between cause factors and effects described in a paragraph from the Literature Review section of the research paper:

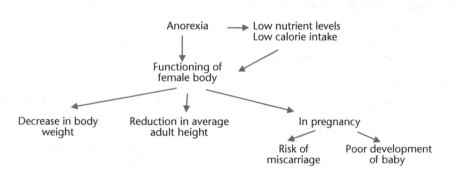

Explicit use of cause-effect language and modal verbs

This analysis uses <u>explicit</u> cause-effect language and modal verbs to establish the relationship between the cause and effect relationships in the diagram:

> Eating disorders can have a number of effects on the functioning of the female body. One of the widely known facts about anorexia is a decrease in body weight, but it can also affect the reproductive cycle. It may also affect neonate development which may have a subsequent impact on the development of the [unborn baby]. (Kouba *et al.*, 2005). These effects can include a reduction in birth weight, small head circumference possible preterm births, or increased risk of a miscarriage (Bulik, 1999 cited in Kouba *et al.*, 2005). Findings from a study by Ellison (2003) found that a reduced brain size could be caused by varying levels of nutrient intake during pregnancy. In other studies, low caloric intake during childhood and throughout adolescence has been linked with a reduction in average adult height (Modan-Moses, 2003).

Modal verbs (can, may) and active form of verb

Noun phrase

Evidence with citation

Passive form of verb

Use of other verbs and sentence structures

Example 2 (2nd year Education, arguing that socio-economic class greatly impacts educational attainment)

This paragraph uses causal analysis to develop the idea that culture has an impact on educational attainment. You will notice that the analysis does not use as many or the same explicit cause-effect markers as those used in Example 1. Can you follow the cause-effect development?

> Gramsci (1971) identifies two ways in which culture can affect educational attainment. The first way is cultural hegemony. This is when the dominant culture of society becomes embedded in institutions and accepted by citizens. Gramsci saw cultural hegemony as oppressive as it reproduces social conditions of society, in which one culture is viewed as the more dominant. Cultural hegemony is relatable to educational attainment. This is because students from minority cultures may learn to accept that they cannot compete with the dominant culture, causing them to have lower expectations of educational success. The second way is culture that is related to art and literature, which has been viewed as being the monopoly of the privileged. Gramsci believed that a culturally rich education should be available to all individuals regardless of their socio-economic class position because a rich education would help them to improve their position in society

Other verbs and sentence structures

Example 3 (2nd year Chemical Engineering, on the viability of setting up a methanol plant)

Cause and effect analyses are common in engineering reports. This paragraph is from the section of a feasibility report, which discusses the environmental impact of gas emissions from a methanol plant.

> **Environmental impact**
> [1] Every chemical plant operation brings environmental effects caused by waste gas emissions from the plant. [2] The waste gases discharged from a methanol plant include hydrogen sulphide, carbon monoxide, carbon dioxide and hydrogen. [3] Human health, plant life and animals can be severely threatened if exposed to large amounts of the gases over a prolonged period [4] Hydrogen sulphide (H_2S) has an unpleasant smell and is very dangerous when the gas level in the air reaches over 50ppm. [5] According to Kilburn, Professor at the University of Southern California of Medicine, 'H_2S poisons the brain, and the poisoning is irreversible'. [6] There is medical evidence that exposure to large amounts of H_2S produces neurological symptoms including memory loss and dizziness. [7] Carbon monoxide is also poisonous but it is hard to detect since it is an odourless gas. [9] Carbon monoxide reduces oxygen delivery to body tissues and is risky once the gas level reaches 200ppm.

Conditional sentence with 'if' clause

Adverb clauses with 'when', 'once'

Other verbs

1.   Using cause-effect expressions
(Text from a 2nd year Education essay, arguing that socio-economic class affects educational attainment)

Fill in each box with a suitable cause-effect word or phrase from the options below:

is associated with	result in	could have an impact	leads to
could affect	correlation exists	consequently	

According to Parsons (1957), the idea that mass public education gives every child an equal opportunity is an ideological view of education. He argues that school is, in fact, a place of socialization, where children are conditioned to fill certain roles in society. Secondary school is seen as the basic education that everyone receives. A tertiary education qualification [1. _____] better occupations, status and salaries. Through school, children also learn how socio-economic position [2. _____] certain professions and status. [3. _____], individuals from a wealthy family or whose parents have high-income professions are more likely to have high expectations of themselves. These expectations are likely to [4. _____] success in school. However, an individual from a low income family or whose parents have low income jobs may not have the same high expectations. Their lower expectations [5. _____] their motivation and educational attainment. In fact, research over the years has also suggested that a [6. _____] between socio-economic class and youth dropouts from school. Therefore, education can be seen as a way that individuals' social conditions are reproduced, which [7. _____] on levels of educational attainment.

2.   Using other logical connectors
(1st year History, on how immigration led to changed attitudes and understandings of race)

This causal analysis does not use conventional cause-effect expressions listed earlier (e.g. *causes, leads to, results in*) but relies on other logical connectors and cohesive devices.

Follow the development of the causal analysis by completing the flow chart in the right margin. Fill in the spaces (a) to (d) with a suitable word or phrase from the text.

[1] Prior to great waves of immigrants, understandings of race were largely focused around obvious physical differences which made race an easily categorised and understood concept. [2] However, with increased immigration, understandings of race became more complicated and racial antipathy greatly intensified. [3] This was due, in part, to the economic threat that immigrants posed to long-settled citizens. [4] In America, anti-Asiatic feelings resulted from Chinese immigration in the1840s and Japanese immigration in the late nineteenth century. [5] Asian immigrants were willing to work for very little money and many Americans saw this as a direct threat to the white man's ability to earn money. [6] Therefore, it was commonly thought that cheap Asian labour 'lowered the American standard of living'. [7] Similarly in New Zealand, immigrants were often viewed as threats to economic security for they brought with them economic competition. [8] In fact, anti-Asiatic sentiments peaked at times of economic recession and high unemployment. [9] For example, 1879 and 1888 were years of harsh economic climate and both saw a peak in anti-Asiatic attitudes. [10] Thus, the competition for resources made racist attitudes prominent. [11] In both America and New Zealand, race became understood as a direct threat to the economic livelihood of their citizens.

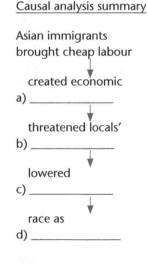

Causal analysis summary

Asian immigrants brought cheap labour

↓

created economic
a) _____

↓

threatened locals'
b) _____

↓

lowered
c) _____

↓

race as
d) _____

3. (Postgraduate Political Studies essay on The State of Food Security: Problems and Solutions)

This diagram is derived from a paragraph describing the effect of climate change on food security. The topic and end sentences are provided. Using the cause-effect analysis technique shown in the examples, develop the middle section of the paragraph from the notes to explain the relationship between climate change and food insecurity.

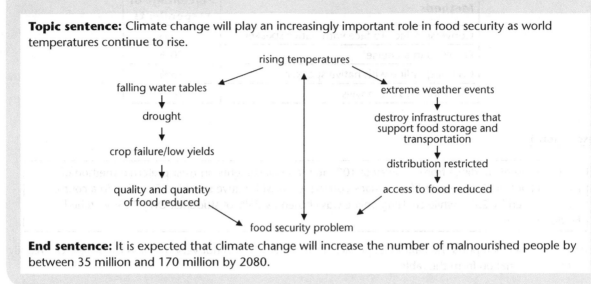

Topic sentence: Climate change will play an increasingly important role in food security as world temperatures continue to rise.

rising temperatures

falling water tables

drought

crop failure/low yields

quality and quantity of food reduced

extreme weather events

destroy infrastructures that support food storage and transportation

distribution restricted

access to food reduced

food security problem

End sentence: It is expected that climate change will increase the number of malnourished people by between 35 million and 170 million by 2080.

5.5 Describing data presented in figures and tables

This technique is used in reports which often include facts and statistics presented in figures (graph, map, chart or drawing) or tables. It involves writing an explanatory text or commentary to accompany the visuals. The data or graphic information may be derived from your own experiments or from other sources.

If you include a figure or table in your writing, make some reference to it to justify its inclusion in the report. The description or commentary not only introduces the visual but it also highlights its significance in relation to the aims of the study or experiment. The length and content of the description may vary. It could be a few sentences to support a point made or longer, especially for figures and tables included in the Results section of reports because the description provides a basis for the Discussion section.

How do you describe data?

Describing data is not a matter of repeating the raw data as it appears in the table or figure. Instead, it is about interpreting and commenting on the data. It follows three steps:

Describe purpose and specific content	What does the figure show: the relationship between values, a comparison, trends?
↓	
Interpret the data	What does the data mean? What trends or patterns stand out? Why?
↓	
Comment on the data	How significant are the findings in relation to the aims of the study or experiment?

How does the three-step technique work?

Example 1 Read two descriptions of Table 1:

Table 1 Four methods of learning English

Methods	Percentage of respondents
Conversing face-to-face with native speakers	45%
Enrolling in a course	20%
Chatting online with native speakers	25%
Watching English movies	10%

Description 1

> Table 1 presents findings from a survey of 100 international students on their preferred method of learning English. 45% selected face-to-face conversations with native speakers. Enrolling in a course was preferred by 25%, while chatting online was chosen by 25% of students. Only 10% watched English movies.

Description 1 merely reports the data as it appears in the table, which is not very useful as the reader can readily extract this information from the table.

Description 2 combines description, interpretation and commentary to highlight significant data, patterns or trends:

Description { Table 1 presents findings from a survey of 100 international students on their preferred method of learning English from four options. The most popular method was face-to-face conversations. Nearly half of the respondents favoured face-to-face conversations with native speakers. Using modern

Interpretation

The highlighted words compare trends and point out what is significant.

{ technologies to communicate also featured strongly, with about a quarter of the respondents preferring online interactions. The more formal method of learning English by enrolling in a course was less favoured, with only one fifth of the respondents selecting it. The more passive and solitary nature of watching movies was the least preferred method, accounting for only 5% of respondents. The results suggest

Comment { that activities that involve learning through spontaneous interactions are more popular ways of improving English.

Percentages expressed as proportions

The following example from a third year year Political Studies essay shows the practice of referring to visuals effectively. The reference is brief but the three elements – describe, interpret, comment – are still visible. The visuals relate directly to the central idea of the paragraph.

Example 2 (3rd year Political Studies essay on 'The State of Food Security: Problems and Solutions')

Two figures are included in the paragraph which explains the financial cause of food insecurity.

The financial cause of food insecurity has two dimensions; <u>poverty and the price of food.</u> Poverty and food security share a strong correlation; poverty causes an inability to purchase food, and limits a country's ability to invest in enhanced food production, creating a self-reinforcing cycle. In similar fashion, spikes in the international price of food can be the difference between a household being able to afford to buy food, and hence be food secure, or not being able to afford sufficient food. The FAO's Food Price Index graph indicates that prices spiked between 2007 and 2008 and again between 2010 and 2011, reaching an all-time high in February 2011.[2] Figure 1 illustrates the clear link between food prices and malnutrition.

> Central idea

> Describes, interprets and comments

Focus on style and language

Describing graphic information is about reporting facts accurately and without judgement. When describing data, avoid over-using hedging words such as *seems to, somewhat, fairly, apparently,* or emotive language such as *extremely, strongly* or *obviously.* These words reflect a subjective rather than an objective response and may show your uncertainty about the description.

The following language and vocabulary charts summarise some style and language expressions which can help you describe graphic information.

Chart 1: Range of visuals in terms of use and language

Notice in particular the language focus for each type of visual and data:

Visual	Type of data	Use	Language (see Chart 2)
line graph	chronological or a continuous data set	displays trends and compares changes over time	language of movement and time expressions
bar graph	data in different categories or groups	compares trends/patterns between groups	percentages and proportions, comparison and contrast language
table	independent values	provides a summary of findings, not trends	
pie chart	parts of a whole	compares parts of a whole	
process	steps in a logical sequence	describes how something works from beginning to end	time expressions (*As ... When ... After ... While ... As soon as*)
cycle	interaction between connected elements	describes how something works	logical connectors of sequence (*Firstly, The first stage*)
flow chart or matrix	usually text	shows process and/or relationship between ranks or levels	cause-effect language, sequence connectors

Chart 2: Some useful expressions and sentence structures

Verbs stating purpose

The graph shows | provides | gives | compares summarises | displays | presents

Verbs analysing or interpreting data

The findings reveal | demonstrate (that) | indicate (that) | suggest that

Referring to the graph

The graph shows ...

According to Table 1, there was a sharp ...

As Table 2 shows, the ...

NOT:

As we/you can see in the graph, it shows ...

Describing trends or changes over time

Upward movement	Downward movement	Degree of rise/fall/change
increase rise climb	decrease decline fall	highest point/peak fluctuate sharp rise gradual/ slight rise remain constant/stable/steady flatten out level off

Expressing percentages

According to the graph, 20 per cent of women reported that (**NOT** *20 percentage* of women)

A small percentage of women (**NOT** A small *per cent* of women)

There was a 20 per cent increase in sales. (**NOT** There was a *20 percentage* increase)

Sales increased by 20 per cent. (**NOT** Sales increased by a *per cent of 20%*)

45 per cent of participants used this method of learning English. (**NOT** *There are 45 per cent of participants* used this method of learning English)

Expressing percentages as proportions

Expressing a percentage as a percentage of change rather than exact data can show that you are interpreting the magnitude of the data and highlighting significant trends.

Percentages	Proportions and comparison/contrast language
90%	Ninety per cent	Nearly all	The vast majority of	Nine-tenths of
60%–70%	more than half; nearly two-thirds
increase of 45%	almost doubled
decrease of 45%	almost halved
40%	less than half
10%	a low percentage	a few	a small minority	one tenth of
0–5%	marginal increase/fall
A 20%; B 45%	The percentage of B was two times higher than	twice that of A; There was almost twice as many.	doubled
A 20%; B 22%	The same number of	Nearly the same number of

Expressing quantities

2.7 million people live in the capital city. (**NOT** 2.7 <u>millions</u> people)
5,000 people lived below the poverty line. (**NOT** <u>5 thousand</u> people)

Common sentence structure errors (especially with sentences beginning with 'There is/are'):

According to the graph, <u>there were</u> 75 per cent of people bought something online.

Correction: According to the graph, 75 per cent of people bought something online.

There was a 20 per cent increase in <u>the number of people walked</u> to work.

Correction: There was a 20 per cent increase in the number of people **who** walked to work.
The number of people **who** walked to work increased by 20 per cent.

PRACTICE ACTIVITY 5.5

1. (3rd year Biological Sciences laboratory report, on the effect of temperature on heart rate.)
The graph below presents one of the main findings of the experiment.

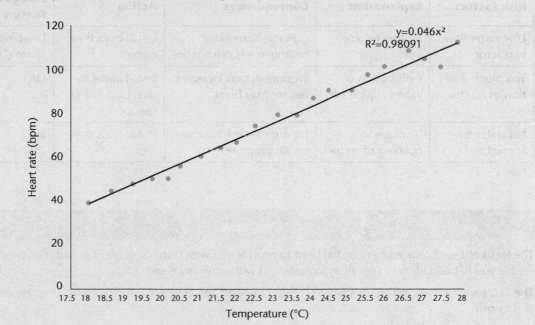

Read the description and answer the questions below it:

[1] Figure 1 shows the relationship between heart rate and water temperature. [2] It shows that there is a positive relationship between heart rate and temperature, with heart rate increasing as temperature increases. [3] This trend conforms to an exponential trend-line with an R^2 of 0.98 suggesting that the trend-line explains 98% of the variation in the data. [4] Regression analysis provided a *P-value* of 7.919×10^{-16}, displaying clear evidence of a relationship between the two factors. [5] There is a slight drop in heart rate after 26.5°C, which is expected when the organism starts to shut down. [6] The crabs were only taken to a temperature that caused them stress. [7] Therefore, the thermal limit for this species is not defined by this study and no break point is seen in the data.

a) Which sentence(s) ...
describe the purpose and specific content?   _____
interpret the data?   _____
comment on the data?   _____
c) Give three evaluative expressions (adjectives, adverbs, verbs) which indicate interpretation:
_____; _____; _____

2. (2nd year Chemical Engineering: a feasibility report on the viability of setting up a methanol plant)

The data in the Table 2 consists of textual information. It summarises the results of a HAZOP (Hazard and Operability) study. (HAZOP is a standard tool commonly used in Engineering feasibility studies to evaluate potential hazards and gather data to support recommendations for improving process safety.)

Write a description of about 60 words to accompany the table. Use the three-step approach (describe, interpret, comment) to avoid repeating words in the table.

Table 2: Summary of HAZOP study on the shift reactor

Risk factors	Explanation	Consequences	Action	Safeguard features
Low water flow in reactor	rupture in pipe inlet	Leakage, flammable hydrogen gas catches fire	Install mass flow meter	Level indicator alarm (LIA)
Too much water flow in reactor	malfunction of valves at pipe inlet	Pressure in tank increases, reactor may burst	Install outlet to direct gas out of reactor	LIA
No water flow in reactor	blockage in opening of rector	Pressure in tank increases, causing rupture	Install mass flow meter	LIA

REVIEW

The focus of *Developing your writing* has been to provide you with techniques, models and frameworks to enable you to build ideas in your essay logically and with confidence and skill.

The TEC paragraph model enables you to construct unified and coherent paragraphs of adequate substance and length.

Expansion and elaboration techniques ensure that each sentence advances the theme in a specific way that helps the reader understand the topic completely. Each technique makes different demands on language use. In full-length essays, a combination of expansion techniques are often used to develop different body paragraphs (see *Part V Putting it all together*).

The extent of the expansion or elaboration of ideas is determined by the word limit set for the assignment. In university writing contexts, it is important to be guided by these length restrictions. Writing over the limit could incur a penalty which usually means a reduction in the final mark or grade.

Using suitable cohesive devices is essential to ensure that the development of ideas can be easily followed (see also *Part I, Unit 4 Coherent flow of ideas*).

Unit 5.5 has not focused on how to present data or graphic information. For guidelines on these aspects, refer to the standard referencing style guides used in your subject area. Most of these guides provide explicit advice on such matters as where to place titles and how to use captions.

Part IV

Presenting a Point of View: Argumentation

Argumentation is the action of reasoning systematically with the aim of persuading others to accept your point of view or thesis on an issue. Essay writing in the Arts, Humanities and Social Sciences, in particular, is often about issues. Issues are topics that people have different opinions about. Therefore, you can expect your thesis to be challenged.

Argumentative writing was introduced in Part II in the unit on essays. Part IV examines this type of writing in more detail. In developing a clear argument in support of your thesis, you will also employ different techniques to elaborate on ideas (see *Part III Developing your writing*). In particular, you will learn effective strategies and language to add an argumentative quality to your writing.

Main units

Unit 1 The elements of argumentation
Unit 2 The issue and thesis statement
Unit 3 Structuring the argument
Unit 4 Building the argument
Unit 5 Argumentative essays for study

UNIT 1 **The elements of argumentation**

Key topics

1.1 The topic and issue
1.2 The elements of argumentation

Academic arguments require careful analysis of the topic and the issues it raises. In academic contexts, argumentation is not about being right or wrong or pointing out that something is either true or false. However, a thesis is usually expected and needs to be justified with logical reasoning and good judgement.

Instructions for argumentative essay assignments are framed differently from those in analytical and discursive essays. In order to develop a clear argument, it is therefore important to understand how the topic or problem for discussion is presented in the question.

1.1 The topic and issue

The issue may be presented as a <u>quotation</u> or a <u>statement</u> that expresses an opinion:

"Art is corrupted by technology". Do you agree? (Anthropology)

> Read the full essay at the end of Part IV

Jo Smith suggests that contemporary film studies should examine how digital technologies affect film form and style and our understanding of narrative. Discuss this claim in relation to one or more film texts or genres. (Film, Television and Media Studies)

The issue may be presented as a <u>question</u>:

Should marijuana be legalised? (Law)

Should we use force to intervene to protect and/or improve the lives of others? (Political Studies)

> Read the full essay at the end of Part IV

To what extent was Japan's modernisation following the Meiji an imitation of Western developments? Explain the reasons for your view. (History)

Do you think it is possible for entrepreneurship to be taught? (Business)

Both statements and questions require a point of view. The purpose of writing is the same – to persuade the reader that your view is the reasonable one. However, the argumentative style may differ, depending on whether a thesis-led approach or a discussion-led approach is used to develop the argument. We will examine these two approaches in more detail in Unit 2, which looks at strategies for developing an argumentative style.

So, what are the challenges?

If this is the first time you have written argumentative essays, you may have the following concerns:

1. How do I show that I am stating my point of view?
2. How can I show that I am presenting an argument and not a description or discussion?
3. Are argumentative essays organised differently from other essays?

1.2 The elements of argumentation

The following diagram summarises the main elements involved in developing an argument:

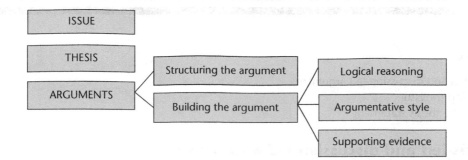

Explanation of elements

The **ISSUE** is the <u>topic</u> that requires your response. The topic is usually arguable. Explaining the issue helps the reader to understand how and why the issue causes disagreement or opposing points of view. In undergraduate academic assignments, two points of view on the issue are usually presented.

The **THESIS** is your <u>point of view or position</u> on the issue. It is a specific statement which tells the reader how you will respond – whether largely agreeing or disagreeing, for example. The thesis is usually stated in the introduction following the explanation of the issue.

ARGUMENTS are the <u>reasons</u> you give to justify your thesis.

Structuring the argument refers to the organisation of the main arguments in the body of the essay. Two organisational patterns are described in Unit 3.

Building the argument (see Unit 4) refers to the development of each argumentative point with

- logical reasoning and use of logical connectors (see also *Part I, Unit 4 Coherent flow of ideas*).
- argumentation strategies and use of appropriate language of argument to distinguish it from writing that is more discursive or descriptive.
- relevant supporting evidence, which could include <u>direct quotations</u>, <u>paraphrases</u>, <u>summaries</u>, <u>examples</u>, <u>research-based evidence</u> and reference to relevant theory or readings from your course.

⚠ When presenting supporting evidence:

- Integrate it smoothly into the text or sentence.
- Use conventions for citing sources correctly.
- Introduce evidence clearly so that the reader can distinguish between your opinion and other people's opinions. This can be achieved by using author tags and reporting verbs, for example, 'Smith (2009) argues' or an introductory phrase such as 'According to Smith (2009)'.

(See also *Part I, Unit 2 Conventions for using sources.*)

UNIT 2 The issue and thesis statement

Key topics

2.1 Thesis-led and discussion-led arguments
2.2 Explaining the issue
2.3 Writing the thesis statement

2.1 Thesis-led and discussion-led arguments

These are two basic approaches to undergraduate argumentative essays. A thesis-led argument usually has a thesis statement in the introduction which identifies your position on the issue clearly. In developing the argument in the body of the essay, you set out to <u>defend</u> your thesis, using persuasion and reasoning. The thesis is usually restated in the conclusion, which reviews the main arguments that support the thesis.

A discussion-led argument adopts a more balanced approach by presenting information on opposing views in a more even way. The thesis statement may be absent or not stated clearly in the introduction. In the conclusion, both views are summarised. However, the reader expects some <u>decision</u> regarding the topic to reach a satisfactory closure to the discussion.

The approach you choose affects the way you present your arguments and use language and other argumentation strategies.

2.2 Explaining the issue

Explaining the issue clearly is important because it prepares the reader to accept your thesis. It includes providing an appropriate context or <u>lead-in</u> to the issue. The purpose of explaining the issue is to establish clearly why there is disagreement. In undergraduate academic arguments, two opposing views may be presented as follows:

- the other view (the view you will argue against)
- your view (the view you support)

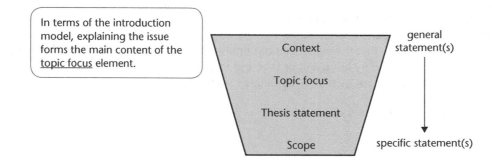

In terms of the introduction model, explaining the issue forms the main content of the <u>topic focus</u> element.

Context — general statement(s)

Topic focus

Thesis statement

Scope — specific statement(s)

How does it work?

The examples below show that it is possible to construct an effective introduction to an argument using these basic principles and the introduction model.

Example 1 (1st year Philosophy, on the Harm Principle and raising the tobacco tax)

The concept of harm reduction has application in a number of policy areas including tobacco sales. Increases in tobacco taxes are widely regarded as a highly effective strategy for reducing tobacco use and its consequences. The government's main argument for raising the tax on tobacco sales is that tobacco 'has no redeeming qualities' and 'the aim ... is to stop its use entirely' ('Time to Quit,' 2010). Some people may view the government's decision as undemocratic and a violation of human rights. In his essay *On Liberty,* Mill (1956) examines the grounds on which interference in the freedom of individuals to act as they wish is morally justifiable. He proposed an answer to this dilemma with his harm principle, which states that 'the only purpose for which power can be rightfully exercised over any member of a civilized community, against his will, is to prevent harm to others. His own good, either physical or moral, is not sufficient warrant' (Mill, 1956, p. 13). In this essay, I will argue that, according to Mill's Harm principle, raising the tax on tobacco sales is not a restriction on the liberty of those who purchase cigarettes.

Annotations:
- Refers to author
- CONTEXT (lead-in to issue)
- TOPIC FOCUS (issue) Two views: a) Government's view b) Mill's view
- THESIS statement (This tells the reader clearly which view is supported)

Example 2 (2nd year Political Studies, responding to this question: Should we use force to intervene to protect and/or improve the lives of others?)

The example shows that, despite some language challenges, there is a sense that the student is <u>building</u> the introduction in a systematic manner. There is no thesis statement.

The twentieth century was the century of human rights and humanity. Awareness of these matters were rapidly raised in the international community. After the Second World War, humanitarian law and humanitarian judgement were substantially improved. A number of international treaties relating to human rights were made one after another, including the protection of human rights, the elimination of racial discrimination and gender discrimination, and the banning of torture. These actions imply that the violation of human dignity and imply that any violation of this dignity is unacceptable even in armed conflict. Intervention using armed force would therefore be viewed as a legitimate action because protecting the dignity of humans and the right to life is a humanitarian act. However, there are those who argue that legitimising humanitarian intervention does not solve the problem. It does not identify or eradicate the root of the problem. This essay outlines some of the key arguments against legitimising a humanitarian intervention, using armed force in particular, and discuss the counter-arguments against intervention.

Annotations:
- Logical connectors
- CONTEXT provides lead-in to the issue
- TOPIC FOCUS Two views: a) forceful intervention is legitimate; b) forceful intervention is not legitimate
- SCOPE

The two example introductions approach the issue differently. Example 1 states the thesis clearly. The essay uses a thesis-led approach. Example 2 does not provide a thesis statement. The essay uses a discussion-led approach, which is explained in the last sentence (SCOPE element). Both express argumentative intent using 'will'. Whether this is appropriate or not is addressed in Unit 4, which looks at different argumentation strategies.

Some common problems

Using a model and some basic principles as explained above can help you build an effective introduction to your argument and avoid the following problems:

- Not establishing a sufficient context as a lead-in to the issue. The context tells the reader why you are writing about the issue, so it is useful to establish it clearly.
- Repeating the claim or quotation in the question. This is not a useful strategy because it does not say anything new or tell the reader that you have understood the issue clearly.
- Being too emotive or emphatic.

Example The following introduction from a Music essay shows some of these problems:

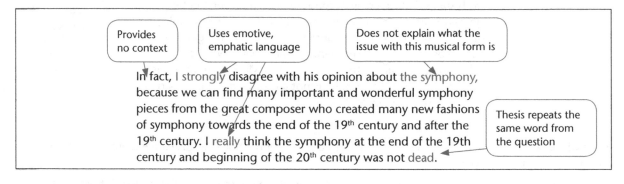

Main problems with the argumentative style

- The introduction does not prepare the reader well for the arguments to follow. There is no context for the claim made by Wagner. The issue is not explained.
- Repeating the same word used in the claim does not provide useful information and leaves many questions unanswered. For example, what did Wagner mean by 'dead' exactly and how does it relate to the symphonic form? Why did he make such a statement? Why was the nineteenth century significant?
- The response contains emotive and extreme language, as shown by the highlighted words.

2.3 Writing the thesis statement

The thesis statement usually follows the explanation of the issue. It states your point of view or position on the issue. A thesis statement is essential in academic arguments to let the reader know how you are going to respond to the question.

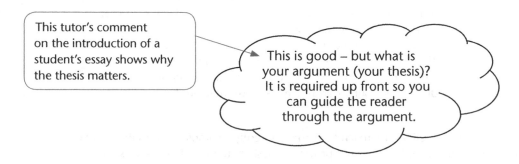

However, as we saw in the two examples in 2.2, the thesis may be presented differently depending on whether the argument uses a thesis-led or discussion-led approach.

Five problems with thesis statements:

➡ Confusing fact with opinion (thesis)

FACT The following sentences are general and commonplace statements of fact.	**OPINION** The underlined expressions evaluate the issue and indicate your thesis (which you have to defend with supporting **evidence** in the body of the essay).
e.g. *Liquid crystal displays are sensitive to high temperatures and moisture.* ⇨	*A critical weakness of liquid crystal displays (LCDs) is their strong sensitivity to high temperatures and moisture.*
e.g. *Overseas travel has both advantages and disadvantages.* ⇨	*Despite some initial difficulties arising from cultural difference, overseas travel provides valuable experiences for the mind, body and soul.*
e.g. *There is no simple answer to the issue of legalisation of marijuana.* ⇨	*The issue is a complex one but in the main, the legalisation of marijuana has far riskier outcomes for society than benefits.*

➡ Confusing scope with opinion

SCOPE This tells the reader what your essay is about.	**OPINION** This tells the reader that you think Friedman's view is too limited and that other aspects of corporate social responsibility need to be considered.
e.g. *This essay will evaluate arguments between the views of corporations and Friedman's opinion about corporate social responsibility and eventually develop a personal stance about how businesses should practise.* ⇨	*This essay will argue that modern business practices reflect a wider application of corporate social responsibility which embraces more than just profit maximisation, as Friedman proposed.*

➡ Repeating the question or claim statement

REPETITION Repeating the question or using words from the question is not useful because it does not show that you have understood the issue.	**NO REPETITION** This thesis statement explains the term 'dead' and some examples of how the symphonic form has survived beyond the nineteenth century.
e.g. *In fact, I disagree with Wagner's opinion that the symphony would be 'dead' by the end of the nineteenth century.* ⇨	*Wagner claimed that Beethoven's Ninth Symphony had exhausted the symphonic form, but it continued to thrive with more innovative styles in orchestration, arrangement, tonality and harmony in the twentieth century.*

➡ Writing a vague thesis

VAGUENESS is caused by using non-specific vocabulary ('better') and overgeneralisation ('everyone'). It is more difficult to justify a vague thesis.	Using **CONCRETE WORDS** and identifying a particular group of people makes the thesis statement clearer and more specific.
e.g. *This essay will argue that paying a living wage is better than a minimum wage. It benefits everyone.* ⇨	*The living wage gives people of lower income better financial resources and enhances their ability to manage their lives more successfully and with greater independence.*

→ Using emotive language and personal pronouns

EMOTIVE LANGUAGE The use of personal pronouns and emotive or extreme language give a subjective tone to your argument and therefore is less acceptable to the reader.	**OBJECTIVE STYLE** Removing personal pronouns and emotive language reflects a more objective and academic argumentative tone.
I strongly disagree with the Smithsonian Institute's view and _I am_ going to talk about what is _wrong_ with that view.	The Smithsonian Institute's view does not acknowledge the historical context and the effects of the bombing on the cities many generations later.

PRACTICE ACTIVITY 2.1

A Explaining the issue

1. (Introduction from a 1st year Anthropology, responding to this claim 'art is corrupted by technology')

> [1] The use of technology within the music industry has been controversial from its very conception. [2] Technologies now entrenched into popular music culture were initially regarded with suspicion and considered emotionally dishonest (Frith, 1986). [3] Using technology to make music has been criticised as inauthentic, alienating to audiences, and opposed to art and nature (Frith, 1986). [4] However, many do not consider the positive effects technology can have on the creation and experience of music. [5] Points that are commonly overlooked are how accessible music is made through technology [...] and the innovative uses and explorations that can be made through technology. [6] Far from being corrupted, art can be enhanced and explored in different ways, as well made more accessible.

   a) Is there an adequate context (lead-in) to the issue? YES ☐ NO ☐
   b) Which sentences explain the other view: Sentences [   ] to [   ]
   c) Which sentences explain the student's view: Sentences [   ] to [   ]
   d) Which sentence states the thesis: Sentence [   ]

2. (Introduction from 2nd year History, responding to this statement: 'Japan's modernisation following the Meiji period appeared to imitate Western developments'. Do you agree?)

> [1] Many aspects of Japan's modernisation following the Meiji appeared to imitate Western developments. [2] Many Western institutions and systems were adopted such as a police force and Western-style factories. [3] In this essay I will argue that the usual purpose of such adoptions was not to imitate the West but rather to enhance Japanese power by adapting Western ideas to advance Japanese values. [4] In some areas, however, the West was clearly imitated, particularly in aspects of culture and the daily lives of some groups. [5] These imitations were temporary, however, and their scope was limited. [6] I will begin by discussing the motivations of Japan for the adoption of Western developments and then demonstrate how the Japanese used these developments to advance their values using the examples of learning from the West and education.

   a) Is there an adequate context (lead-in) to the issue? YES ☐ NO ☐
   b) In a few words, explain the other view. _____

c) In a few words, explain the student's view. _____

d) Which sentence(s) states the thesis? Sentence(s) [ ]

3. (Introduction from 2nd year Business, responding to this question: 'Do you think it is possible for entrepreneurship to be taught?')

> [1] The question of whether it is possible for a person to learn to become an entrepreneur has vexed numerous scholars. [2] For many decades, entrepreneurs have been seen as individuals who are born with specific set of personality traits and abilities that enable them to recognise and exploit business opportunities. [3] A person without these innate attributes simply cannot be educated to become an entrepreneur. [4] However, there is sufficient evidence to suggest that a person does not need to have a set of specific personality traits in order to become an entrepreneur. [5] Anyone who can learn to behave entrepreneurially can become an entrepreneur. Research also shows that it is possible for aspiring entrepreneurs to learn to acquire entrepreneurial soft-skills, such as the ability to think creatively and take calculated risk through participation in activities that are designed to simulate real entrepreneurial experience. [6] This essay will explain the reasons why, contrary to the widely-accepted myth, it is possible for entrepreneurship to be taught to aspiring entrepreneurs.

a) Is there an adequate context (lead-in) to the issue? YES ☐ NO ☐
b) What is the other view? _____ _____
c) What is the writer's view? _____ _____
d) Is there an explicit thesis statement? YES ☐ NO ☐

B Writing thesis statements

Evaluate the following thesis statements by ticking a box (or more, if it applies) in the right margin.

Example:

(from 1st year Anthropology: responding to the claim that 'art is corrupted by technology') *Far from being corrupted, through technology, art can be enhanced and explored in different ways, as well as made more accessible.*	☐ Gives scope ☐ Repeats the question ☑ Clear thesis ☐ Vague or general thesis ☐ Uses emotive language/Personal pronouns

NOW YOU TRY

1. (From 2nd year Education, responding to this claim: 'Egalitarian ideals of modern democratic society suggest that massed public schooling provides every individual an equal opportunity and access to education')

This essay will argue that this claim is false and that socio-economic class greatly impacts educational attainment.	☐ Gives scope ☐ Repeats the question ☐ Clear thesis ☐ Vague or general thesis ☐ Uses emotive language/ personal pronouns

2. (From 1st year Management, responding to Milton Friedman's claim that "there is only one social responsibility of business – to use its resources and engage in activities to increase its profits without deception or fraud")

[...] Finally, my contrast opinion about the quote will be shown.	☐ Gives scope ☐ Repeats the question ☐ Clear thesis ☐ Vague or general thesis ☐ Uses emotive language/ personal pronouns

3. (From 2nd year Law, responding to this question: Should marijuana be legalised?)

[...] Finally, Part IV will conclude that marijuana should not be legalised.	☐ Gives scope ☐ Repeats the question ☐ Clear thesis ☐ Vague or general thesis ☐ Uses emotive language/ personal pronouns

4. (From 2nd year Political Studies, debating whether the Second World War was a 'good war')

Hence my purpose here is to illustrate that while World War II was not the best war, in the total sense of the 'Good War Myth', it was undoubtedly still a good war for the majority of Americans who experienced the war from America.	☐ Gives scope ☐ Repeats the question ☐ Clear thesis ☐ Vague or general thesis ☐ Uses emotive language/ personal pronouns

REVIEW

The introduction model discussed in Part III is also a workable framework for developing effective introductions for argumentative essays. A clear context is essential to orient the reader to the argument by explaining what the issue is and why there is disagreement about it.

There is usually an explicit thesis statement that clearly identifies your position on the issue. It prepares the reader for the direction you will take in the main body of the essay.

After you have written your thesis statement, TEST it by asking these questions:

- Is it clear to the reader why there is disagreement on the issue?
- Can the reader distinguish between the common view and my view?
- Is the expression of the thesis overly personal, subjective, extreme and emotional?
- Can I justify (prove) my thesis? (This is a good question to ask because you cannot justify your thesis if you have not stated it clearly.)

UNIT 3 Structuring the argument

Key topics

3.1 Separate or 'Block' pattern
3.2 Paired or 'Point-by-point' pattern
3.3 Separate and paired patterns combined

Argumentative essays have the basic structure of an academic essay, with an introduction, main body paragraphs and a conclusion. Building an argument is also more successful if the principles of paragraph construction based on the TEC model are applied (see *Part III, Unit 4 Paragraph structure and construction*).

When thinking about argument structure, you are concerned about the following:

- Which arguments should I present first: my reasons to support my thesis or the opposition to my thesis?
- Should I present all the positive arguments together and then proceed to all the negative arguments?

3.1 Separate or 'Block' pattern

The arguments for and against the thesis are developed separately (i.e. in separate 'blocks'):

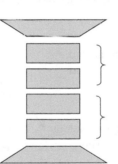

INTRODUCTION
context, issue, thesis, scope

BODY

A block of arguments in support of your thesis

A block of arguments opposing your thesis

CONCLUSION
summary, restatement of thesis

This is a manageable organisational structure for students writing argumentative essays in English. The following outline is derived from the headings used in a 2nd year Law essay, responding to the question 'Should marijuana be legalised?' A report format is used (i.e. uses numbering) but the structure has a separate ('block') organisational pattern:

I   Introduction

II Strengths of legalising marijuana
    A. Medicinal marijuana
    B. Revenue boost
    C. Improvements in criminal justice
       and law enforcement

    Block 1: Arguments <u>for</u> legalisation

III Weaknesses of legalising marijuana
    A. Health effects
    B. Gateway pattern
    C. Increased chance of use among
       children

    Block 2: Arguments <u>against</u> legalisation

IV Conclusion

3.2 Paired or 'point-by-point'

This pattern facilitates a more persuasive and classical style of argumentation. For the same point, both views are presented, using a concession-counter-argument strategy (referred to as the 'YES, BUT' strategy, which will be examined in more detail in the next unit).

How does the strategy work?

For each argumentative point, you begin with the view which opposes your thesis or in which you acknowledge the opposition (concession/yes), followed by your view (counter-arguments/but).

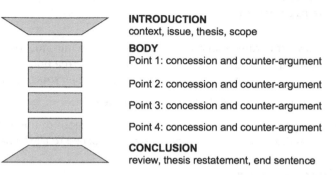

INTRODUCTION
context, issue, thesis, scope
BODY
Point 1: concession and counter-argument

Point 2: concession and counter-argument

Point 3: concession and counter-argument

Point 4: concession and counter-argument

CONCLUSION
review, thesis restatement, end sentence

The following example from a 1st year Anthropology essay arguing against the claim that 'art is corrupted by technology' uses the paired pattern to organise the argument and the concession-counter-argument strategy consistently to begin each argumentative point:

Introduction Thesis	... Far from being corrupted, art can be enhanced and explored in different ways, as well made more accessible.
Body Point 1	A commonly raised argument concerning technology is that it is an inauthentic form of music; ... This viewpoint overlooks the fact that ...

— Concession
— Counter-argument

Point 2 — Part of the negativity around music technology is the idea that it alienates audiences. ... This viewpoint does not consider the wide range of uses technology has in music production and consumption today ...

— Concession
— Counter-argument

Point 3 — Music technology is often considered inauthentic and a corrupting force on art because it means singers do not have to do any work. ... However, technologies such as auto-tune are not automatically bad ...

— Concession
— Counter-argument

3.3 Separate and paired pattern combined

Example (1st year Academic English course, arguing in favour of a living wage). The student uses both separate and paired patterns to organise the argument. The first block of paragraphs presents all the arguments in favour of a living wage. The second block presents arguments against a living wage but uses a paired pattern and the concession-counter-argument strategy:

Introduction Thesis with scope	… This essay will argue that paying the living wage provides consumption efficiency, increases productivity of employees and contributes to economic growth.	
Body 1st block: 3 reasons in support of living wage	First of all, having enough funds to live on means that the government can reduce social costs caused by poverty and low wages. … . Secondly, paying the living wage has productivity benefits as it encourages workers' participation in production. … Moreover, living wage leads to business success as people spend more and it stimulates economic growth. …	Sequence markers introduce the reasons
2nd block: Opposing argument 1 Counter-argument 1 Opposing argument 2 Counter-argument 2	In spite of such advantages, opponents claim that businesses would raise prices to maintain efficiency of the company. … . However, when the productivity of workers grows, … Furthermore, some people insist that businesses could … reduce working hours resulting in unemployment and poverty. … . However, workers who do not have adequate money would lose motivation to participate in production as well as efficiency would be down. …	Contrast markers show concession – counter--argument strategy

Which organisational pattern to use?

Both patterns are acceptable as long as the structure is clear, the reasoning is coherent and elements of argumentation are used. The separate or 'block' organisational pattern can be more manageable for students writing short argumentative essays for the first time. However, in longer essays with more argumentative points, the paired or 'point-by-point' pattern is more effective.

PRACTICE ACTIVITY 3.1

Identifying organisational pattern. (2nd year Political Studies essay responding to this question: 'Should we use force to intervene and protect the lives of others?')

Below are the opening sentences from the five body paragraphs of the student's essay. Read and answer the questions following the extract.

BODY 1	Advocates for intervention argue that forceful intervention is justified if a sovereign country fails to protect its own people.
BODY 2	Another point in support of forceful intervention is that there are some cases it is only option left to alleviate human rights violation.
BODY 3	However, realists and supporters of non-intervention claim that there is no basis for humanitarian intervention according to international law.
BODY 4	Non-interventionists also argue that there is no agreement about what constitutes extreme human rights violations among international communities.
BODY 5	The strongest argument against legitimising forceful intervention is that it does not solve the root of the problem.

1. Which paragraphs (give the paragraph numbers) are in favour of armed intervention? _____
2. Which paragraphs are against armed intervention? _____
3. Write the word which signals the opposite view. _____
4. What organisational method is used to structure the argument?
   SEPARATE | PAIRED | COMBINATION
5. Is the concession-counter-argument strategy used? YES ☐ NO ☐

UNIT 4 Building the argument

Key topics

4.1 Process of logical reasoning
4.2 Appropriate argumentative style: some challenges
4.3 Argumentation strategies: problems and alternatives

4.1 Process of logical reasoning

In logical reasoning, you want to make sure that the reader can follow the line of reasoning. One way to achieve this is to use <u>logical connectors</u>. These are words or phrases that help to organise your argument into logical segments. They may be used at the start of a sentence or in the middle.

Below is a quick review of some logical connectors according to purpose (see the full list in *Part I, Unit 4 Coherent flow of ideas*).

Purpose	Example
Adding or reinforcing ideas	*in addition, … moreover, … another … above all, … furthermore, …*
Contrasting	*however, … on the other hand, … in spite of, … although …, despite …*
Enumerating (introducing ideas in logical order)	*first of all, … secondly, … finally*
Showing similarity	*similarly, … in the same way, … equally …, the same as …*
Exemplifying or illustrating	*for instance, … for example, … such as …*
Showing result or logical consequence	*thus, … therefore, … consequently, … as a result, … subsequently*

In the example below, different types of connectors are used to help the reader follow the reasoning.

Example (1st year History essay, on how immigration has led to changes in racial attitudes and understandings of race. It argues that competition and cohabitation, not physical differences, made racial attitudes prominent.)

Racial tensions undoubtedly increased with the coming of immigrants to both New Zealand and American shores throughout the nineteenth and twentieth centuries. Prior to great waves of immigrants, understandings of race were largely focused around physical differences. For example, racial discrimination was placed on Native Americans and Maori, and sustained through the clearly visual differences between the two. Whilst physical differences were not the sole determinants of race, such explicit differences made race an easily categorised and understood concept. With the influence of immigration, however, understandings of race became more complicated, and racial antipathy greatly intensified. This was due, in part, to the economic threat that immigrants posed to long-settled citizens. In America, anti-Asiatic feelings resulted from Chinese immigration in the1840s and Japanese immigration in the late nineteenth century. Asian immigrants were willing to work for very little money and many Americans saw this as a direct threat to the white man's ability to earn money. [4] Therefore, it was commonly thought that cheap Asian labour 'lowered the American standard of living'. [5] Similarly in New Zealand, immigrants were often viewed as threats to economic security for they brought with them economic competition. [6] Thus, the competition for resources that the cohabitation of races brought made racist attitudes prominent.

Types of logical connectors

- Exemplification
- Contrast
- Contrast
- Result/logical consequence
- Comparison
- Result/logical consequence

Fill in each box with a suitable logical connector from the table. Use the <u>purpose hints</u> in the right margin to help you choose. (Review the list of logical connectors on the previous page, if you need to. If the purpose is the same, find another word from the list.)

<u>Purpose hints</u>

1. [_____] area in which Western influence was sought is in the area of education. Education was seen by the Japanese as a great source of Western power and high levels of literacy were required to develop Western knowledge in Japan. 2. [_____], the Meiji introduced a universal education system in 1872. The structure of the system was based on that of the French while the curriculum was originally based on that of America, with an emphasis on scientific knowledge. 3. [_____], by 1878, the values that were being taught had become a concern. They were considered too individualistic and liberal for the government, who wanted to promote a sense of nationalism and loyalty to the Emperor. 4. [_____], many school textbooks had been translated directly from books published in Western countries and lacked relevance to Japan's society or geography. 5. [_____], the state gradually took over the selection of school textbooks, with increasing importance placed on the development of traditional moral and nationalist values. [...]

1. addition
2. result
3. contrast
4. addition
5. result

⚠ Using too many logical connectors can cause confusion because you are providing too many signals close together. Check that you are not using a logical connector in every sentence. Give the reader time to consider each point. In the examples, most of the connectors occurred at the beginning of the sentence. To avoid this, introduce some variety to your sentence structures (see *Part I, Unit 5*).

4.2 Appropriate argumentative style

An academic argument is the result of considered analysis of an issue, taking into account other people's opinions and evidence.

Some challenges

When presenting an argument, you want to

- show conviction (show that you believe in your ideas);
- show authority (show that you have knowledge of the topic and are in control of the reasoning process);
- be emphatic without sounding extreme or overly emotional; and
- be seen to be fair and reasonable without sounding uncertain about your position on the issue.

The following example shows some of these challenges for students writing argumentative essays for the first time. Personal pronouns (*I, my*) and emotive and extreme language (*wonderful, great, wrong*) are inappropriately used to show conviction and emphasis:

Extreme language

<u>Introduction</u> (actual length)
In fact, I disagree with his opinion about the symphony because there [many] important and wonderful symphonic pieces from the great composers who created many new forms of symphony towards the end of the nineteenth century.

Emotive and extreme language to show emphasis

Personal pronouns

<u>Conclusion</u> (last two sentences)
In conclusion, I personally think Wagner's statement that the symphony would be dead is [totally] wrong. ...
<u>My</u> argument proves that the symphony is not dead!

Inappropriate punctuation

4.3 Argumentation strategies

One way to avoid sounding extreme, biased and unreasonable is to use <u>qualification</u> (or hedging) strategies. Qualification is the act of making something less extreme or absolute. It does not weaken your arguments; instead, it displays <u>caution</u>, making your statements more accurate and your reasoning more acceptable to your reader.

Consider for example the following sentences on the effects of climate change. Which sentence presents the view more effectively?

1. Climate change <u>will</u> have <u>many</u> <u>devastating</u> effects on the <u>whole</u> world in <u>five years'</u> time.
2. Climate change <u>could</u> have <u>serious</u> effects in <u>some</u> parts of the world in the <u>coming decades</u>.

In sentence 1, the use of the emphatic modal verb (*will*), an emotive evaluative adjective (*devastating*), heightened intensifiers (*many, whole*) and an exact time frame (*in five years*) combine to create an extreme and absolute point of view.

On the other hand, the underlined hedging expressions in sentence 2 create a more accurate and reasonable assessment of the situation.

 Overusing qualification or hedging can create uncertainty and cause the reader to question the strength of your arguments. The extent of hedging also depends on whether your argument is led by the thesis or by discussion. In a thesis-led argument, you may use less hedging to avoid sounding unsure about your own arguments. In a discussion-led argument you may use more hedging because you want to provide a more balanced view and information.

Three qualification strategies

- *Yes, but* strategy
- Intensifiers (adverbs and adjectives mainly) to vary the degree of force or intensity of what you are saying
- Modal verbs to vary the degree of certainty (absolute certainty, probability, possibility or uncertainty).

We will examine how each strategy works, show some problems with using it and suggest some solutions.

Strategy 1: The *Yes, but* strategy

The *Yes, but* strategy is commonly used in thesis-led arguments. It is used to show the reader that you have thought about the issue and considered different viewpoints, thus making it easier for the reader to accept your reasoning and thesis.

The strategy has two elements: concession and counter-argument.

- In <u>concession</u>, you acknowledge or accept the opposing arguments. You anticipate possible opposition. You are saying '**Yes**, I can see why some people might think this' or '**Yes**, I accept that some of the opposing arguments are valid and supportable'.
- In <u>counter-argument</u>, you respond to the opposition. You are saying '**But** here is another view'. You then proceed to explain why, give your reasons and support with evidence from research. The aim is to show that your view is more reasonable.

The *Yes, but* strategy has a clearly defined structure and use of language. Notice the <u>boxed expressions in bold</u> introducing the concession and counter-argument in these examples:

Concession ⟶	**It is true that** every individual has the right to smoke,
Counter-argument ⟶	**but** there is undeniable medical evidence which proves that second-hand smoking is harmful. The freedom of non-smokers also needs to be considered.
Concession ⟶	**Some critics argue** that Beethoven did not invent the motif and sonata form and that he inherited them from Haydn and Mozart.
Counter-argument ⟶	**However, there is no doubt that** Beethoven greatly extended them, writing longer and more ambitious movements.

Here are more ways of expressing concession – counter-argument:

> There is no denying that … . | However, …
>
> Some critics/Proponents of … point to the fact /claim that … but …
>
> Some scientists believe that … | On the contrary, …
>
> Despite the fact that … | Although there is clear evidence that … .
>
> A commonly raised argument against/for … is that … | However, …
>
> While it could be argued that … | This view overlooks or ignores the fact that …
>
> One objection to … is that …

How does the *Yes, but* strategy work?

Example (1st year Philosophy, arguing that the raising of the tax on the sale of tobacco is opposed to John Stuart Mill's Harm Principle, which values liberty above all else).

This is a <u>discussion-led</u> argument. The student's thesis is not stated explicitly in the introduction but in the conclusion, as shown below:

> <u>Introduction</u> (last sentence):
> In this essay, I will discuss whether, under the harm principle, Mill would have believed the Government's decision to raise the tax on tobacco sales to be a legitimate restriction upon the liberty of those who purchase cigarettes.
>
> <u>Conclusion</u> (last sentence):
> I believe it is fair to say that Mill would not agree with nor approve of the raise of tax on the purchase of tobacco.

This is the first argumentative point.

Yes → It could be argued that raising the tax on tobacco sales is not a paternalistic interference on smokers' liberty as preventing them from smoking will also prevent others from having to come into contact with harmful second hand smoke. Another argument on a similar vein is that smokers will eventually cost the health system a lot more than non-smokers due to the increased health risks in smoking, which would have a negative impact on the taxpayer. I **But** → do not believe that these are particularly compelling arguments, however, as there are already many laws in place preventing people from smoking in certain places to protect others from the harmful effects of second hand smoke; breathing in a small amount of smoke when passing someone smoking on the street is very unlikely to have harmful effects. Also, the fact that smokers tend to die sooner, and so cost less in later life healthcare such as rest homes, essentially balances out the cost for smokers and non-smokers on the health system. Therefore, we can safely assume that the main reason the tax is being raised is to dissuade people from smoking for their own benefit, thus making it a paternalistic interference.

Anticipates what the opposition might say

Logical connectors to show reasoning process

Provides 2 counter-arguments

<u>Variation in use of strategy</u>

Using the *Yes, but* strategy for every argumentative point can make your essay sound monotonous and formulaic. The following examples show some variations in using the strategy.

Example 1 (2nd year History on 'The Good War myth').

This is a <u>thesis-led argument</u> with a clearly stated thesis in the introduction: ' ... while World War II was not the best war, in the total sense of the "Good War Myth", it was undoubtedly still a good war for the majority of Americans who experienced the war from America'.

The following body paragraph presents one positive outcome of the war. It does not follow the *Yes, but* strategy. You can see that concession (*Yes*) is not immediately followed by a counter-argument (*But*).

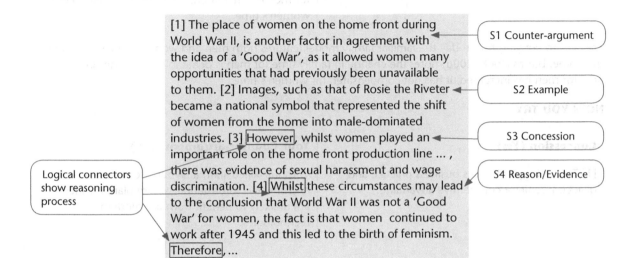

[1] The place of women on the home front during World War II, is another factor in agreement with the idea of a 'Good War', as it allowed women many opportunities that had previously been unavailable to them. [2] Images, such as that of Rosie the Riveter became a national symbol that represented the shift of women from the home into male-dominated industries. [3] However, whilst women played an important role on the home front production line ... , there was evidence of sexual harassment and wage discrimination. [4] Whilst these circumstances may lead to the conclusion that World War II was not a 'Good War' for women, the fact is that women continued to work after 1945 and this led to the birth of feminism. Therefore, ...

- S1 Counter-argument
- S2 Example
- S3 Concession
- S4 Reason/Evidence

Logical connectors show reasoning process

Example 2 (2nd year Political Studies responding to this question: 'Should force be used to intervene and/or improve the lives of others?')

This is a <u>discussion-led argument</u>. It presents each view and its reasons. The *Yes, but* strategy is not used, but there is evidence of other argumentation strategies, which we will look at next.

[1] Advocates for intervention by armed force argue that it is necessary if a sovereign country fails to protect its citizens such as in the case of genocide. [2] When a state fails in this duty, it loses its sovereign rights. In addition, with the existence of the Universal Declaration of Human Rights and [...]the legitimacy of accusing a country of violating human rights has become stronger. [3] With the establishment of the United Nations, the fundamental principal is to guarantee human rights and dignity. [4] In fact, it could be argued that infringement of these principles is equal to an invasion. [5] Therefore, in their perspective, NATO's 11-week bombing against Yugoslavia in 1999 was justified because if NATO had not acted, the Yugoslavian regime would have continued its brutal repression of the Albanian population. [6] In the face of an imminent 'humanitarian catastrophe', armed force was the only option.

- S1 Introduces one view
- S2-5 Explain with reasons
- S6 Concludes the point

Evidence of other strategies of argumentation

1.   Construct concession – counter-argument structures. You may need to write two sentences:

Example

Concession (*Yes*)	Counter-argument (*But*)
Today the familiar family model features both men and women working outside the home.	Hook (2006) notes, the change in family time for men is debatable. Even though unpaid work time for men has increased, it has not compensated for women's time.

There is no denying that today the familiar family model features both men and women working outside the home, but as Hook (2006) notes the change in family time for men is debatable. Although unpaid work time for men has increased, it has not compensated for women's time.

NOW YOU TRY

Concession (*Yes*)	Your Counter-argument (*But*)
[1] Technology enhances business practice and give companies a competitive advantage.	Without skilled staff, a favourable infrastructure, and effective information system plan, businesses are unlikely to benefit from the modern technologies.
[2] Women are clearly participating in more paid work.	Women are also retaining responsibility for the unpaid domestic work, which indicates that women are in reality working much more than their husbands.
[3] Privately-operated prisons reduce expenditure of tax-money.	The main objective of the private sector is to maximise profitability. In the prison context, this could lead to reduced rehabilitative, food and health services.

2.   Spot the *Yes, but* strategy.
(Text from 2nd year History, on the extent to which Meiji Japan's modernisation was an imitation of Western developments)

Argumentative thesis: 'In this essay I will argue that the usual purpose of such adoptions was not to imitate the West but rather to enhance Japanese power ... These imitations were temporary, however, and their scope was limited.'

This example shows the conventional approach to the strategy. Identify the concession (*YES*) – counter-argument (*BUT*) sentences in the following paragraph. Write the sentence number(s) in the right margin:

[1] It is true that the Japanese did imitate many aspects of everyday life. [2] In fact, the government actively encouraged the Westernisation of all aspects of culture as it was considered 'civilized'. [3] Western clothing became popular and was even made compulsory for government officials in 1872. [4] Western hairstyles were considered increasingly fashionable and the eating of beef became popular. [5] The government also promoted modern, Western, music education and supported artists using Western style painting techniques. [6] Indeed, these developments even led some groups of the Japanese population to view Japanese traditions as backward and uncivilized. [7] However, this feeling was not universal. [8] The peasantry in particular found it difficult to adjust to the developments. [9] A younger generation of Japanese were also concerned that too much emphasis was being placed on westernisation and felt that these practices and values should only be used by Japan if they were to Japan's benefit. [10] There was also a sense of fear amongst the population that Western influence would lead to a loss of cultural identity.	Concession (*Yes*) sentence: [　] Support sentences: [　] Counter-argument (*But*) sentence: Support sentences: [　]

Strategy 2: Intensifiers

Intensifiers are words used to indicate the effect on the force of the verb. This strategy involves heightening or lowering the effect on the force of what you are saying.

The table below shows intensifiers (mainly adverbs, but some adjectives, verbs and other phrases) on a scale of intensity or emphasis. In general, avoid overusing intensifiers at the high end of the scale and the words marked with an asterisk (*). They can give your writing an emotive and informal style which is inappropriate for university contexts. (Review academic style in Part I, Unit 1.)

Scale of intensity or degree of force			
high degree of intensity			**lesser/limited degree**
Extreme/Maximum	**High/Booster**	**Emphatic**	**Qualification/hedging**
Ly-ADVERBS absolutely, always, completely, entirely, inevitably, fully, thoroughly, virtually, totally, barely, hardly, scarcely	Ly-ADVERBS badly, greatly, extremely, sadly, strongly, tragically, unfortunately	Ly-ADVERBS *actually, admittedly, certainly, clearly, definitely, evidently, *essentially, indeed, *obviously, *really, *simply, undoubtedly	ADVERBS especially, only, slightly, *potentially, generally, commonly, particularly, almost, nearly, often, mainly
DETERMINERS PRONOUNS all, every, many PHRASES in all respects, never, not at all	DETERMINERS PRONOUNS most ADJECTIVES/ NOUNS *dramatic, *tremendous, *massive, *remarkable, *wonderful, *thousands, *millions	PHRASES even, still, in fact, far more, *more and more, *of course, (may) well, a great deal, to a large extent, by far, *very	VERBS appear, indicate, seem, suggest PHRASES to some extent

How does the scale of intensity work?

Use the scale to determine if you have used too many intensifiers at the upper end of the scale, thus heightening the effect of what you are saying. Consider the evidence and determine if your statements need qualification. For example, depending on your assessment of the cause of a fire, you could make one of the following statements:

> The fire <u>is</u> caused by faulty wiring. [ABSOLUTE]
> The fire is <u>entirely</u> caused by faulty wiring. [ABSOLUTE]
> The fire is <u>clearly</u> caused by faulty wiring. [EMPHATIC]
> The fire is <u>mainly/largely</u> caused by faulty wiring. [QUALIFICATION/HEDGING]
> The evidence <u>suggests</u> that faulty wiring caused the fire. [QUALIFICATION/HEDGING]

 Intensifiers feature prominently in thesis-led arguments, in which defending the thesis is important. However, avoid using too many intensifiers at the heightened end of the scale. Intensifiers marked with an asterisk are informal and often over-used. Instead, aim to use <u>concrete adjectives</u> and <u>active verbs</u>.

Some problems of use

- <u>Overusing intensifiers</u>

When intensifiers are overused, they become meaningless and lose their impact. For example, the addition of the intensifier 'very' in sentence (a) below does not make much difference to the message. Sentence (b) conveys the message with more conviction and authority.

    a)   It is a <u>very</u> efficient system and will definitely save energy in the long run.
    b)   The system is efficient and will save energy in the long run.

Overusing intensifiers at the heightened end of the scale can result in over-generalisation or oversimplification of the issue. The subjective tone and emotional appeal can also become too heightened, as seen in the following example:

OVERUSE OF INTENSIFIERS

[HIGH/BOOSTER]   [EXTREME]

I am strongly against offshore drilling. In my view, it is totally unnecessary
because there are actually many eco-friendly alternatives, which are far more
suitable.

[EMPHATIC]   [EXTREME]   [EMPHATIC]

The same view can be expressed without the distraction caused by using too many intensifiers, personal reference or emotive language.

BETTER   With the eco-friendly and sustainable alternatives available today, offshore drilling is not necessarily a viable option.

- <u>Overusing qualification or hedging</u>

Overqualification and using intensifiers at the lower end of the scale of intensity can create too much uncertainty and cause the reader to wonder if you are convinced about what you are saying. In academic arguments, overqualification may also indicate a lack of research and reading for the assignment.

[OVERQUALIFICATIION]

There is some evidence to suggest that eco-friendly alternatives are generally
better for the environment than offshore drilling.

BETTER The evidence from research into alternative energy sources in the past five years has highlighted the environmental hazards caused by offshore drilling.

Some solutions or alternatives

- Remove or replace with active verbs, nouns and concrete adjectives:

Overused intensifying adverbs	Alternatives: remove or replace
Very difficult/really difficult *Really difficult* *Extremely difficult*	<u>with active verbs</u>: *challenges, demands* <u>with concrete adjectives</u>: *challenging, taxing,* *exhausting, physically/ mentally demanding*;
Prior to *great* waves of immigrants ...	with <u>concrete nouns</u>: Prior to the rapid *increase/* *rise in the number* of immigrants;
Smoking can *potentially* increase the risk of lung cancer.	with adjective and noun: Smokers have a *higher* *risk of* contracting lung cancer.

- In general, avoid overusing these verbs: *seems, appears, suggests, indicates, potentially*.

  e.g. The research findings *indicates/suggests* that the new machine can *potentially* decrease energy costs by at least 30 per cent.

BETTER According to research findings, the new machine can decrease energy costs by at least 30 per cent.

- Expand your academic vocabulary to replace vague and simple nouns and adjectives e.g. *things, good, bad, great*.

  e.g. The new machine will improve *things* in many areas.

BETTER The new machine will improve operational processes in the packaging and assembling sectors.

PRACTICE ACTIVITY 4.3

1. <u>Identifying intensifiers</u>. The following paragraphs rely on intensifiers to show emphasis. By referring to the scale of intensity table, identify the highlighted intensifier in each of the following paragraphs. The first one has been done as an example in each case.

   a) (Thesis-led argument from 1st year Anthropology, arguing against the claim that 'art is corrupted by technology')

A [1] commonly raised argument concerning technology is that it is an inauthentic form of music, and that technologies such as synthesizers and drum machines do not require any skill to use. There is a discourse around music that only if you know how to play a 'real' instrument are you a 'real' artist, and technology corrupts this idea of music as real, authentic art (Théberge, 1999). This viewpoint overlooks the fact that instruments themselves are a form of technology. [2] Even singers require microphones so that they can reach their entire audience. Despite the fact that technology is used as an aid for these things, it could be argued that a certain degree of skill is [3] still required to be able to master them. The artist must learn to play the instrument, and only once they have done this can they use it to create their music. [4] Of course, what is [5] often not considered is the skill needed to create or enhance music using technologies such as synthesizers. [6] Indeed, as Warner points out, 'gaining intimate, practical knowledge of specific pieces of equipment is highly time consuming' (Warner, 2003, p. 33).	[1] qualification [2] [3] [4] [5] [6]

b) (Thesis-led argument from 1st year History on the 'Good War' myth)

This is the introductory paragraph, which relies on intensifiers at the heightened end of the intensity to state the thesis and clarify the central issue of the argument:

The Second World War has lived on in the memories of Americans as the 'Good War'. The American society remembered that It was a war that fought for freedom and democracy against the [1] clear evils of the world.]Whilst the reality of World War II may not fully endorse such a myth and memory, it [2] certainly does not mean to say that it was not a 'good war' for America. [3] Indeed, for [4] many Americans, it was a war that stimulated a dormant economy, challenged and brought about change in the lives of the minority groups of America. Whilst for [5] some, the war was [6] most certainly not good, for [7] many it brought about crucial change in the post war years. Hence, my purpose here is to illustrate that while World War II was not the best war, in the total sense of the 'Good War Myth', it was [8] undoubtedly still a good war for the majority of Americans who experienced the war from America.	[1] emphasis [2] [3] [4] [5] [6] [7] [8]

2. Remove or replace unnecessary intensifiers or construct a new sentence.

Consider whether the <u>underlined intensifier</u> is necessary or over-used. Remove it if you think it is unnecessary; replace it with a more concrete or specific adjective or noun; or write a new sentence structure.

Example: Prior to the great increase in the number of immigrants, understandings of race were largely focused around clearly obvious physical differences.

Remove	Prior to the increase in the number of immigrants, understandings of race were focused around physical differences.
Replace	With the significant increase in immigration, understandings of race became defined by more than just physical differences.
Construct a new sentence	Before immigration increased, understandings of race were defined by physical difference.

NOW YOU TRY:

a) Breathing in a small amount of smoke when passing someone smoking on the street is very <u>unlikely</u> to have harmful effects.

_____

b) The fact that smokers tend to die sooner <u>essentially</u> balances out the cost on the health system.

_____

c) With the influence of immigration, however, understandings of race became more complicated and racial antipathy <u>greatly</u> intensified.

_____

d) It can be <u>safely</u> assumed that the main reason the tax on tobacco sales is being raised is to <u>basically</u> dissuade people from smoking for their own benefit, thus making it a paternalistic interference.

_____

e) A <u>commonly</u> raised argument concerning technology is that it is <u>potentially</u> an inauthentic form of music.

_____

Strategy 3: Modal verbs

Another argumentation strategy is to use varying <u>degrees of certainty</u> to show the reader that you are not stating your ideas in absolute terms. One way to indicate the degree of certainty is to use <u>modal verbs</u> (*must, have to, should, will, can, would, could, may, might*). Other expressions of certainty include *It is possible that ... It is likely to ... It is certain that, ... probably*).

The following assignment questions use modal verbs (in *italics* here) to frame the question, which often causes students to use them in their arguments:

Should marijuana be legalised? (Law)

To what extent *should* the NZ Courts take International Law into account when developing and applying the Common Law? (Law)

Do you think it is *possible* for entrepreneurship to be taught? (Business)

Bush and Bush (1994) argue that ethical and moral issues resulting in controversy *will* always surround advertising because of the nature of the creative process. Do you agree? (Film, Television and Media Studies)

Modal verbs on a scale of certainty

The following table presents the main modal verbs (underlined in example sentences) on a scale of certainty, from absolute certainty to least certainty. Understanding the degree of certainty expressed by a specific modal verb can give you more control over the argument building process.

Modal verbs	Scale of certainty	Examples
MUST SHOULD	**Duty, Obligation**	A local body endowed with power by parliament <u>must</u> correctly understand the law. An applicant <u>should</u> have the opportunity to challenge judicial material.
WILL	**Absolute** certainty (certain result-for assertions/claims)	Some people argue that creative advertisers <u>will</u> always attract controversy. (You can just use the active verb 'attract')
CAN	**Theoretical** possibility (or general possibility)	Socio-economic or class position <u>can</u> affect educational attainment.
WOULD	**Conditional** (if) certainty (probable or likely given certain conditions)	Employees <u>would</u> lose motivation if they were denied promotions or wage increases.
COULD MAY	**Partial** certainty (possible, less likely)	Low wages <u>could/may</u> lead to reduced efficiency and productivity.
MIGHT	**Least** certainty (least likely result)	Some employees on low wages <u>might</u> go on strike.

Apply the scale as a guide to check the way you use modal verbs to build your argument. For example, if you use mainly 'would' or 'may', you show that you are too tentative (uncertain) and lack belief in your own arguments.

Some problems of use

- Overusing modal verbs

Modal verbs are not easy to use. Over-use or incorrect use creates more confusion and makes your argument weak because you are too tentative. This is clearly reflected in the following extract from a 2nd year Law essay, arguing for the legalisation of marijuana.

Are these modal verbs correctly used?

> Advocates for the legalisation of marijuana state that it could allow for a more economical dispensation of law enforcement resources. Approximately $12,000,000 is spent annually to imprison marijuana users in New Zealand. Many believe that legalisation will enable the crime force to spend money on harsher offences. This would also allow the judicial system to focus their resources on more important principles that [4] may need development in the law.

Revision: The modal verbs are replaced by active verbs.

The use of active verbs creates a stronger argument delivered with authority and conviction.

> Advocates for the legalisation of marijuana state that it results in a more economical dispensation of law enforcement resources. Approximately $12,000,000 is spent annually to imprison marijuana users in New Zealand. Many believe that legalisation enables the crime force to spend money on harsher offences and allows the judicial system to focus their resources on more important principles to develop the law in the law.

- Using intensifiers with modal verbs: some problems

The following example shows a common problem with using modal verbs and intensifiers together. In these concluding sentences from a 1st year Anthropology essay, the student is restating her thesis that 'art is not corrupted by technology'. The mix of emphasis, partial certainty, qualification and absolute certainty is confusing and weakens the conclusion:

> [EMPHASIS] [PARTIAL CERTAINTY]
>
> Rather than corrupting art, then, technology could be considered a form of art in itself. Just because it is a different means of musical expression than instruments which are considered more traditional does not mean that technology will destroy art as we know it. [...] Considering these factors, I disagree with the statement that art is corrupted by technology. Technology is merely a new platform for artistic growth and exploration.
>
> [LOW INTENSITY]   [ABSOLUTE CERTAINTY]

Be more assertive when restating your thesis in the conclusion. The following revision projects a more confident and assured tone:

[VERB TO BE]

Rather than corrupting technology, then, technology is a form of art in itself. It is a platform for artistic growth and exploration which adds a new dimension to traditional art forms by providing a new platform for artistic growth and exploration.

[ACTIVE VERB]

Example Modal verbs are incorrectly used in this paragraph from a 1st year Academic English essay, arguing in favour of paying a living wage.

There is a lot of uncertainty and confusion between 'would' and 'could' for example. Notice the corrections in the right column.

Another argument against the living wage is that it [1] would cause businesses to compensate by reducing working hours, thus resulting in unemployment and poverty. McCrate (2003) argues that businesses which approve a living wage [2] would have to pay higher payroll taxes. For the purpose of making large profits, these businesses [3] would inevitably have to find other ways to cut costs, such as by regulating working hours. Workers affected by loss of income [4] would lose motivation to participate in production and this [5] would affect their efficiency. Pollin (2007) argues that when there is a high demand for their products, firms actually [6] would tend to work harder to meet that demand. Similarly, if companies pay a living wage, employees [7] would be more willing to work more actively in partnership with management.	[1] → causes [2] → have [3] → have [4] → may lose [5] → could affect [6] → tend [7] → will be

Explanation of corrections

[1], [2]   The modal verb is replaced by the active verb 'causes'. Assertions or claims can be established with a higher degree of certainty.
[3]   'would' is removed to indicate a certain result or prediction.
[4]   'may' replaces 'would' to indicate some doubt. It is possible.
[5]   'could' replaces 'would' to indicate the ability.
[6]   active verb in the present simple tense 'tend' replaces the more uncertain 'would tend'.
[7]   'will' replaces 'would' for an emphatic conclusion to the argument.

Read the revised paragraph below. You will notice the comments have more conviction and authority.

Another argument against the living wage is that it causes businesses to compensate by reducing working hours, thus resulting in unemployment and poverty. McCrate (2003) argues that businesses which approve a living wage have to pay higher payroll taxes. For the purpose of making large profits, inevitably businesses have to find other ways to cut costs, such as by regulating working hours. Workers affected by loss of income may lose motivation to participate in production and this could affect their efficiency. Pollin (2007) argues that when there is a high demand for their products, firms actually work harder to meet that demand. Similarly, if companies pay a living wage, employees will be more willing to work more actively in partnership with management.

⚠ The present simple tense can replace the future 'will' to express future events without the intensity or force.

Fill in each numbered box with the correct verb from the two verb options given.

(from 1st year Business, responding to this question: 'Do you think it is possible for entrepreneurship to be taught?')

It is true that there are aspects of entrepreneurship that 1. _____ easily communicated. Soft skills such as thinking creatively and taking calculated risks 2. _____ difficult to teach. Due to the difficulty associated with teaching these skills, some believe that these skills 3. _____ be taught to aspiring entrepreneurs and that successful entrepreneurs are simply born with these specific skills. However, research has shown that it 4. _____ for students to acquire entrepreneurial soft-skills through participation in activities that simulate real-life entrepreneurial experience. A study based on the personal testimonies of entrepreneurs concluded that soft-skills 5. _____ acquired through a combination of their personal experience and by observing the actions of more senior entrepreneurs. Clearly, then, entrepreneurial skills, such as the ability to think creatively, 6. _____ taught to students. Hence, it 7. _____ possible for an individual to learn to be an entrepreneur through education.

[1] are not | may not be

[2] are | may be

[3] cannot | could not

[4] is possible | would be possible

[5] might be | could be acquired

[6] will be | can be

[7] would be | is

UNIT 5 Argumentative essays for study

Up to this point, we have looked at elements of argumentation using short extracts of student writing. This unit brings all these elements together in full-length essays. The essays have been selected to illustrate two approaches to argumentative essays: thesis-led and discussion-led. The approach you choose affects the overall argumentative style and use of the argumentative strategies examined in the earlier units. The first three essays use a thesis-led approach with varying degrees of intensification and qualification. The last essay uses a discussion-led approach.

The essays are presented in their original structure and organisation and with mostly original content. The main change is in the length. Omissions are indicated with three dots. References at the end of the essays are not included. Footnotes are presented at the bottom of the first page of essays which use a footnote referencing style.

Guide to annotations

Left-margin annotations show the argument structure: introduction, body and conclusion and use of the TEC paragraph model, especially the T (topic sentence) and C (comment) elements (review in *Part III, Unit 4 Paragraph structure and construction*).

Right-margin annotations focus on the building of the argument, development techniques (review in Part IV, Unit 5), academic style, argumentation strategies and integration of evidence from research.

Highlights in the main text Expressions in colour point to features of academic, informal and argumentative style (i.e. use of intensifiers, modal verbs). Boxed words highlight the flow of ideas in the reasoning process (i.e. use of logical connectors, author tags, reporting verbs, introductory phrases).

At the end of each essay, you have the opportunity to assess the overall effectiveness of each essay and review these elements of argumentation:

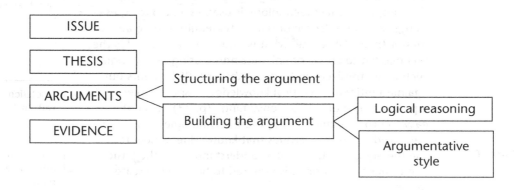

ESSAY 1 Thesis-led argument

SUBJECT AREA: Anthropology   **YEAR:** First   **LENGTH:** 1563 words

REFERENCING STYLE (excludes reference list): APA (Author, Year system)

ASSIGNMENT QUESTION: Agree or disagree with this claim: 'Art is corrupted by technology'

ARGUMENT STRUCTURE		REASONING & STYLE
INTRODUCTION MODEL **Lead-in to topic** **Two views** **Thesis**	The use of technology in the music industry has been controversial from its very conception. Even technologies now entrenched in popular music culture, such as the microphone, were initially regarded with suspicion and were often considered emotionally dishonest (Frith, 1986). Using technology to make music has been criticised as inauthentic, alienating to audiences, and opposed to art and nature (Frith, 1986). It is essentially viewed as a corrupting force on an authentic art form. However, many do not consider the positive effects technology can have on the creation and experience of music. Points that are commonly overlooked are how accessible music is made through technology, the knowledge required to use this technology, and the innovative uses and explorations that can be made through technology. Far from being corrupted, art can be enhanced and explored in different ways, as well made more accessible.	
BODY TEC MODEL Argument 1 **T skill factor** **C reinforces T**	A commonly raised argument concerning technology is that it is an inauthentic form of music [and that] technologies such as synthesizers and drum machines do not require any skill to use. There is a discourse around music which dictates that only if you know how to play a 'real' instrument are you a 'real' artist, and technology corrupts this idea of music as real, authentic art (Thé berge, 1999). This viewpoint overlooks the fact that instruments themselves are a form of technology. Instruments such as electric guitars require amplifiers to be plugged into, and even singers require microphones so that they can reach their entire audience. It could be argued here, though, that despite the fact technology is used as an aid for these things, a certain degree of skill is still required to be able to master them. Of course, what is often not considered is the skill needed to create or enhance music using technologies such as synthesizers. Indeed, as Warner (2003) points out, "gaining intimate, practical knowledge of specific pieces of equipment is highly time consuming" (p. 33). It is not as easy to produce music using these technologies as is often perceived. He further argues that knowledge of how to use the equipment, as well as understanding of the basic components of music ... is required to be able to create music.	*Yes, but* strategy Degrees of qualification Quotation with citation Paraphrase from same source

Argument 2	Rather than corrupting art, technology could be considered a form of art in itself. Technologies such as synthesizers and samplers are simply different ways of creating sound to express a certain feeling or mood within a musical track. They are different means of musical expression than instruments which are considered more traditional, but this does not mean that technology will destroy art as we know it. Instead, they allow musicians to further explore different ways of creative expression. As Théberge (1999) notes, he once witnessed a rock musician refer to his electric guitar as a "real instrument" – as opposed to a synthesizer – and although this might be a common conception now. Frith (1986) gives an example of how Bob Dylan was rejected by the folk movement for 'going electric' in the 1960s Technology and people's opinions on it are always going to grow and change; the fact that the way art is produced evolves over time does not mean it is any less authentic or emotionally honest than that which came before it.
T technology an art form	
C reinforces T	
Argument 3	Part of the negativity around music technology is the idea that it alienates audiences. Musicians are relying on technology to create music that contains no emotion for audiences to relate to and connect with (Frith, 1986). This viewpoint does not consider the wide range of uses technology has in music production and consumption today, or even the part it plays in live music. As Théberge (1999) points out, 'too often technology is thought about in terms of machines rather than in terms of practice,' (pp. 216–217). Technology is often used to refer to a few selected things as opposed to its use in a general sense, which undermines the importance of technology in the music industry (Théberge, 1999). For instance, the use of the microphone in live performances allows artists to create a feeling of intimacy. Allowing audiences to experience live music in such a large group brings people together, not alienate them. Similarly, the wide distribution of music through CDs, and MP3s on the internet, makes music accessible to more people (Bishop, 2005). Through services such as iTunes, music listeners can gain access to almost any type of music … The artist Lady Gaga's recently released song 'Born This Way' – a dance music track – became the fastest selling musical track in iTunes history (Reisinger, 2011). This is an example of the fact that simply because music uses certain technologies does not mean it cannot be authentic, or that it is in any way alienating. It is possible to put thought, emotion, and feeling into music as well as be a popular artist who uses synthetic music technologies.
T connection with audience	
C reinforces T, links to thesis	
Argument 4	Music technology is often considered inauthentic and a corrupting force on art because rather than putting effort into singing, musicians rely on a technology such as autotune to correct any imperfections (Tyrangiel, 2009). However, autotune can, in fact, have the opposite effect. In his article on autotune, Tyrangiel (2009) talks about the artist T-Pain who found a novel use for it. By changing the parameters on the autotune machine, T-Pain was able to find a unique voice effect that
T innovative use of technology	

Annotation callouts:
- Author tag and reporting verb before quotation
- Emphatic style
- Yes, but strategy
- Specific examples
- Degrees of qualification with intensifiers and modals
- Specific example

was not commonly being used in popular music at that time. This innovative use of autotune in his music made him famous and his songs instantly recognizable (Tyrangiel, 2009). With technology, artists are able to explore different means of expression and artistic production and create a sound which would not have been possible without the use of a particular technology. In her song 'The Red Shoes,' Kate Bush uses 'technologically produced music and sounds that highlight the rhythmic repetition and the peculiarities of her voice' (Gordon, 2005, p. 38). The singer has often been quoted talking about how she considers her music to be 'serious' music, that it is about art and creativity (Gordon, 2005). She is not simply using technology out of laziness or cheap gimmickry. Part of the attraction of live shows is being able to connect with their audience through creative use of technology.

> Specific example

> Emotive, informal language

C reinforces T

CONCLUSION MODEL

Technology, then, has a wide variety of uses in the music industry. Whether it be distribution and consumption of music, aid in live performance, or simply experimenting with new sounds, it is fair to say that technology and the music industry are inextricably linked. However, technology cannot be a stand in for everything; artists are still pushed to use their natural abilities. Technology is not the all corrupting force that it is sometimes considered to be. The development of new technologies means new ways for artists to express themselves; it means new ways to connect with audiences and to create art. Considering these things, I disagree with the statement that art is corrupted by technology. It is a new platform for artistic growth and exploration.

> Persuasive force to finish argument

> Informal language

Restates thesis

> Vague vocabulary, personal reference

End sentence points to future

YOUR RESPONSE

1. Which organisational method is used to structure the argument? PAIRED SEPARATE
2. In terms of paragraph structure, the use of the TEC model is clearly evident. YES NO
3. How would you describe the use of the following strategies?

Yes, but strategy	FREQUENT USE | SOME USE | LIMITED USE
Intensifiers	FREQUENT USE | SOME USE | LIMITED USE
Modal verbs	FREQUENT USE | SOME USE | LIMITED USE

4. Overall, how effective is the argument? Use this checklist of features to rate the essay. Put a tick (✓) in the box if the essay displays the feature successfully and a ✗ if it does not:

   ☐ provides an adequate context   ☐ develops argument with logical reasoning

   ☐ identifies opposing views on the issue   ☐ provides relevant evidence

   ☐ states thesis in the introduction   ☐ uses an appropriate argumentative style

   ☐ has a clear paragraph and argument structure ☐ restates thesis in a strong conclusion

ESSAY 2 Thesis-led argument

SUBJECT AREA: Business   **YEAR:** Second   **LENGTH:** 1467 words

REFERENCING STYLE (excludes reference list): APA (Author, Year system)

ASSIGNMENT QUESTION: Do you think it is possible for entrepreneurship to be taught? Develop a clear argument that indicates your view on the question, and justify your choice using appropriate evidence and examples.

STRUCTURE & ORGANISATION		REASONING & STYLE
INTRODUCTION MODEL Two views	The question of whether it is possible for a person to learn to become an entrepreneur has vexed numerous scholars. For many decades, entrepreneurs have been seen as individuals who are born with a specific set of personality traits and abilities that enable them to recognise and exploit business opportunities. A person who is not born with these innate attributes simply cannot be educated to become an entrepreneur. However, there is sufficient evidence to suggest that anyone can learn to behave entrepreneurially … Research also shows that it is possible for aspiring entrepreneurs to learn to acquire entrepreneurial soft-skills, such as the ability to think creatively and take calculated risks through participation in activities that are designed to simulate real entrepreneurial experience. This essay will describe the competing theories about entrepreneurship and the most common argument used to justify the idea that entrepreneurs must have a specific set of inherent personality traits. Then this essay will explain the reasons why, contrary to the widely-accepted myth, it is possible for entrepreneurship to be taught to aspiring entrepreneurs.	Use of emphatic 'will' is unnecessary
Scope **Thesis**		
BODY TEC MODEL Argument 1 **T two theories**	There are two competing theories about the definition of entrepreneurship. Traditionally, entrepreneurship is defined in terms of the personal characteristics that distinguish entrepreneurs from non-entrepreneurs. Proponents of this theory believe that entrepreneurs are individuals who are more creative, more extroverted, more confident, and more optimistic than the average population (Fisher & Koch, 2008, p. 1). Those who are not born with these entrepreneurial traits simply cannot become an entrepreneur, even if they have been trained to think and behave like an entrepreneur (Thompson, 2004, p. 246). There are, however, some scholars who reject the traditional approach of defining entrepreneurship. Instead, these scholars believe that entrepreneurship is a behaviour as opposed to a set of innate personality traits. For example, Spinelli and Adams (2012) defined entrepreneurship as 'a way of thinking, reasoning, and acting that is opportunity obsessed, holistic in approach, and leadership balanced for the purposes of value creation and capture' (p. 87). Proponents of the behavioural approach of defining entrepreneurship believe that it is possible to teach individual to act and think entrepreneurially because its foundation lies in concept and theory rather than intuition.	Extended definition

Argument 2	To this day, there is still no consensus on the definition of entrepreneurship. The widely-accepted belief is that all entrepreneurs share a similar set of personality traits which enable them to become successful entrepreneurs such as passion, vision, risk-taking, fearlessness and tenacity. However, real life observations of entrepreneurial behaviour suggest that these personality traits do not automatically determine a person's ability to become a successful entrepreneur. Real life entrepreneurs have a wide variety of personality traits and not all successful entrepreneurs possess the same personality traits. For instance, in a study of 250 British entrepreneurs, 52% described themselves as being risk averse, even though it is commonly believed that successful entrepreneurs are individuals who are not afraid of taking risks (Kim, 2012). As Lee (cited in Spinelli & Adams, 2012) once said, real-life entrepreneurs can be 'gregarious or low key, analytical or intuitive, charismatic or boring, good with details or terrible, delegators or control freaks' (p. 42).

T real life entrepreneurs

Yes, but strategy

Brief reference to study

Quotation with citation

C reinforces T

Argument 3	Creativity and innovation have often been cited as the most important characteristics of an entrepreneur. However, according to Allen (2012), there are many individuals who create an innovative product and still fail to commercialise their invention due to their lack of business skills to market the product. This example shows that in order to be a successful entrepreneur, a person must know how to think and act entrepreneurially. According to Drucker (1985), entrepreneurship is the practice of innovation, by which entrepreneurs search for change, responds to it and exploits it as an opportunity for a business or service. Successful entrepreneurship also needs communication, team-building skills and domain experience or 'on-the-job' training, supported by peer mentoring and practice. Unlike personality traits, these skills can be learnt and taught through new methodologies and tools with structured educational components created by entrepreneurs for entrepreneurs. For example, entrepreneurs must have a sound knowledge of business and management skills such as the ability to create a business plan. These skills are relatively easy to teach to students and are widely taught by educational institutions (Henry et al., 2003, p. 90).

T other skills

Yes, but strategy

Author introductory phrases

Reasoning supported by five logical connectors

C reinforces T

Argument 4	It is true that soft skills such as those mentioned above are not easy to teach. However, in his book, *Innovation and Entrepreneurship: Practice and Principles*, Drucker (1985) identifies innovation a specific tool of entrepreneurship. He argues that a feature of innovation is that it can be observed in the actions of people or institutions and therefore it can be learnt. Other researchers also suggest that students can acquire and improve their entrepreneurial soft-skills of thinking creatively and exploiting opportunities by participating in activities that are designed to simulate real-life entrepreneurial experience (Haase & Lautenschlager, 2011, p. 157; Rasmussen & Sorheim,

T definition of innovation

Yes, but strategy

Summary of research with citations

2006, p. 188). A study based on the personal testimonies of entrepreneurs indicates that real entrepreneurs acquire their soft-skills through combination of their personal experience and by observing the actions of more senior entrepreneurs (Rae & Carswell, 2001, pp. 156–157). There is evidence which suggests that this method of teaching entrepreneurship can improve an individual's entrepreneurial soft-skills. Students participating in studies where they are required to participate in simulated entrepreneurial activities such as managing a pop-up shop and creating new products reported that their ability to think creatively, take risks, and work effectively in a team improved over the course of the program (Robinson & Stubberud, 2014; Bell, 2015). Additionally, Swedish universities where entrepreneurship is taught using activities-based learning have reported high company start up rates among their graduates (Rasmussen & Sorheim, 2006, p. 193). The evidence suggest that entrepreneurial skills, such as the ability to think creatively, can be taught to students, even though it cannot be communicated easily. Hence, it is possible for an individual to learn to be an entrepreneur through education.

Summary of research with citations

Specific example

C repeats thesis

CONCLUSION MODEL

In conclusion, there is sufficient evidence to suggest that a person can learn to become an entrepreneur through education. Despite the enduring belief that entrepreneurs must possess a specific set of innate personality traits, real life observations suggest that a person can become an entrepreneur without being born with the ideal entrepreneurial personality traits. Additionally, even though it may be difficult to teach entrepreneurial soft skills such as the ability to think creatively and take calculated risks, there is evidence to suggest that students can acquire and improve those skills by participating in activities that simulate real-life entrepreneurial experience. Therefore, it is possible for an individual to learn to become an entrepreneur through education. As such, entrepreneurship is "capable of being presented as a discipline, capable of being learned, and capable of being practised" (Drucker, 1985, p. 23).

Little variation in thesis restatement

Degrees of certainty with modal verbs and language of possibility

Thesis restated twice

Quotation to end conclusion

YOUR RESPONSE

1. Which organisational method is used to structure the argument? PAIRED SEPARATE
2. In terms of paragraph structure, the use of the TEC model is clearly evident. YES NO
3. How would you describe the use of the following strategies?

   Yes, but strategy   FREQUENT USE | SOME USE | LIMITED USE
   Intensifiers   FREQUENT USE | SOME USE | LIMITED USE
   Modal verbs   FREQUENT USE | SOME USE | LIMITED USE

4. Overall, how effective is the argument? Use this checklist of features to rate the essay. Put a tick (✓) in the box if the essay displays the feature successfully and a ✗ if it does not:

☐ provides an adequate context
☐ identifies opposing views on the issue
☐ states thesis in the introduction
☐ has a clear paragraph and argument structure

☐ develops argument with logical reasoning
☐ provides relevant evidence
☐ uses an appropriate argumentative style
☐ restates thesis in a strong conclusion

5. Has the student defended the argumentative thesis effectively in the conclusion? YES   NO

ESSAY 3 Thesis-led argument (but has features of discussion)

SUBJECT: History   **YEAR:** First   **LENGTH:** 1455 words

REFERENCING STYLE (excludes reference list): Footnote (on first page only)

ASSIGNMENT QUESTION: To what extent was Japan's modernisation following the Meiji an imitation of Western developments? Explain the reasons for your view.

STRUCTURE & ORGANISATION		REASONING & STYLE
INTRODUCTION MODEL Thesis Extent of imitation explained Scope	Many aspects of Japan's modernisation following the Meiji appeared to imitate Western developments. Many Western institutions and systems were adopted such as a police force and Western-style factories.[1] In this essay, I will argue that the usual purpose of such adoptions was not to imitate the West but rather to enhance Japanese power by adapting Western ideas to advance Japanese values. In some areas, however, the West was clearly imitated, particularly in aspects of culture and the daily lives of some groups. These imitations were temporary, however, and their scope was limited. I will begin by discussing the motivations of Japan for the adoption of Western developments and then demonstrate how the Japanese used these developments to advance their values using the examples of learning from the West and education.	Emphatic personal style – not necessary
BODY TEC MODEL Argument 1 T motivation for imitation	The primary motivation for the adoption of Western developments in Japan was to correct the 'unequal treaties' of the 1850s and regain sovereignty.[2] The aim was 'fukoku kyohei', or to 'strengthen and enrich' the nation.[3] While the treaties meant that the threat of Western colonisation was no longer imminent, Japan had nevertheless been forced to accept limits on its sovereignty. According to one treaty, for example, Westerners in Japan were subject to their own laws rather the laws of Japan. Following the Meiji Restoration, the government realised that becoming westernised was the only way for Japan to compete with the West and to regain power and sovereignty.	Footnote referencing, footnote at bottom of the page Logical connectors to clarify explanation

[1] Mikiso Hane, *Modern Japan: A Historical Survey,* Boulder, 2001, pp. 103–109.
[2] Michael Barnhart, *Japan and the World since 1868*, London, 1995, p. 5.
[3] Hane, p. 92.

C reinforces thesis

The Japanese did not just want to be equal with the West, they wanted to be superior. This sentiment is typified in a slogan of the time, that urged that Japan attempt to *'oitsuke, oikose'* or 'catch up, overtake'. This did not mean that the Japanese wanted to become completely westernised, however. Japanese traditions and values remained an important part of society and the government knew that any developments could not be viewed as being 'un-Japanese' by the population.

> Logical connectors to clarify explanation

Argument 2

T selection process

The process of selecting which aspects of western development to adopt was meticulously planned in order to ensure that Japan's own culture was not perceived as being undermined by Western influence. One example of this selection is the way in which the Japanese went about learning how to implement Western modernization. In 1871, a party of Japanese diplomats departed on a tour of the United States, Western Europe and Britain where they met with heads of state and investigated all aspects of laws and constitutions; education; and finance, trade, industry and communications. The trip provided the wealth of knowledge needed to implement Western developments in Japan. It also allowed the government to choose which aspects of Western development would be of most use in advancing Japan's status in the West. The Japanese then spent large sums of money hiring foreign experts to advise them on the best way to implement the changes they desired. These experts were employed in a wide range of activities but were always supervised by Japanese officials and were only hired for as long as it took for Japanese people to learn their skills. They were called *'oyatoi gaijin'* or 'hired foreigners', a term that suggest the Japanese viewed these experts with superiority and contempt rather than respect and exemplifies the way in which the Japanese used Western developments to suit their own purposes.

> Process description as evidence of selective imitation

C reinforces thesis

Argument 3

T evidence of imitation-education

One area in which evidence of imitation was clearly visible was in the education system. Education was seen by the Japanese as a great source of Western power. While Japan already had an education system of sorts and a large proportion of the population had some ability at reading and writing, the government decided high levels of literacy were required to be able to develop Western knowledge in Japan. Subsequently, the Meiji introduced a universal education system in 1872 ... The structure ... was based on that of the French while the curriculum was originally based on that of America, with an emphasis on scientific knowledge.

> Yes, but strategy

However, although Japan set out to create a Western-style education, by 1878, the values that were being taught had become a concern. They were considered too individualistic and liberal for the government, who wanted to promote a sense of nationalism and loyalty to the Emperor. In addition, many school textbooks had been translated directly from books published in Western countries and lacked relevance to Japan's society or geography. As a result, increasing importance was

> Logical connectors track the reasoning process

placed on the development of traditional moral and nationalist values and the state gradually took over the selection of school textbooks. These values were eventually set out in the 1890 *Imperial Rescript on Education* which placed an emphasis on filial piety, or respect for parents and ancestors, loyalty to the Emperor, benevolence and righteousness. So, although the Japanese initially imitated the system and values of education in the West, they subsequently modified it to suit their purposes, that is improving literacy and the skills required for modernization while at the same time promoting a sense of moral duty and nationalism amongst their population.

C reinforces thesis

Logical connectors track the reasoning process.

Informal connector

Argument 4

T evidence of imitation- everyday life

The Japanese did imitate many aspects of everyday life. The government actively encouraged the Westernisation of all aspects of culture as it was considered 'civilized'. Western clothing became popular and was even made compulsory for government officials in 1872. Western hairstyles were considered increasingly fashionable and the eating of beef became popular. The government was also involved in the promotion of modern, Western, music education and the introduction of Western melodies and harmonies into schools as well as providing support to artists using Western style painting techniques. A well-known symbol of this move towards the westernisation of culture and daily life was the *Rokumeikan*, a hall that was built by the government and by government officials to hold Western style social events such as balls, especially popular during the 1880s. However, the peasantry in particular found this adjustment difficult. A younger generation of Japanese who had been brought up to accept Western developments were also concerned that too much emphasis was being placed on westernisation and felt that these practices and values should only be used by Japan if they were to Japan's benefit. There was also a sense of fear amongst the population that Western influence would lead to a loss of cultural identity and a sense of a 'Japanese essence'. The government eventually responded to these concerns by turning to the promotion of nationalism by emphasising the role of the emperor as a symbol of Japanese culture values, again reflected in the *Imperial Rescript on Education*. So, although many aspects of Western daily life were imitated in Japan for a period of time, there was a strong reaction amongst parts of the population to these changes and there was a return to cultural conservatism in later years.

Yes, but strategy

Yes, with evidence

But, with evidence

CONCLUSION MODEL

Restates thesis

Following the Meiji restoration, the Japanese did appear to imitate Western developments to some extent. Closer examination, however, reveals that for the most part, these developments were carefully selected and adopted to suit the purposes of the Japanese government. Periods of indiscriminate imitation were limited both in time and scope and were followed by a return to emphasis on Japanese values and identity. As a result, Japan successfully used Western developments to become a modernised nation and avoid colonisation by the West while retaining its own identity and values.

Review is too general. Mention specific developments to remind reader what they were

YOUR RESPONSE

1. Which organisational method is used to structure the argument?   PAIRED SEPARATE

2. In terms of paragraph structure, the use of the TEC model is clearly evident. YES NO

3. How would you describe the use of the following strategies?

Yes, but strategy	FREQUENT USE | SOME US E | LIMITED USE
Intensifiers	FREQUENT USE | SOME USE | LIMITED USE
Modal verbs	FREQUENT USE | SOME USE | LIMITED USE

4. Overall, how effective is the argument? Use this checklist of features to rate the essay. Put a tick (✓) in the box if the essay displays the feature successfully and a ✗ if it does not:

    ☐ provides an adequate context   ☐ develops argument with logical reasoning

    ☐ identifies opposing views on the issue   ☐ provides relevant evidence

    ☐ states thesis in the introduction   ☐ uses an appropriate argumentative style

    ☐ has a clear paragraph and argument structure   ☐ restates thesis in a strong conclusion

5. Has the student defended the argumentative thesis effectively? YES NO

    _____

    _____

    _____

    _____

ESSAY 4: Discussion-led argument

SUBJECT: History   **YEAR:** Second   **LENGTH:** 2230 words

REFERENCING STYLE (excludes reference list): Footnote (on first page only)

ASSIGNMENT QUESTION: Should we use force to intervene and improve or protect the lives of others?

STRUCTURE & ORGANISATION		REASONING & STYLE
INTRODUCTION MODEL Context Issue Two views	The twentieth century was the century of human rights and humanity. Awareness on these matters were rapidly raised in the international community. After the Second World War, humanitarian law and humanitarian judgement were substantially improved. A number of international treaties relating to human rights were made one after another, including the protection of human rights, the elimination of racial discrimination and gender discrimination, and the banning of torture. These actions imply that any violation of this dignity is unacceptable even in armed conflict.[1] Intervention using armed force would therefore be viewed as a legitimate action because protecting the dignity of humans and the right to life is a humanitarian act. However, there are those who argue that legitimising humanitarian intervention does not solve the problem.	Introduction model used Footnote referencing with footnote at the bottom of the page

---

[1] Nicholas J. Wheeler, Saving strangers: Humanitartian intervention in international society (NY: Oxford University Press, 2000), 28.

Scope	It does not identify or eradicate the root of the problem. This essay will outline some of the key arguments against legitimising a humanitarian intervention, using armed force in particular, and discuss the counter-arguments against intervention.
BODY TEC MODEL **T 1 definition** **T 2 For intervention: first argument**	To begin with, it is important to define the keyword in the question. 'Force' basically implies two meanings in this context: armed force and non-armed force, which is an economic sanction. The basic purpose of economic sanctions is to restrict foreign trade and finance or withhold economic benefits such as state aid from targeted states in order to accomplish broader security or foreign objectives. For example, as part of the six-party talks in 2007 over North Korean nuclear disarmament, an important incentive for North Korea in agreeing to denuclearise its nuclear facilities was the promise of aid. The problem arises in the case of using armed force since it is basically illegal for a single actor to use force in the international community unless it is for self-defence and unless it is sanctioned by the United Nations Security Council (UNSC). The main issue in this essay is whether it is legitimate for a single country to use armed force to intervene in another sovereign state. Only if the UNSC acknowledges that there is a threat to peace, can forceful intervention be legitimised.

Extended definition (annotation, bracketing the paragraph above)

T 2 For intervention: first argument **T 3 For intervention: second argument**	Advocates for intervention argue that forceful intervention is needed if a sovereign country fails to protect its own people. Wheeler argues that sovereignty is derived from a state's responsibility to protect its citizens, but it is not absolute, so when it fails in this duty, it loses its sovereign rights. When outsiders do not intervene to give relief, the persecuted people are therefore unlikely to receive any aid at all. Nakanishi claims that with the existence of the Universal Declaration of Human Rights and the International Covenant on Civil and Political Rights, the legitimacy of accusing a country for violating human rights has become stronger. Furthermore, Mogami states that the fundamental principle of the UN is to guarantee human rights. Therefore, infringement of these rights is as equal to an invasion. The intervention by NATO in 1999 was viewed as legitimate because of the severe acts of violation against human rights by the Yugoslavians.

Author tags and reporting verbs (annotation)

Specific example (annotation)

Logical connectors to show reasoning (annotation)

T 3 For intervention: second argument	Another argument for intervention is that in some cases forceful intervention is the only option left to alleviate suffering on a large scale. In the case of the NATO intervention in Kosovo, President Milosevic had repeatedly failed to comply in earlier resolutions. The UK representative Greenstock stated that in order to avoid a human catastrophe on a large scale, intervention by force was acceptable ... The international community was morally obligated to act. It was deemed to be better than non-action. If NATO had not intervened in Kosovo, the Yugoslav regime would have continued its brutal repression of the Albanian population of Kosovo.

Specific example (annotation)

T 4 Against intervention: first argument

However, realists and supporters of non-intervention claim that there is no basis for humanitarian intervention in International Law. They argue that the autonomy of a state and the necessity of non-interference as a principal for order in international relations. In their view, the primary concerns are security and order among states. Therefore, the common good is best preserved by maintaining a ban on any use of force without authorisation from the UNSC. Ayoob argues that humanitarian interventions should not be carried out under the provision of Chapter VII of the UN Charter since the circumstances of human rights violations usually do not fall within the scope of threats to international peace and security. He also states that Chapter VII was intended to augment the states sovereignty and protect them for external aggression and unwanted in tarnation into their domestic affairs. As such, humanitarian interventions underline the very purpose for which the charter was written.

> Reference to the law

T 5 Against intervention: second argument

In addition, the realists claim that intervention has possibilities to be abused. They claim that actors could act selectively. According to Nakanishi, there are only certain countries with the capacity and willingness to intervene. In such cases, the problem of arbitrariness arises. Actors can decide if intervention is worth the risk of placing their own people in danger. Therefore, intervention depends on the motivation of countries rather than legitimacy. This selectivity is shown in the non-intervention in the Rwanda genocide in 1994 ... because the region's problems were viewed to be of insufficient importance for UNSC interests. Another example is NATO's intervention in Kosovo1999 which was carried out without UNSC authorisation. Again, these cases illustrate that that intervention is not purely based on humanitarian reasons. States choose cases for forceful intervention. Although the international community is bound by International law to help oppressed people, the problem remains if countries arbitrarily takes action without the agreement from the UN. In fact, allowing forceful intervention in the name of humanitarian intervention could jeopardise the legitimacy of intervention.

> Specific example

> Reference to previous example

T 5 Against intervention: third argument

Non-interventionists also argue that the concept of forceful intervention is not easily defined since there is no agreement among the international communities about what constitutes extreme human rights violations.(Footnote) ... Human rights are constructed within a specific cultural context and are not universal and there is a diverse array of cultures and ideas. Faced with such diversity, powerful states could impose their own culture on weaker states, resulting in less understanding among states and throwing the international community into disorder. Without clear rules and procedures for using armed force, humanitarian intervention will always be based on the cultural values of the powerful states.

> Modal verbs express degrees of certainty

T 5 Against intervention: fourth argument

The most critical argument against intervention, according to the realists, is that legitimising humanitarian intervention does not really solve the root of the problem or eradicate it. There are normally some fundamental issues behind large scale human rights violations or conflict. NATO's intervention in Kosovo alleviated the suffering of the Albanian people. However, ten years after the intervention, reconciliation between ethnic communities in Kosovo has still not been achieved. Today, crime and corruption are rampant and there is virtually no existing economy ... According to Nakanishi, problems should be solved by the countries concerned. He argues that the principle of sovereignty is to stimulate a self-awareness and recognition of fundamental human rights. Today, sovereignty is seen as an obstacle to the protection of human rights, although it is a crucial element of human rights that people have the right to choose the political actors to govern them. It could be argued that intervention deprives individuals and groups within a state to exercise the right to self-determination. Above all, the protection of state autonomy and freedom of its inhabitant should have priority over intervention. A far more sustainable and practical alternative to intervention is to assist these states to develop long-term peaceful measures and establish a realistic structural framework to identify the root of the problem. Intervening by force only gives temporary solutions.(137)

Evidence of argumentation strategies and emphatic style

CONCLUSION MODEL

Explicit signal used

Brief review

In conclusion, the use of armed force on humanitarian grounds brings controversy. Even though advocates for intervention claim that the responsibility to protect innocent people should be transferred to the wider international community, the risk of abuse is potentially high. Intervention may be motivated by selfish interests. Therefore, it is important to establish clear rules and procedures and criteria for using armed force; otherwise humanitarian intervention will always be based on the cultural values of the powerful states. To end this controversy, it is important to set a minimum threshold condition for using force to intervene in other sovereign states, including clear rules, procedures and criteria especially relating to the decision to intervene, its timing and modalities. If there is no mutual understanding of humanitarian intervention among the international community, the controversy will never end.

Comment rather than explicit thesis

Extreme language unnecessary

YOUR RESPONSE

1. Which organisational method is used to structure the argument? PAIRED SEPARATE
2. In terms of paragraph structure, the use of the TEC model is clearly evident. (This means that each paragraph begins with a Topic sentence and its theme, continues with Expansion of the topic using different techniques and ends with a final comment on the topic.) YES NO

3. How would you describe the use of the following strategies?

YES BUT strategy	FREQUENT USE | SOME USE | LIMITED USE
Intensifiers	FREQUENT USE | SOME USE | LIMITED USE
Modal verbs	FREQUENT USE | SOME USE | LIMITED USE

4. Overall, how effective is the argument? Use this checklist of features to rate the essay. Put a tick (✓) in the box if the essay displays the feature successfully and a ✕ if it does not:

☐ provides an adequate context
☐ identifies opposing views on the issue
☐ states thesis in the introduction
☐ has a clear paragraph and argument structure

☐ develops argument with logical reasoning
☐ provides relevant evidence
☐ uses an appropriate argumentative style
☐ restates thesis in a strong conclusion

REVIEW

You can see from the sample essays that writing in an argumentative style can be achieved relatively successfully by applying some basic principles and strategies. Overall, all four essays show good essay and paragraph structure and use development techniques and citation conventions effectively. The argumentative style and strategies vary depending on whether the argument is thesis-led or discussion-led.

Below is a brief summary of some strengths and weaknesses:

- Essay 1 has a classical argumentative style. It relies mainly on intensifiers at the heightened end of the scale of intensity. The *Yes, but* strategy is used to develop each argumentative point. The writing is assured and arguments are supported by specific and relevant examples. In some parts, however, the tone is overly emotive and there are some informal language lapses.
- Essay 2 uses less persuasive force, employing more qualification and hedging strategies. In some parts, however, modal verbs are overused, creating a less assured tone. It presents a clear thesis, which is repeated with little variation.
- Essay 3 displays more caution than persuasion in assessing the extent of Japan's imitation of western developments. The writer shows a clear understanding of the words 'To what extent' in the question and uses the *Yes, but* strategy effectively. The conclusion is too general with the word 'developments' repeated several times.
- Essay 4 takes a more balanced and exploratory approach, presenting both views using a block or separate pattern. The use of argumentation strategies is moderate. It does not present a thesis in the introduction, which is acceptable in discussion-led arguments. The reader can conclude that using forceful intervention presents more problems because there are more arguments against it than for it. However, a direct statement that addresses the question 'Should we use force to … ? would give a more satisfactory ending to the discussion.

Part V

Putting it all Together

Part V brings together the principles of academic writing in relation to essays that are more exploratory, that is, requiring <u>analysis</u> and <u>discussion</u> rather than persuasion or argumentation in defence of a thesis (see Part II for features of these essays).

In general, the essays included here show features of good writing in these key areas:

- clear essay and paragraph structure
- relevant and coherent development of ideas
- appropriate academic writing style
- correct in-text citations and integration of evidence to support ideas.

⚠ In-text citations and referencing styles follow subject-area practices. Always check conventions with your department or in your course handbook.)

Guide to annotations

<u>Left margin annotations</u> show the overall essay structure and key structural elements (Introduction, Body and Conclusion) and use of the TEC paragraph structure (mainly the topic sentence (T) and comment (C) elements).

<u>Right margin annotations</u> comment on the development techniques used to develop the body paragraphs. Some annotations alert you to effective use and integration of evidence, citing conventions and inappropriate academic style.

<u>In the main text</u>, the boxed expressions refer to cohesive devices and linking words used to introduce evidence. The highlighted expressions indicate style features.

End of essay references are not included. Instead, the focus here is on how evidence is integrated and cited in the essay itself. Some changes to expression and the length of the body paragraphs were necessary. The original length of each essay is given.

At the end of each essay, you have the opportunity to assess its effectiveness and review the principles of academic writing covered in the book.

ESSAY 1 **Analytical: comparison and contrast**

SUBJECT AREA: Film, Television and Media Studies   **YEAR:** Second   **LENGTH:** 2154 words
REFERENCING STYLE: MLA (Author page system)
ASSIGNMENT QUESTION: Using close reading and research, compare the ways in which two films use historical setting to comment on contemporary issues.

STRUCTURE & ORGANISATION		DEVELOPMENT & STYLE
INTRODUCTION MODEL Context Topic focus Thesis	The genre label 'historical film' is one of several used to describe films with narratives set wholly or partly in the past (Chapman 2). ... Other labels include costume, period or heritage film. These films put fictional characters in historical settings and provide glimpses of a past era. The accuracy of their representation of the past may be debatable but the visual accuracy of the setting achieved through mise-en-scène of authentic period objects and costume enable these films to reflect on social attitudes of the period in a specific and vivid manner. The following is an exploration of how two historical films, *The Last Samurai* and *Gosford Park, ...* construct images of the past that cause the audience to reflect on issues of class, intercultural and transnational relations, which still have relevance today.	Defines terms Uses film vocabulary and technique
BODY TEC MODEL T 1 Setting Film 1 C comments on significance	Both films are set in important periods of history. *The Last Samurai* is set in 1870s Japan during the Meiji Restoration, which was an important period in Japanese history. It was marked by strides towards modernization and signalled the end of the privileged Samurai class and way of life. The settings for the film's narrative are epic, moving from battle scenes to the formal court of Emperor Meiji and tranquil scenes of rural Japan. The opening scene shows how setting is used to introduce the film's main themes of contrasting cultures and ideologies in a dramatic way. It begins with panning shots of the rural landscape and the solitary figure of the samurai leader, Katsumoto in meditation atop a mountain. The tranquillity is suddenly interrupted by Katsumoto's vision of a battle with a foreign and mightier force, symbolised by the face of a roaring tiger. By referring to the American Civil War setting, the film also shows Algren's disenchantment with the U.S. army. These settings also have undertones of Western superiority and orientalism (Roan 183).	Explains by referring to history Links to question Displays knowledge of film techniques

Setting Film 2	*Gosford Park* does not have such epic settings, but the setting of 1930s Britain is also significant, particularly in relation to the crumbling of its rigid class system with the outbreak of the Second World War in 1939. The entire action takes place in a wealthy English country house, in which exist two social worlds: the downstairs world of the domestic servants and the upstairs world of their employers. Unlike the varied settings of *The Last Samurai*, the single location provides greater opportunities for observations of the two worlds. The camera shifts between these two clearly defined settings to show the contrast between them: the lavish furnishings, artefacts of wealth, languid days and dinners of the upstairs world, and the dim, simple and busy world of service downstairs. Many shots in the film are	*Explains by referring to history*
		Uses adjectives of comparison
		Displays knowledge of film techniques
C comments on significance	viewed through a door or window, further highlighting the two separate social worlds.	
T2 Film narrative – point of view	Both films are concerned with class and cultural differences. In *The Last Samurai*, the film narrative of East-West dynamics is mainly from the point of view of a disillusioned American Civil War captain Nathan Algren, who writes about his experiences in 1870s Japan in his journal entries. Algren is placed in different settings for his encounters with the Japanese and Samurai	*Mentions one film and the other to show comparison on the same point*
Last Samurai	culture in particular. He is changed by his experiences. The problems of cultural clashes are suggested through mise-en-scène. Emperor Meiji's monologue near the end of the film urges his subjects to 'not forget where [they] came from' and he abandons the treaty negotiations with the United States. However, the motive for his actions comes from Algren.	
Gosford Park	On the other hand, the narrative of *Gosford Park* is told from the point of view of the new lady's maid and what the servants know and hear while serving upstairs. Higson describes *Gosford Park* as the "new heritage film" (243). It is different from the conventional heritage films which Monk identifies as having a "particular aesthetic approach to the visualisation of the past", which presents a 'museum look' of England and its inhabitants	*Supports with quotations*
C links to thesis and question	(185). However, except for the visual decadence of the McCordle estate, nostalgia is not the central theme. Both films, therefore, use setting to explore social issues.	
T3 Class/culture clash Gosford Park	The cultural and class differences are explored differently in the films. In *Gosford Park*, the two social settings do not mix, although they exist in the same house. Instead, the contrast between them is heightened to point out the absurdities of class distinction and hierarchical rules. The rain mise-en-scène of the opening scene introduces this view vividly. A yellow Rolls Royce arrives at the McCordle estate for one of the dinner guests. While she is escorted to the car under cover of an umbrella, her lady's maid stands in the pouring rain … The servants are 'nobodies' to their employers. This view is expressed by the head housekeeper who declares: 'I am the perfect servant, I	*Illustrates with specific examples*

have no life'. The 'upstairs' characters, however, are shown to be brutal, selfish and fickle. This criticism of the ... upper-class society is conveyed through the sympathetic portrayal of the 'downstairs' characters ... who are shown to be ultimately wiser. ... For example, the new lady's maid is shown to be closer to solving the murder of Sir William than the incompetent and pretentious Inspector. The film narrative after the murder seems to suggest a change in power relations, but the hierarchy and class distinction remain the same through the 1930s.

C links to thesis and question

Logical connectors create flow

T Class/culture clash *Last Samurai*

In contrast, in *Last Samurai*, Eastern and Western cultures clash through the experiences of the main character, who abandons his own culture for Japanese values and way of life. Unlike *Gosford Park*, the film presents a more ambivalent look at Japanese class systems and particularly the samurai way of life. The samurai leader Katsumoto learns of American 'history' through Algren's journal entries, which allow him, as well as the audience, to develop empathy for Algren. The friendship between Algren and Katsumoto is a story about clashing cultures, but it is presented as one of mutual respect and acceptance. The closing scene in the film shows Algren arriving back at the rural village, which is viewed in a long shot. His assimilation into Japanese culture is now complete. It is an idealistic and romantic view but the tranquil nature scenes of rural Japan hint at nostalgia for a gentler past and traditional values.

Uses contrast language to heighten comparison

Illustrates with example and film technique

T4 Period authenticity

Period authenticity is important in historical settings. In both films, there is attention to detail in the use of costumes and period artefacts. The aim is not only to recreate the mood and feelings of the period but also to comment of behaviour and class. In Gosford Park, furnishings are an index of wealth and status, and costume plays a role in establishing class difference. In the upstairs world, for example, the guests change clothes several times during the course of the day to avoid being caught wearing the same dress or the same clothes more than once. When the American guests at the McCordle estate appeared in the hunting scene in inappropriate clothes, instead of the traditional tweed jackets, they were viewed as vulgar by the British guests. In the Last Samurai, the mise-en-scène of Algren proudly putting on samurai clothes symbolises his transformation and adoption of Japanese culture. This contrasts vividly with the portrayal of Algren at the beginning of the film as a disillusioned soldier in his dusty army uniform.

Points out similarities

Gosford Park

Last Samurai

Exemplifies with specific details from each film

CONCLUSION MODEL

As evidenced above, historical settings are not just ornate backdrops, but serve as vehicles for social critique on class and cultural issues that still resonate with contemporary concerns.

Repeats key words to remind reader of the question

Reviews { It may be argued that the landscape shots in the *Last Samurai* conform to a classically orientalist image of Japan, which is 'aestheticized, unchanging, pastoral, and ahistorical' (Roan187). However, these seemingly positive depictions of Japan's scenery lose some of their credibility in light of undertones of imperialism which can be ascertained from the film. In *Gosford Park* there is a similar issue of intercultural dissonance between the British and the Americans. In both films therefore, there are undercurrents of uneasy intercultural and class relations, which

Restates thesis ——▶ still exist today although in different forms.

Mentions both films again

YOUR
RESPONSE

1. Which of the following methods best describes the organisation of the comparison-contrast analysis?   PAIRED | SEPARATE

2. The TEC paragraph structure is effectively used in the body paragraphs.   YES ☐   NO ☐

3. How does the writer display subject (film) knowledge? _____

4. Is the comparison and contrast consistently shown throughout the essay?   YES ☐   NO ☐

   How is this achieved?

   _____

   _____

5. In your view, has the student answered the question effectively?   YES ☐   NO ☐

6. We looked at techniques for developing ideas and expanding topic sentences in Part III, Unit 5. Which techniques are used in this essay? Circle the main technique (s) from these options:

   SPECIFIC EXAMPLES | EXTENDED DEFINITIONS | COMPARISON | CAUSE-EFFECT

SUBJECT AREA: Music   **YEAR:** First   **LENGTH:** 1093 words

REFERENCING (excludes reference list): Footnote (shown on first page only)

ASSIGNMENT QUESTION: Write a response to a musical composition of your choice.

STRUCTURE & ORGANISATION		DEVELOPMENT & STYLE
INTRODUCTION MODEL Gives brief context Thesis and scope	The third movement of Webern's *String Quartet op.5* explores the notion of musical time and defies the classical presumption that music must have harmonic progression to define a clear trajectory. Webern instead creates this trajectory through the use of counterpoint in structure, pitch organisation, timbre and rhythm.	
BODY TEC MODEL **T1 Main elements** **C links to thesis**	The movement has three sections and a short coda, each with a distinct texture. Section A (b.1-8) is characterised by C# pedal and interjections from the upper strings that produce a dissonant harmony. The key role of this section is to introduce the idea of atonal three-note intervallic cells, hence defining the harmonic language of the movement. Section B, beginning in b.9, contains the first melodic entry over sparse, disjointed quavers and introduces the [0 -4 -1] cell.[1] The third section, C, is characterised by contrapuntal interplay of sections A and B. Here, off-beat quavers and intervallic cells from Section A contrast the violin melody and semiquaver/quaver rhythm introduced in B ... The coda restates the [0 -4 -1] cell from the first melody ... and returns to the C# 'tonic' on the final note. The movement therefore develops towards a climax through integration of a limited number of rhythmic, melodic and harmonic motifs.	Evaluates, interprets (shows analytical response) Footnote referencing with footnote at the bottom of the page
T2 First element **C links to thesis**	At first glance, the C# pedal in the cello in b.1-6 appears to provide a tonal centre. However, it is harmonically isolated from the upper parts, and could be interpreted as a timbral effect – this is the lowest note playable on the cello without using a naturally resonant open string, and consequently has a very distinctive tone. C# is a non-functional tonic in that it plays little part in the harmonic language of the movement, but it does act as an aural flag for climactic moments, such b.7 (marking the transition into Section B). The return to C# in the final unison suggests that C# is a tonic of sorts. This is another way that Webern demonstrates that though musical time must necessarily pass, a movement need not have harmonic progression to be coherent.	Uses evaluative language to show response

---

[1] The intervallic cells and the [0 -4 -1] notation are defined in the 'Key to Colour-Coding of Intervallic Cells', attached.

T3 Composition

Pitch organisation through three-note intervallic cells is the harmonic language Webern has defined, and which is crucial to the contrapuntal nature of this work. These cells are built from thirds (major and minor) and semitones. The [0 3 2] cell is one of the most commonly used, and usually appears in imitative pairs a perfect fifth apart in pitch and a quaver apart in time, such as in b.4 between the first violin (D) and the viola (A). In sections A and B, this cell usually appears as the first three notes of the larger six-note cell [0 3 -10 -2 -8 -4]. The cell is also stated in b.18-19 as an ostinato figure, with the viola imitating the second violin, again displaced by a quaver. The quaver displacement of the [0 3 2] cell gives a sense that the cell is perpetually looping, creating dissonances and demonstrating that a motif can provide climactic drive even if it does not develop melodically. Imitative counterpoint at 'tonic' and 'dominant' might be expected to give a sense of tonal stability. Instead, the distinct atonal harmonic language Webern has defined and the juxtaposition of several melodic cells (such as the [0 3 2] ostinato against the [0 -4 -1] ostinato in b.18-19)

C links to thesis → provide harmonic tension and lead to the unison climax.

> *Uses evaluative language to show response*

> *Explains, Interprets*

T4 Second element

The [0 -4 -1] melodic cell has a unifying function. Introduced in b.9 as the first three notes of the melody, it returns as a staccato ostinato in the cello at b.15, contrasting the legato first violin melody. In the penultimate bar, [0 -4 -1] is used simultaneously in all four voices to begin the unison climax of the movement. This cell persists without melodic extension, unifying the sections of the movement ... Other intervallic cells are used throughout the work ... to highlight important transition bars, such as b.6 and b.8. Where cells combine, a climax is created, signalling the end of a section ... These pitch clusters break the work into three-note fragments ... , giving an aural impression

C links to thesis → of brief, disconnected moments in time that combine into a coherent trajectory due to their intervallic unity.

> *Uses specialised vocabulary – displays subject knowledge*

T5 Third element

Webern employs a wide range of timbres in this work switching frequently between am Steg, col legno, arco and pizzicato. Relatively melodic lines tend to be emphasised by the use of arco, for example in the first violin in b.12-14 and b.17-21, while passages that contribute more to rhythmic drive than melodic line such as the cello ostinato in the opening six bars are often marked pizzicato. The use of contrasting timbres highlights the counterpoint and prevents several independent lines becoming aurally indistinguishable. Distinct timbres are not exclusive to a particular pitch cluster, but the timbre often changes at the same time as the intervallic cell changes, and never part way a cell. This aurally highlights the counterpoint and the changing motifs of the harmonic language, which

C links to thesis → might otherwise be missed given the speed at which it is performed. It also acts as a reminder that change is occurring as musical time elapses.

> *Interprets evaluates*

T6 Fourth element

The rhythms of this movement fall into three motifs within the 2/2 time metre – a semiquaver followed by a quaver, constant quavers and offbeat quavers. Constant quaver movement and the opening crotchet ostinato (an augmented form), push the movement onwards in musical time and unify the movement. Frequent off-beat pizzicatos and the presence of dynamic accents on traditionally weak beats (such as the ff chords on the sixth quaver beat of b.3) create a hemiola that is further highlighted by imitative [0 3 2] quaver displacement.

> Describes how device works

In b.15-17, the unrelenting quaver motion and hemiola produced by offset imitative cells builds tension until the climactic release into rhythmic and melodic unison in b.22-23. This, along with what is essentially a half-movement-long **C links to thesis** ──► crescendo, is the most striking method Webern uses to create direction and climax without harmonic or motivic development.

> Explains, evaluates

CONCLUSION MODEL

In just 23 bars, Webern defines an atonal harmonic language and uses this as a springboard from which to explore ideas of musical time and create forward motion without traditional harmonic or melodic progressions. It is the counterpoint between intervallic cells, rhythmic motifs, timbres and sections that gives this movement its drive and clear trajectory.

> Repeats key words from the introduction

YOUR RESPONSE

1. Which of the following methods best describes the organisation of the response essay and analysis?   CHRONOLOGY | DIVISION | LOGICAL ENQUIRY

2. How does the writer display subject (music) knowledge? _____

3. The word 'response' means 'to react to something'. It includes explaining, interpreting and evaluating. Is there evidence of 'response' writing in the essay?   YES ☐   NO ☐

   Find three examples of this style from the essay: _____

   _____

4. In terms of length, both the introduction and conclusion are below the percentage guideline of 8–10 per cent of the total length. As a reader, which elements of the introduction and conclusion model would you like included? (Review these models in Part III, Unit 3.)

   _____

   _____

5. Is the TEC paragraph model used effectively throughout?   YES ☐   NO ☐

6. In your view, has the writer answered the question?   YES ☐   NO ☐

ESSAY 3 **Analytical and discursive**

SUBJECT AREA: Art History   **YEAR:** First   **LENGTH:** 1485 words

REFERENCING STYLE (excludes reference list): Footnote (on first page only)

ASSIGNMENT QUESTION: Discuss the ways in which the work of Edouard Manet deviated from traditional practice in 19thC France as part of the emerging avant-garde. Consider matters of content (subject matter), technique and social and exhibition context.

STRUCTURE & ORGANISATION		DEVELOPMENT & STYLE
INTRODUCTION MODEL	Émile Zola, a friend of Manet, saw him as one of the 'masters of the future but a child of his own time.'[1] Indeed, Manet is now regarded by many as the father of modernism. He was a realist with his content, but developed the impressionist technique, both of which reacted against the traditions of the French	Uses emphatic style
Context	Royal Academy. However, Manet did not ignore the Academy completely, as Reyburn comments, 'Manet … was a sphinx-like figure, on the one hand outrageously confronting the salon and its audience, on the other craving its acceptance.'[2] Indeed, Manet saw the Salon as the 'true field of battle' where 'one must measure oneself'.[3]	Uses many short quotations (some could be paraphrased)
BODY TEC MODEL **T1 Social context**	Manet never studied at the École des Beaux Arts, beginning tuition instead under the French master Thomas Couture, who influenced his choice of contemporary realism, once proclaiming, 'I did not make you study the old masters so that you would always follow trodden paths.'[4] Newly emerging private galleries, more than a hundred of which opened in Paris in the early 1860s, allowed artists such as Manet to explore avant-garde subjects and techniques outside the established demands of the Salon. Many of Manet's works were displayed in private galleries; however, his painting *Olympia* was exhibited in the Salon in 1865, and *A Bar at the Folies-Bergère* in 1882, showing he could not reject tradition completely.	Explains Manet's deviation Footnote referencing style (footnotes at bottom of page)

[1] Anne C. Hanson, *Manet and the Modern Tradition* (New Haven: Yale University Press, 1977), 3.
[2] Scott Reyburn, *The Art of the Impressionists* (London: The Apple Press, 1998), 22.
[3] Manet quoted in Scott Reyburn, *The Art of the Impressionists* (London: The Apple Press, 1998), 22.
[4] Ibid, 23.

T2 Subject-matter This battle with tradition is evident in his early work, such as *Olympia* completed in 1862, and persisted through to his last works, such as *A Bar at the Folies-Bergère* in 1882. In *Olympia,* Manet referenced academic practice by depicting a nude, and by echoing traditionally accepted works, such as Titian's *Venus of Urbino* and Ingres' *La Grande Odalisque* and *Odalisque with a Slave. Olympia* is almost identical to these earlier works in the placement and choice of subject, showing Manet's attempt to appease academic taste. Titian's *Venus of Urbino* glances suggestively at the viewer, subverting the usual modest, submissive looks of the Venus Pudicas at the time. Manet plays on this, depicting Olympia as a reclining, high-class prostitute ... glaring shamelessly at the viewer and confronting them with the reality of her work ... However, Olympia was a modern-day Parisian prostitute. Manet's avant-garde approach ... in making the nude a modern working girl, meant that *Olympia* was received with public outrage, with one critic commenting that 'art which has sunk so low is not worthy even of censure'. Manet's innovative and bold look at the moral uncertainties of Parisian life angered the conservative Salon audience, who expected the Academy's usual scenes of history, grand, noble themes, allegories, rural landscapes, and aristocratic portraits. Not only did Manet ignore the social milieu favoured in Academy paintings but also the proletariat in Courbet's. By depicting the middle-class, and in the case of *Olympia,* by portraying a contemporary prostitute, he confronted their conservative nature, and their sexual taboos, which led many men to solicit the company of prostitutes. This is enforced by the flat space in *Olympia,* which brings the viewer forward into the painting as a voyeur or potential client.

Compares with other works

Gives visual details

Repeats key word to emphasise deviation

Exemplifies with concrete details

C links to subject matter and thesis

T3 Subject-matter As with *Olympia, A Bar at the Folies-Bergère* also presents social commentary on the middle-class. Here, the barmaid appears divorced from the viewer. The mirror behind shows she is conversing with a customer, yet her expression is vacant and disconnected; she is 'so still that she has more in common with the lovingly painted objects on the bar than with the noisy humanity behind her.' Indeed the application of paint connects the girl and objects, both detailed in longer, more carefully applied brushstrokes, whereas the crowded bar, reflected in the mirror behind, is painted in impressionist style. This shows Manet's views on the true nature of the social relationships forged by the middle-class in these new situations, as '[h]is reserve toward representation of emotion and his immersion in the aesthetic side of social life can be taken as examples of modern detachment paralleling that of the protagonists in many of his works.'

Supports style with visual details

Vague/wordy quotation (paraphrase instead)

C links to thesis with quotation

T4 Subject-matter

A Bar at the Folies-Bergère was additionally avant-garde by featuring modern places. During Manet's life, France underwent several political changes, the most influential on the impressionists being the second empire, under Emperor Napoleon III (1851–1870), when much of Paris was rebuilt by Baron Haussman, creating new indoor and outdoor social spaces. Industrialisation created the nouveau riche, the emerging bourgeoisie, and regimented working hours, which allowed time for socialising, pastimes and visiting the new social spaces. This new arena fascinated the impressionists, including Manet, and became the subject of many of their paintings, such as Manet's *Music in the Tuileries Gardens* (1862) and *At the Cafe* (1878).

> Explains influence on artist

T5 Technique

Another element that upset traditional viewers was Manet's scandalous technique. Traditionally, painting involved chiaroscuro, in which the images are built up carefully by the gradual contrast of light and shade, allowing for soft and subtle nuances to create the impression of depth and relief. Traditionally, artists would start their paintings with a dark undercoat to give the illusion of depth. Such is the case in Alexandre Cabanel's *The Birth of Venus* (1863), where naturalistic tonal modelling builds the flowing, rounded form of Venus in soft muted colours. The paintwork appears to have been breathed onto the canvas, as the brush marks are barely visible. Manet did away with transitions between tones, replacing them with expanses of colour. This resulted in the subject appearing harshly lit, as in the jarring pallor of *Olympia* and her stark white sheets. Manet abandoned this in favour of off-white undercoat, which makes his paintings luminous. This was at the expense of convincing depth, as is noticeable in *Olympia*, where the back wall with its hanging fabric appears uncomfortably close to Olympia.

> Uses contrast to emphasise deviation from tradition

C reinforces deviation, links to thesis

However, Manet was not interested in depicting a false reality, preferring to focus on themes, social commentary and the painterly qualities of art.

T6 Technique

Form has also been outlined in thick dark lines, influenced by Courbet's work and Japanese prints, which had been discovered by the painters of Manet's generation and embraced as being free from the traditions of the academy. Such painterly qualities are exemplified by Manet's application of paint, for as Gardener mentions, he used 'art to call attention to art'. Traditionally, paints were applied flat on the canvas, except for highlights which were painted more thickly to aid the impression of depth. Manet deviated from convention and applied both highlights and dark colours thickly. This experimentation was begun years earlier by Theodore Gericault and Courbet. Manet, however, took it further by making the texture of paint more obvious, often using this seemingly hurried technique to depict whole

> Compares with other techniques to reinforce deviation

scenes, as in *Music in the Tuileries Gardens,* or in sections, as in *A Bar at the Folies-Bergère.* Here the mirrored crowd is painted loosely with a thick application of paint, giving a sense of movement that contrasts with the barmaid's stillness. Manet's radical approach can be seen by comparing his work to Ingres' *Madame Moitessier, Seated* (1856), where the whole painting – from the foreground to the background, the reflection to the finer detail – is rendered with the same precision and fine brushstrokes.

> Shows knowledge of subject

CONCLUSION MODEL

Reviews avant-garde style

Émile Zola may have been correct in his statement about Manet as a 'child of his own time' for Manet's exploration of modern social themes of alienation and the moral uncertainties of Parisian life are inspired by the world and era in which he lived. This, along with Manet's experimentation and development of technique, is what makes his art truly innovative and influential in the avant-garde movement, for, 'The power of [his] pictures lies in the degree to which their realism is social as well as visual.' While Manet persisted in trying to exhibit his work in the Salon, he also sought out less traditional venues. His work inspired the art of Degas, Cézanne and Monet. Although such artists would further explore his subject matter and develop his techniques, their work, and indeed the impressionist movement, would not have been the same without Manet.

> Repeats quotation from introduction

> Uses different words to sum up deviation

End statement points to Manet's influence

YOUR RESPONSE

1. Which of the following methods best describes the way the main topics [T] are organised? DIVISION | LOGICAL ENQUIRY | CHRONOLOGY

2. How is subject knowledge displayed in the essay? _____

3. There are four short quotations in the introduction. Based on what you have learnt about using quotations in Part I, Unit 2, which quotations would you use and which would you paraphrase? _____

4. There is some use of emotive and informal language in T5. Can you find some examples of this? _____

5. In your view, has the writer effectively shown how Manet deviated from traditional practice? YES ☐   NO ☐

6. Which techniques are predominantly used to expand ideas in each body paragraph? Choose from these options:

EXTENDED DEFINITIONS | EXAMPLES | QUOTATIONS | COMPARISON-CONTRAST | VISUAL ANALYSIS

SUBJECT: Sociology   **YEAR:** First   **LENGTH:** 1193 words

REFERENCING STYLE (excludes reference list): Footnote (on first page only)

ASSIGNMENT QUESTION: 'Choose any type of text. Provide an analysis of your chosen text using theory that has been covered in the course. You may wish to concentrate on a certain aspect of the text such the depiction of gender, ritual, class or ethnicity, or discussing how the text relates to theories of production or consumption.' (**NOTE:** The student's 'text' is an art work.)

STRUCTURE & ORGANISATION		DEVELOPMENT & STYLE
INTRODUCTION MODEL Context Topic focus	Artist Andy Warhol, leader of the 1960s 'Pop Art' movement, created work that paralleled the consumer culture of the time. One of his most famous works is *Campbell Soup Cans*, produced in 1963. The work consisted of thirty-two almost identical images, each of a different flavoured can of Campbell's Soup. While being simplistic in style, it has proved to be a complicated and ambiguous piece, with its meaning being up for interpretation.[1] Although the text can be easily related to the consumer driven society of the 1960s, employing sociological theory helps to develop a deeper understanding of the text to determine how *Campbell Soup Cans* reflects, glorifies or even mocks the mass-consumption of the modern era.	Directly connects artist and text to consumer culture Footnote referencing style with footnote at the bottom of the page.
BODY TEC MODEL T1 The 'text' C reminds reader of the question	When analysing the meaning produced by *Campbell Soup Cans*, it is important to employ semiotics. Semiotics allows meanings to be understood through the study and interpretation of signs.[2] A sign has two different forms; its *signifier* and its *signified* meanings. The signifier is the literal form that the sign takes. In *Campbell Soup Cans* the signifier is the cans of soup, and the words 'Campbell's Soup' written on them. The second component; a sign's signified meaning, is the concept represented by the signifier.[3] Understanding the signified in *Campbell Soup Cans* is considerably complex due to the ambiguous nature of the text. [4] ... Due to this, it is necessary to look behind the context of the painting and employ sociological theory to produce a significant analysis of the text.	Defines meaning of text using theory Rather vague. State clearly complex and ambiguous nature

---

[1] Caroline A. Jones (1991). Andy Warhol's "Factory": The Production Site, Its Context and its Importance on the Work of Art. Science in Context, 4, doi: 10.1017/S026988970000017X, pp.119, 127.

T2 Relevance of text

Warhol produced much of his artwork in the 1960s and embraced the consumer driven society of the time. In doing so he mirrored industrialised production and consumption in the production of his art. He named his studio the 'factory' and, instead of traditional painting methods, he used the process of silk screen. This method involved mechanically printing images, a method chosen specifically by Warhol for 'he wanted something ... that gave more of an assembly line effect'. The text is therefore industrialised, impersonal and mechanically created, imitating the nature of mass production. In addition, Warhol chose a famous icon of the assembly line for his subject matter. The brand of 'Campbell's Soup' is presented in the text, without any other distracting subject matter, and is repeated thirty-two times, making the brand 'large and formidable.' Brands are symbols of mass-production. They allow consumers

C reinforces relevance

to distinguish between the vast amounts of increasingly available mass-produced products. In using a mechanical mode of production and presenting subject matter with strong connotations with mass-production, Warhol directly responded to the dominating presence of brands and consumption in society.

> Gives four examples of how the artist and the 'text' relates to production and consumption

T3 Identity

It is not uncommon to use art to comment on society and human behaviour. Throughout history, artists have used their painting to reflect expressions of the self and society. In his painting *Campbell's Soup Cans,* Warhol makes observations about individual and social identities. By using a product brand as the sole image, Warhol suggests that consumption is the religion of the modern era. People create their identity through their purchases; the choices they make about specific commodities supposedly define the consumer's identity. Furthermore, the repeated images of the cans reflect the limitations of a consumer identity. The thirty-two cans are essentially the same; they were made using the same method and take the same form, only exhibiting minor variations. According to the theory of standardisation, the masses are drawn into believing that there are intrinsic differences between products, when in reality they are consuming products with only superficial differences. This suggests

C reinforces identity link

that the identities which people attempt to create through choosing particular products are in fact artificial. The repetition of imagery captures this idea; the cans are virtually identical, but consumers pick one and let it become a defining factor of their sense of self.

> Explains connection between the artwork and identity

> Relates to theory

T4 Consumer behaviour

Whilst it is evident that *Campbell Soup Cans* reflects a consumer society, it is not necessarily created to paint a positive or negative picture of consumption. In fact, we can presume that it was largely neutral due to Warhol identifying himself as being merely a 'machine'. However, interpreting *Campbell Soup Cans* using the theory of 'false needs' presents the image as a satirical text mocking consumption's influence over the masses. The theory assumes that consumers are 'cultural dupes' manipulated to see trivial items as necessities. 'False needs' are placed on an individual by producers and advertisers to encourage consumption. Prior to the Industrial Revolution, people consumed products of their own labour. To consume soup, one would have grown ingredients and subsequently made the soup. But in modern society, ... we are manipulated into believing that we are too busy to grow and cook. Therefore, we buy products that are advertised as being tailored specifically for our busy lifestyles. Whilst food is a necessity, industrially produced food is not and therefore it constitutes a 'false need'.

Relates consumer behaviour to theory

Uses contrast

Uses personal pronouns (we, our)

CONCLUSION MODEL

No signal used but repeats a comment from the introduction

Although Warhol elevated the status of a Campbell's Soup Can by making it art, he did not glorify it. *Campbell Soup Cans* is a soulless and lifeless work of art suggesting that a can of soup amongst other products is ultimately meaningless. Consumer society, on the other hand, has glorified products, promoting them to necessities, when in reality they are trivial results of modernisation. In Warhol's life, and in his paintings, consumer driven society is clearly reflected. The repeated imagery in *Campbell Soup Cans* highlights consumption's dominance and the notion that identities are being based solely on purchasing power. In turning a common brand into art, Warhol challenges us to question branded products and the dangers they pose to society. Ultimately, *Campbell Soup Cans*' signified meaning alludes to the associated processes of production and consumption in a capitalist economy and a consumer society inevitably driven by false needs and brands.

Repeats key words (highlighted here) to remind reader of the question

C reinforces consumer behaviour

End statement points to the future

YOUR RESPONSE

1. Which of the following methods best describes the way the main topics [T] are organised? DIVISION | LOGICAL ENQUIRY | CHRONOLOGY

2. The question requires the use of theory to analyse the text. How many theories are used in the analysis?
_____

3. There are some lapses into informal writing style such as the use of personal pronouns in one of the body (T) paragraphs. Can you identify the paragraph?　　　　　　　　　　　　　　　T [ ]

4. The conclusion brings all the issues together effectively. How is this achieved?
_____

5. In your view, has the writer effectively related the art work and the artist to the theories of production and consumption?　　　　　　　　　　　　　　　YES ☐　NO ☐

ESSAY 5 **Discursive**

SUBJECT: Sociology **YEAR:** Second **LENGTH:** 2048 words

REFERENCING STYLE (excludes references): APA (Author, Year system)

ASSIGNMENT QUESTION: 'Popular representations suggest that today's fathers make significant contributions to childcare and other housework duties. Drawing on recent sociological research discuss the accuracy of such representations and consider whether a gendered division of labour still exists in childcare and housework.'

STRUCTURE & ORGANISATION		DEVELOPMENT & STYLE
INTRODUCTION MODEL Brief context	The organisation of modern families has changed over time, with men and women participating in paid work to provide for family. With both in paid work, who performs the unpaid work that sustains day-to-day living? This research essay critically discusses the notion that men make significant contributions to childcare and other household duties. It will do this by first addressing a brief history of changes to the family organisation ... and describing two dominant views. Secondly, it draws on statistics from ... to argue the notion of men's significant participation in unpaid work. Thirdly, there is a discussion on the practice of 'doing gender' which describes how men and women participate in gender roles influenced by society ... It will also discuss the power relations between men and women, which comes from inequalities of income, policy, tradition and attitudes. Lastly, this essay highlights research that explain why men do not participate as much as women in unpaid work.	Poses a question (avoid this style)
Scope element of the model mainly		
BODY TEC MODEL T1a	**History and Two Views** Men's involvement in family life has changed significantly over time, from the close family unit of production to the industrial age, when men left daily family life to seek wage labour (Hook, 2006). According to Hook, this led to the separation of men's and women's labour: the men as breadwinners, the women as caregivers. However, the dominant role of the breadwinner began to be challenged during the mid twentieth century ... Today, the familiar family model features both men and women, working outside the home but, the change in family time for men, is under debate. Hook notes that even though unpaid work time has increased for men, 'it has not compensated for women's decline nor reached parity with women's time' (p. 1).	Uses appropriate connectors to track changes
		Quotation with citation
C sums up Craig's view		

T1b

Craig (2016) describes two main views on how modern households manage paid and unpaid work. The 'gender convergence' view is that there is a decrease in specialisation of activity between the sexes. This view assumed that when women entered the paid workforce, unpaid work of the home would have naturally evened out between genders (Hook, 2006; Craig & Mullana, 2001). ... . The oppositional view argues working women are dividing their time more efficiently to accommodate both paid and unpaid work, while men specialise only in the paid market. Craig argues that, in reality, although women participate in paid work, they are also 'retaining responsibility of the unpaid domestic work', which indicates woman are in actual fact 'working much more than their husbands' (Craig, 2016, p. 51).

Paraphrase with citation

C concludes with reason

T1a

Who's doing the important work?

Everyday human existence requires the essentials of life reproduced by unpaid labour that feeds, clothes, shelters and cares for the family. These are 'just as important to the maintenance of society as the productive work that occurs in the formal market economy' (Coltrane, 2000, p. 1209). Coltrane analysed a range of American research using different methodology. He compared results from 1965–1985 and concluded that men's participation in unpaid work doubled from two hours to four hours per week, while women's unpaid work reduced from 24 to 16 hours per week. Other similar research showed a slight reduction in women's contribution to housework while men's participation increased gradually. Coltrane argues that this finding is not an accurate representation because men contributions were at a lower level to begin with. Coltrane concluded that 'the average woman, still does about three times the amount of routine housework as the average man' (pp. 1211–1212).

These short quotes could be paraphrased

C assesses evidence

Provides statistical evidence from different research

T2b

A Statistics New Zealand's (2006) overview found that overall 98 percent of women performed unpaid work compared to 86 percent of men. Unpaid work in the home such as cooking, cleaning, household repairs and gardening was performed by 89 percent of women compared to men at 82 percent. 35 percent of women engaged in the unpaid care of children with men at 27 percent ... An OECD report on unpaid care work also supports the fact there is an unequal distribution of care responsibilities and women are disproportionately 'spend[ing] two to 10 times more time on unpaid work care than men' (OECD, 2014, p. 1)

Quotation

T3a

The assignment of gender and power relations

Representations of participation in unpaid work need to be viewed from the way gender is constructed ... Maloney and Fenstermaker (2002) use the work of Butler (1997a) to illustrate that gender is a ritual performance and its powers come from continual 're-iterated, re-citational and re-signification' (p. 198). ... This is evident in the way children are 'gendered' from birth by parents and society ... . and expected norms of behaviour and activities are carried into adulthood. West and Zimmerman (2002) argue that the division between men's and women's work reflects differences in 'feminine and masculine attitudes and behaviours that are prominent features of social organization' (p. 5). In addition, they argue that the differences created between men and women are not biological, but constructed 'to reinforce the essentialness of gender' (p.13). Gender then becomes a way of behaving and performing according to 'institutional arrangements that are based on sex category' (p. 22).

C comments on gender and equality

Quotations could be paraphrased to clarify meaning

T3b

It has also been suggested that gender differences can affect power relations in the family structure. Dermott (2008) reports that in British homes, men still contribute larger proportions of income to family, at approximately 67 percent. Even in cases of dual income families, only a quarter shows that women contribute more than 45 percent of couples' total income. According to Dermott, women's inability to contribute more paid work is due to accepting shorter working hours and therefore a lower pay structure ... Unequal labour markets also cause women to specialise in unpaid work and men in paid work. They affect 'relative resources and household bargaining power, reinforcing attitudes about appropriate gender roles' (Craig & Mullana, 2011, p. unknown).

C comments on power relations

Provides statistical evidence

T4a

Why Men don't

... Understanding why men do not participate in unpaid work requires some reflection into the past. Burgess (1997) provides a historical context of fatherhood from tribal times, where men were intentionally kept away from children for practical means ... because of the concern that if men became emotionally attached to their children, they would become ineffective in performing hard physical work and going to war ... Gauntlett (2002) suggests that the media portrayals of men and women in activities also reinforce the gender ideologies ... In a study of 720 television commercials, Bartsch et al. (2000) found that women were twice more likely to feature in advertisements for domestic products than men.

Refers to various views in different ways (e.g. with author tags and reporting verbs to begin the sentence or with citation at end of sentence)

T4b

Finally, there is research that suggests that some mothers 'actively prevent fathers from doing more with their children through 'gate-keeping and hampering [men's] involvement'. It suggests women may do this to retain control of the home domain where they feel the most expert (Craig & Mullana, 2011. Focusing on traditional gender roles, these perspectives claim that housework tasks have different meanings and standards for men and women. The cleanliness of the home and children's appearance is a reflection of a woman's competence as a wife and mother, not her husband's. Because of this, women

C sums up reason → may have high standards and are hesitant to relinquish control and trust their husband to perform housework and care tasks. (Bianchi et al., 2000).

CONCLUSION
MODEL

Reviews main findings

End sentence points to future

Conclusion

This essay has critically discussed the notion that fathers today are participating more in the unpaid work of childcare and housework duties. Statistics from research show that male participation has increased over time. However, it is difficult to determine if men's participation in housework in the modern era is significant or accurate, because their contributions are still nowhere near parity with women's participation. The findings from evidence from different studies suggest that women in paid work are still continuing to do more work at home. Determining the accuracy of men's participation is further complicated by gender roles assigned from childhood, which continue to influence gendered behaviours into adulthood. In addition, as a result of institutional and state policies, women have continued to experience inequality resulting in less power to negotiate unpaid work of the home, and men as breadwinners still dominate the family organisation.

Reminds reader of the question

YOUR
RESPONSE

1. Which of the following methods best describes the way the essay is organised?
    DIVISION | LOGICAL ENQUIRY | CHRONOLOGY

2. Each of the main headings in the body of the essay is developed in two paragraphs (e.g. T1a, T1b), each with a central theme.
    a) Explain why by applying the principles of paragraph construction. _____
    b) What is the theme of T1a? _____
    c) What is the theme of T1b? _____

3. The discussion refers to sociological research. Give two examples of how this is done:
    a) _____
    b) _____

4. The thesis is clearly stated in the introduction.   YES ☐   NO ☐

5. Discursive essays present balanced information and explore different perspectives.
    Is this done well in the essay?   YES ☐   NO ☐

6. The question asks if the representation of men's increased participation in unpaid work is accurate and if a gendered division of labour still exists. In your view, does the writer address this question in the conclusion?   YES ☐   NO ☐

SUBJECT AREA: Management   **YEAR:** Second   **LENGTH:** 1590 words

REFERENCING STYLE (excludes references): APA (Author, Year system)

ASSIGNMENT QUESTION: <u>Analyse</u> the organisational culture at a firm of your choice, indicating whether the firm manufactures a culture or if it is generated naturally by employees. <u>Discuss using relevant theories</u> and <u>analyse</u> the firm's culture from a <u>mainstream</u> and <u>critical perspective</u>.

STRUCTURE & ORGANISATION		DEVELOPMENT & STYLE
INTRODUCTION MODEL	Culture is an important organisational facet and plays a vital role in influencing employee behaviour and a firm's success. Organisational culture is defined as 'the shared values and beliefs that provide the norms of expected behaviour in an organisation' (Hogan & Coote, 2014, p. 1). The critical perspective maintains that organisational culture is constructed naturally by employees and not something that management can manipulate (Knights & Wilmott, 2012). It creates a weaker culture because the same values are not shared by all employees (Saffold III, 1988). The mainstream perspective advocates that organisational culture plays a pivotal role in a firm's success. It describes culture as something an organisation 'has'; it is manufactured by management to unite staff and create a common goal (Knights & Wilmott, 2012). Kermally (2005) argues that in a firm with a strong manufactured culture, it is	
Context using key words		Lead-in to discussion by defining 4 key terms in the question
Topic focus ——→	easier to know what behaviour is expected as opposed a culture in which the behaviours and attitudes emerge naturally. This	
Scope ——→	essay analyses the culture at Mars Incorporated, an American global manufacturer of pet care products, confectionery, drinks and health products. It draws on the theories of Schein (1989), Handy (1999) and Peters and Waterman's (1982) 7s framework for culture and management. It concludes	
Thesis ——→	that the manufactured culture at Mars has led to its overall success.	
BODY TEC MODEL	Schein (1983) identifies three levels of culture which are based on his belief that an organisation's culture has visible and inviable element. The first level refers to the visible artefacts which reflect a shared purpose and mission in employees. At Mars Incorporated, the artefacts are suits and lab coats that employees wear, posters of the Five Principles that constitute the foundation of its organisational culture – quality, responsibility, mutuality, efficiency and freedom (Marketline, 2015) – displayed on the walls, the computer screens dispersed throughout the offices that update staff on current financials [...] (Cubiks, 2010).	
T1 Schien's theory		Explains theory
		Relates theory to practice

The second level, espoused values, are the expectations of the acceptable behaviours of members in an organisation. According to Knights and Wilmott (2012) espoused values are difficult to measure or 'see' but individuals are conscious of them. At Mars, these values exist in the family atmosphere created by the Mars owners who view their staff as family members and the business as the staff's legacy. Another espoused value is the equality of opportunity within the organisation, regardless of gender or ethnicity (Cubiks, 2010). This lack of discrimination encourages employees to constantly improve their skills, knowing that any promotion will be awarded solely on the basis of merit. Mars encourages interactions with other staff through the use of social rooms and by using escalators instead of elevators (Morand, 1998). This facilitates informal face-to-face contact among staff and nurtures the 'family' atmosphere.

Relates theory to practice

C links Mars culture to theory

T2 Schien's theory

Schien's third level of culture refers to deeply rooted values that staff share. Knights and Wilmott (2012) describes this as the psychological contract of implied expectations of the organisation and employees of each other. These expectations also include the organisation's relationship with society and its corporate social responsibilities. According to Crainier (2014), in Mars Incorporated, basic assumptions could be the idea that the owners expect their staff to be creative, constantly thinking and improving their skills, whilst the staff expect Mars to reflect the vibrant, exciting nature of its brands. There is also evidence that Mars initiates programs that aim to create a sustainable environment and helping the community (Kaplan & Adamo, 2013). Crainer describes experiences of employees who have taken part in the Mars Volunteer and Ambassador Programs where employees contribute to the well-being of their communities or visit Ghana to understand the process of growing cocoa beans.

Uses opinion as evidence

C evaluates Mars' performance

T3 Handy's theory

Kermally (2005) explains that all organisations can be divided into one of four of Handy's cultures, based on the organisation's history, structure, ownership and environment. Mars fits into the task culture, where the key values are expertise and teamwork (Knights & Wilmott, 2012). This culture thrives in competitive and volatile markets or industries such as the food industry in which Mars operates (Knights & Wilmott, 2012). In this culture, creativity is vital and strong communication is essential to anticipate and adapt to change (Kermally, 2005). Crainer (2014) explains that Mars employees receive a mentor during their first year to introduce them to the culture. The open floor plan layout of the offices at Mars encourages communication and further emphasises the teamwork aspect of this culture. Furthermore, Mars employs individuals who are innovative and independent (Robison, 2008). These practices are essential in a task culture that operates in rapidly changing markets.

Explains task culture at Mars with specific examples

C links Mars' performance to theory

Peters and Waterman, as described by Van de Ven (1983), identified seven major organisational components that successful organisations have – strategy, structure, systems, skills, staff and style (referred to as the 7s model). One of these is the hands-on, value-driven characteristic that managers must work among subordinates, instead of dictating over them (Knights & Wilmott, 2012). Morand (1998) explains that at Mars, the CEO's desk is in the middle of the floor, which creates a sense of collegiality and shared authority among colleagues, whilst demolishing any hierarchies. This leads onto the next characteristic which is that of simple form and lean staff. This promotes the abandoning of hierarchies, seen at Mars through their 'universal first naming' implied policy, where titles are abolished (Morand, 1998). Another value is the productivity through people, emphasising the importance of the employee as a resource (Van de Ven, 1983). The Mars owners are actively involved in the business and regularly work among staff and praise or reward them for any success (Crainer, 2014). This positive reinforcement increases employee pride and motivation. These three qualities are visible in Mars and according to Van de Ven (1983) create a singular optimal culture or way of carrying out practices that all staff share and believe in.

> Gives example of Mars' 'manufactured culture'

C links Mars' performance to model

T5 Mars' Manufactured culture

At Mars, The Five Principles were created by the owners and are reinforced in every place, task and employee at Mars (Mars Incorporated, 2003). This produces a top-down, manufactured culture, generated by senior management and followed by staff. Management's informal directions and rules about the culture are what create the shared homogenous beliefs that all employees have (Saffold III, 1988). Saffold III (1988) explains that an advantage of this strong culture is that it generates an irreplaceable energy that empowers staff towards greater performance, contrary to some arguments that the mainstream approach of a strong culture may cause complacency and reduce creativity among staff and cause an organisation to become inflexible or slow to change, reducing its competitive advantage (Knights & Wilmott, 2012). However, these factors are miniscule at Mars. According to Robison (2008) independence and originality are rewarded in Mars employees. Additionally, Crainer (2014) states that being in the unstable food industry, complacency is non-existent and Mars continuously adapts to retain competitive advantage.

> Uses evidence to show the strength of manufactured cultures

> Uses author tags to refer to research

C reinforces success of Mars' culture

T5 Manufactured culture

Kaliprasad (2006) states that high-performance cultures promote teamwork and commitment to the organisation. The owners and managers at Mars instil the 'family' culture into their staff by emphasising that everyone has an equally significant role in the organisation and that the owners' legacy is also the staff's legacy. Robison (2008) explains that Mars managers stress the importance of allowing their employees to perceive their jobs as managing a successful business rather than selling sweets.

	This family culture is what allows Mars to have a geographical presence in more than 74 countries and still remain a single unified team across borders (Marketline, 2015). Santora (2009) continues that the more an organisation's culture values goal-setting, the more it will have a positive impact on its performance and lead to success. It is this goal-oriented culture that has led Mars to be the third largest privately-owned company in the USA (Crainer, 2014). Crainer (2014) continues that even the owners of Mars visit the factories and headquarters every day and are extremely involved in the business. This high degree of involvement, says Baker (1980), allows managers to solve problems faster and leads to greater organisational success. At Mars, this success has made it one of the world's most prominent candy manufacturers.	Gives evidence of success
C reinforces success of Mars' culture		
CONCLUSION MODEL **Reviews but with general comments**	This essay has explored the idea of organisational culture and its different aspects in relation to Mars Incorporated. Schein's model and Handy's task culture assessed the different aspects and characteristics of Mars' culture. Peters and Waterman's study was analysed and Mars was found to personify the characteristics that successful businesses contain. Mars' success was found to be associated with the culture that the original founders created and subsequent owners have implemented through the years. Mars' organisational culture rooted on the foundation of the Five Principles reflects the mainstream perspective that a manufactured culture unifies staff towards a common professional purpose and has contributed to its success.	Could mention some specific characteristics

YOUR RESPONSE

1. Which of the following methods best describes the way the essay is organised?
   DIVISION | LOGICAL ENQUIRY | CHRONOLOGY

2. The topic of each paragraph is clear from the first sentence.   YES ☐   NO ☐

3. Is there a consistent relation of theory to the case?   YES ☐   NO ☐
   How do you know this?
   _____
   _____

4. The conclusion has the function of reminding the reader of the main arguments. In this case, the main arguments relate to the specific characteristics of the culture of MARS incorporated.
   Do you think this has been achieved in the conclusion?   YES ☐   NO ☐

5. Is this essay an effective and relevant response to the question?   YES ☐   NO ☐

SUBJECT: Health Sciences   **YEAR:** Second   **LENGTH:** 2597 words

REFERENCING STYLE (references not included): APA (Author, Year system)

ASSIGNMENT QUESTION: Is caffeine a drug of abuse?

STRUCTURE & ORGANISATION	DEVELOPMENT & STYLE

INTRODUCTION MODEL

Scope mainly

Introduction

Some people have questioned whether caffeine should be considered a drug of abuse and caffeine dependence included in the Diagnostic and Statistical Manual of Mental Disorders. (Hughes et al., 1992; Nehlig, 1999). This essay will describe the effects of caffeine and where it is found and explore whether caffeine should be considered a drug of abuse. The basis of this consideration will be whether caffeine fits the DSM-IV criteria for substance abuse or dependence, and the abuse liability of caffeine.

> Use of 'will' unnecessary

BODY TEC MODEL
T1

Sources and consumption

Caffeine is the most widely consumed psychoactive substance in the world ... The average intake daily intake of caffeine is estimated at 200–300mg/day (Satel, 2006). (Hughes et al., 1992). A natural alkaloid, caffeine ... is found in a number of plants including ... which are used to make beverages] such as ... The amount of caffeine found in these foods and beverages varies widely. Coffee contains ...

T2

Properties of caffeine

Caffeine is a psycho-stimulant ... Once ingested, it is absorbed rapidly ... It readily crosses the blood-brain barrier ... Caffeine is metabolised in the liver ... The half-life of caffeine is variable and influenced by factors such as cigarette smoking, sex, age, pregnancy and use of oral contraceptives ...

> Provides facts

T3a

Physiological and behavioural effects

Caffeine's primary mechanism of action is as an adenosine receptor antagonist ... found in the brain ... Generally, caffeine has biphasic effects, with low doses producing desirable stimulation and high doses unpleasant side effects. Behavioural effects include ... In higher doses, caffeine can cause anxiety, insomnia, tremors and seizures. Effects on other body systems include elevated blood pressure, increased respiration, increased metabolic rate and increased gastric acid secretion. (Benowitz, 1990; Fisone et al., 2004).

> Explains causes and effects; uses cause and effect language

T3b

Caffeine is toxic in high doses but only a few cases of death due to excess caffeine intake have been reported ... The risk of intoxication is especially high among children and younger adolescents ... Energy drinks consumed with alcohol can mask the effects of alcohol intoxication and lead to a greater occurrence of alcohol-related problems. (Reissig et al., 2009).

> Explains causes and effects; uses cause and effect language

T4

Criteria for drug abuse classification

There is no standard definition of a drug of abuse. However, important aspects to consider include the ability of the drug to induce physical dependence, the DSM-IV criteria for substance abuse and dependence and the abuse liability of the drug.

> Good lead-in to sub-headings

T4a

Substance dependence

According to DSM-IV, substance dependence is a 'maladaptive pattern of substance use leading to clinical impairment or distress'. These criteria must be fulfilled in a 12-month period for a diagnosis of substance dependence: tolerance, withdrawal, reduction in social activities, desire to reduce use and continued use ... Tolerance is defined as ... Withdrawal is ... Together tolerance and withdrawal constitute physical dependence.

T4b

Substance abuse

DSM-IV criteria for substance abuse are one or more of the following in the last 12 months: recurrent failure to fulfil role obligations due to substance use; recurrent substance-related legal problems; recurrent use in situations in which use is physically hazardous; and continued use despite social or interpersonal problems caused or exacerbated by the substance. (American Psychiatric Association, 2000).

> Explains how the three criteria work

T4c

Abuse liability

Other important aspects to consider when evaluating whether a drug should be considered a drug of abuse are whether the drug is reinforcing and can be discriminated from other substances. The basis or discrimination is the presence or absence of effect or the presence or absence of withdrawal symptoms.

T5
a) First criterion

Is caffeine a drug of abuse?

In terms of substance dependence, caffeine clearly fulfils the DSM-IV criteria for tolerance and withdrawal. In a study by (Hughes et al., 1998), 56% of people in the survey reported desire or unsuccessful attempts to cut down on caffeine use and 50% of those surveyed reported a great deal of time spent using or obtaining the drug. One person reported a reduction in social activities. However, as the study collected data using telephone interviews, it is difficult to tell whether the findings are sufficient to constitute clinical levels of impairment or distress, and whether the criteria for substance dependence are really met. Another study found caffeine dependence amongst teenagers. In the study, participants were selected on the

> Measures caffeine against first criterion

> Refers to two studies

basis that they used caffeine daily and at least one criterion of dependence was reported in a screening interview. 22% of participants were found to be dependent on caffeine. The most commonly fulfilled criteria were tolerance, withdrawal and desire to cut down. (Bernstein et al., 2002) ... However, given the lack of adverse effects as a result of caffeine use, it is difficult to justify including caffeine dependence as a clinical diagnosis in the DSM. It is debatable whether caffeine use can result in clinical levels of impairment or distress.

Decides on first criterion

b) Second criterion

While caffeine clearly fulfils the DSM-IV criteria for tolerance and withdrawal, it is unlikely that it could fulfil the DSM-IV criteria for substance abuse. Caffeine is readily available and socially acceptable and the effects are such that it is unlikely to result in failure to fulfil role obligations, legal problems or interpersonal or social problems. Use is not likely to cause accidents and is not physically hazardous.

Measures and decides on second criterion

c) Third criterion

Abuse liability, or the likelihood that use of a drug will lead to addiction, is determined by the reinforcing properties of a drug. As caffeine is, at best, weakly reinforcing, the abuse liability of caffeine is low. That is, humans and animals will self-administer caffeine in preference to a placebo under some conditions. Caffeine is not as reinforcing as other stimulants such as cocaine or amphetamines and reinforcement is maintained at lower doses. Caffeine differs from other stimulants and, more generally, other drugs of abuse in that it does not activate the mesolimbic dopaminergic pathway in the brain at usual doses. This pathway is thought to be responsible for the high addiction potential of other stimulants such as cocaine. While caffeine does activate this pathway, it only does so in high doses by which time many other brain regions have already been activated. The actions of other stimulants on the mesolimbic pathway are much more specific, acting primarily on this pathway. (Nehlig, 1999)

Measures and decides on third criterion

T6

Reinforcing effects of high doses of caffeine
The undesirable effects of high dose of caffeine are demonstrated using animal studies. Low doses of caffeine cause conditioned place-preference but high doses cause place-aversion. Caffeine appears to be more reinforcing in humans than in animals. Avoidance of withdrawal is thought to be partly responsible for reinforcement, rather than the stimulating properties alone. As caffeine appears to be reinforcing in some animals, the psychostimulant properties are also believed to account for some of the effects. However, it is possible that other aspects of caffeine use are reinforcing rather than the caffeine itself. Coffee is preferred over caffeine tablets in studies, and it is possible that part of the reinforcing properties of coffee and tea are related to enjoyment of the beverage itself. Additionally, tea and coffee are often consumed in social situations which may be reinforcing. (Daly & Fredholm, 1998; Nehlig, 1999).

Compares with other stimulants. Note also the use of qualification strategies (highlighted here)

CONCLUSION MODEL	**Conclusion**	
	While caffeine may meet the criteria for substance dependence in some people, it is unlikely to meet the criteria for substance abuse. The abuse liability is low relative to other stimulants.	Mentions key words
States thesis which answers assignment question	The unpleasant side effects of caffeine mean that it is usually consumed in moderation and is not usually taken in doses that are harmful. Coffee drinking is a social ritual that provides many people with enjoyment and it is important that behaviours such as these are not pathologised without good reason. However, caffeine use, especially in energy drinks should continue to be monitored. The caffeine content of energy drinks should be restricted and labelling required, as people may not be aware of the high doses they contain. It may be that if the current	Adequate length – good balanced review
End sentence points to future	increase consumption of energy drinks continues and harmful effects become evident then caffeine should be considered a drug of abuse. However, at present, this consideration is not justified.	

YOUR RESPONSE

1. Which of the following methods best describes the way the essay is organised?
   DIVISION | LOGICAL ENQUIRY | CHRONOLOGY

2. Are the headings useful?   YES ☐   NO ☐

3. In T5, is the question 'Is caffeine a drug of abuse?' adequately answered?   YES ☐   NO ☐
   Why do you think the writer has employed qualification strategies in answering this question?
   _____

4. In this essay, the criteria [T4] and the measurement of caffeine against each criterion [T5] are discussed
   separately. An alternative organisational method could be to discuss T4 and T5 together (in pairs) – that is,
   describe each criterion and measure caffeine against it in the same paragraph. Which method works best, in
   your view?
   _____

   _____

REVIEW

The purpose of Part V has been to demonstrate that there is a common set of techniques that can be applied to essay assignments in many subject areas.

In the analysis of the essays, the focus has been on aspects of writing outlined in the table below. Use it as a checklist to evaluate your own writing.

Structure and organisation	Development and style
☐ uses a logical organisational method for the main body of the essay	☐ shows understanding of assignment requirements
☐ has good layout and clear structure	☐ uses different techniques to advance a point
☐ applies the introduction model to provide an effective entry into the topic	☐ shows knowledge of subject
☐ uses the TEC paragraph model to develop each main point	☐ shows evidence of research for the assignment
☐ applies the conclusion model to provide a strong ending	☐ employs an academic writing style
	☐ uses correct conventions for citing and using sources

Summary of the key strengths of each essay

- In Essay 1, the use of comparison-contrast language and consistent references to both films provide a unified and coherent development of ideas. The comparative analysis is controlled and displays knowledge of the subject.
- In Essay 2, the elements of evaluation and interpretation show that the writer is not merely describing the musical composition but responding to it. The use of specialised vocabulary shows the writer's depth of knowledge.
- Essay 3 displays features of discussion and analysis. Discussion is shown in explaining how Manet deviated from traditional practice. Analysis is seen in the visual descriptions of the artist's paintings to illustrate a point.
- In Essay 4, the writer systematically connects the art work and artist to production and consumption, using relevant sociological theory to provide a critical analysis of this connection.
- Essay 5 is typical of discursive essays. It provides different perspectives on the issues in the main body of the essay. The thesis is not stated in the introduction but in the conclusion, the writer does address the issue of 'accuracy' posed in the assignment question, thus giving a sense of completeness to the discussion. The TEC paragraph model is applied effectively to begin each new paragraph.
- A key feature of case study essays is relating theory to a practical situation. This is consistently done in Essay 6. The analysis of each aspect of organisational culture begins with a relevant theory and proceeds to show how it relates to the case. The references to the company ('At Mars') may seem repetitive but the strategy works. If you find writing challenging, this approach can give you control over the writing process.
- Essay 7 is a good example of logical enquiry. It also reflects a common practice of using headings, especially in the Sciences and in essays of more than 2500 words long.

Some style issues

1. In some essays, the use of informal language and personal pronouns produces a casual and conversational tone.
2. Several short quotations are used close together (see Essay 5).
3. In some conclusions, the review of the main arguments is too general and therefore less useful to the reader (see Essay 6).
4. The use of headings need careful consideration (see Essays 5 and 7). Headings only identify the topic of each body paragraph in a general way. In addition, the TEC paragraph structure may not be fully used to advance a point. In essay assignments, it is important to maintain coherence throughout. One way to achieve this is to include an explicit topic sentence after the heading. A good test is to read the essay without looking at the headings to see if the beginning sentences of each paragraph introduce the main content clearly.

APPENDIX A **Answers to practice activities**

Part I Essential features of academic writing

Unit 1 Appropriate writing style

Practice Activity 1.1 (pp 3–4)

2 jobs; 3 Like; 4 employers also; 5 and not only that; 6 get; 7 sentence fragment/incomplete sentence; 8 so much; 9 lot of; 10 so; 11 our; 12 sentence fragment/incomplete sentence

Practice Activity 1.2 (pp 9–10)

A Using subordinators

1. Although 'gender' and 'sex' are often considered to be interchangeable, they refer to two different phenomena.
2. Whereas sex refers to the biological differences of male and female, gender refers to the social identities of masculinity and femininity.
3. Because gender is generally based on biological differences, it is assumed to be 'natural' rather than a socially constructed discourse.
4. People are born with a particular sex, while gender identity is something gained over time as a result of socially constructed psychological influences.
5. Since the feminine identity is considered to be more nurturing and caring, it is often the expectation that women stay at home with the children and perform domestic chores.

B Using formal sentences and academic words

b) There may be a change in policy.
c) The issue causes concern.
d) The problem needs urgent attention./The problem needs to be resolved quickly.
e) The role of the manager is to ensure operational efficiency./The manager's role is to monitor operations and ensure efficiency.

C Changing informal to academic writing style

Here is one suggested revision. By removing all obvious informalities, the same content is delivered in a more formal and academic tone.

One benefit of overseas university study is the opportunity to gain new insights and experiences, especially if the university provides special activities for international students. At the University of Auckland, for example, there are many various club activities for international students to participate in. Engagement in these activities also increases contact with the local culture and interaction with native speakers, as new friendships are formed. The Canoeing Club, for example, organises an activity every weekend. Registered members can hire all the canoeing gear at a low cost, which makes such activities affordable for international students. Other clubs such as rock climbing, scuba diving, and surfing also provide unique experiences. In some countries, membership fees are extremely expensive and therefore such clubs inaccessible to most people. In a recent survey conducted by Auckland University's International Students' Centre, the majority of respondents reported that the university's club activities offered them the most valuable overseas experience for their personal and social development.

Unit 2 Conventions for using sources

Practice Activity 2.1 (pp 23–4)

1. a) To Manet, the Salon provided the ideal venue for him to test his artistic skills.
   b) Manet believed that, at the Salon, he would be able to test his skills against other artists.

2. Suggested summary:

In her study of Native North American perceptions of gender, Lang (1996) discovered that it is conflicting to say whether gender is biologically determined. In these tribes, although the men behave and live like women they do not change their physical appearance. The same applies for women who live and behave like men.

3. Suggested revision:

The industrial age changed the conventional family structure when men left the home daily to seek wage labour. **According to Hook (2006),** this led to separation of men's and women's labour: men as breadwinners, women the caregivers. Today's family model features both men and women working outside the home, but **Hook argues** that although unpaid work time has increased for men, 'it has not compensated for women's decline nor reached parity with women's time' **(p. 1).**

---

4. Paraphrase 1 – Unacceptable – some criteria met
✓ Cites source ✗ Retains meaning ✓ Changes text structure ✓ Uses different sentence structures ✓ Changes most words

Paraphrase 2 – acceptable – all criteria met
✓ Cites source ✓ Retains meaning ✓ Changes text structure ✓ Uses different sentence structures ✓ Changes most words

Paraphrase 3 – Unacceptable – most criteria not met
✗ Cites source ✓ Retains meaning ✗ Changes text structure ✗ Uses different sentence structures ✗ Changes most words

Unit 4 Coherent flow of ideas

Practice Activity 4.1 (p 34)

1. reference pronoun 2. repetition with same word 3. repetition with same word 4. repetition with same word	5. logical connector 6. repetition with parallel word 7. reference pronoun 8. repetition with same word	9. repetition with different form of the same word 10. repetition with different form of the same word 11. logical connector 12. repetition of same word

Unit 5 Accurate use of language

Practice Activity 5.1 (pp 43–4)

Grammar

1. Only **a** small number of people are responsible for the project. (missing article)
2. The living wage contributes to _ economic growth. (no article needed)
3. Firms **will benefit** as more products **are consumed**. (two-part verb forms)
4. Over the past few years, the minimum wage **has generated** much debate. (verb forms in present perfect)
5. Recently, there **have** been significant **debates** around **the** world about paying wages as they **affect consumption** and daily **lives** directly. (agreement, plural – s, definite article, agreement, uncountable noun, countable noun (plural))

<u>Sentences</u> Over-long sentences are broken up and and unnecessary words are removed to produce a more direct and clearer writing style.

1. James and Susan bought a second-hand washing machine from Ben on the online auction site, Trade Me, for $150 and paid an extra $40 delivery fee. A month after the purchase, the machine stopped working. Ben has declined the buyers' request to either replace the machine or repair it, so they claim compensation to the amount of $115.
2. This report describes a design solution for the device to enable it to perform all the functions specified in the product specifications.
3. The combination of elements reflects the artist's unique use of different colour tones to add texture and emotion to the work.
4. Various research in the teaching and learning of English in the 1990s concluded that pupils' knowledge and language proficiency could be substantially improved.

Part II Types of university written assignments

Unit 1 Essays

<u>Practice Activity 1.1</u> (pp 51–2)

1. Statue of Liberty.   <u>Suggested order and explanation</u>
   [1] [3] [2]   Description (subject-matter)
   [4] [6] [8] [12]   Analysis (compositional elements – form, shape)
   [11] [10] [5] [7] [9]   Analysis (construction – material, dimensions)
2. Focus on spatial composition: If you are a student of architecture, you might find this task manageable because you have knowledge of the subject from course work. Use the suggested organising principles to help you organise your writing. Follow the logical line of your eye and move across the room in a logical way.

Part III Developing your writing

Unit 2 Methods of organisation

<u>Practice Activity 2.1</u> (pp 82–3)

1. Types of power relationships: Men's superiority over women; Institutional power; Ethnic groups and majority; Man's power over nature.
   Sequence markers: *also, another*
2. 4 socio-economic factors: school; capitalism; culture; teachers
   <u>Comments</u>: Instead of starting with author tags, a more direct way would be to state the socio-economic factor, e.g. *School plays an important role in determining levels of educational attainment. Parson (1959) argues that...*

<u>Practice Activity 2.2</u> (pp 84–5)

1. ORDER: WHAT, WHAT, WHAT, WHY, HOW
2. Logical order: Question [2,5]; Question [4]; Question [3]; [Question [1]; Question [6]

<u>Practice Activity 2.3</u> (pp 86–7)

Body 1: Media image; Body 2: 'Mother' era; Body 3: 'Sex object' era; Body 4: Current status

<u>Practice Activity 2.4</u> (pp 89–90)

1. Paired
2. a) separate; b) Sentence [4] <u>Comment</u>: The separate method is a manageable way to do comparative analysis but the writing can become too descriptive and the comparative details less clear to the reader.
3. One cause and its effects are discussed together in the same paragraph (Paired method)

Unit 3 Introductions and conclusions

Practice Activity 3.1 (pp 95–6)

1. CONTEXT Sentences [1] [2] [3]; TOPIC FOCUS Sentence [4] [5]; THESIS Sentence [7]; SCOPE Sentence [7]
2. a) CONTEXT; b) TOPIC FOCUS; c) SCOPE; d) THESIS (in the same sentence as SCOPE)
3. a) FACTS; b) TOPIC FOCUS Sentence [5] [6]; c) THESIS Sentence [9]

Practice Activity 3.2 (p 97)

1. a) CONTEXT; b) THESIS; c) TOPIC FOCUS; d) SCOPE
2. a) SCOPE; b) CONTEXT (background information/facts); c) TOPIC FOCUS
   Comment: In experimental reports, the thesis is usually not stated in the introduction.

Practice Activity 3.3 (pp 101–2)

<table>
<tr>
<td>

1. ☒ Signal
   ☑ Review
   ☑ Thesis restatement
   ☒ End sentence
     ☐ uses quotation
     ☐ points to larger context
     ☐ links back to thesis/essay question

Comments: Review lists main points. Conclusion is too short. The end sentence relates only to one prime minister.

</td>
<td>

2. ☑ Signal
   ☑ Review
   ☑ Thesis restatement
   ☑ End sentence
     ☑ uses quotation
     ☐ points to larger context
     ☐ links back to thesis/essay question

Comments: Applies model effectively.

</td>
</tr>
<tr>
<td>

3. ☑ Signal
   ☑ Review
   ☑ Thesis restatement
   ☑ End sentence
     ☐ uses quotation
     ☑ points to larger context
     ☐ links back to thesis/essay question

Comments: Applies model adequately.

</td>
<td>

4. ☒ Signal
   ☑ Review
   ☑ Thesis restatement
   ☒ End sentence
     ☐ uses quotation
     ☐ points to larger context
     ☐ links back to thesis/essay question

Comments: The thesis restatement is too subjective. The use of 'seem' makes the conclusion weak. The words 'public discussion and research' are too vague.

</td>
</tr>
</table>

Practice Activity 3.4 (p 104)

1. a) Signal for end; b) THESIS RESTATEMENT (Comment: This sentence is not a restatement, because the thesis was not stated in the introduction. The thesis was dependent on the results of the findings. In report conclusion, the thesis restatement is in fact the THESIS.)
2. a) SIGNAL FOR END; b) END SENTENCE (pointing to future potential of study)

Unit 4 Paragraph structure and construction

Practice Activity 4.1 (pp 109–11)

1. TEC model Correct order: [4] [6] [1] [5] [8] [2] [7] [3]
2. a) Composition; b) Characterisation; c) Clear and attractive text design; d) Use of humour
3. Text A: Most effective accurate topic sentence: b
   Text B: Most effective topic sentence: c
   Text C: Suggested answer: *One of the most important ways that the Second World War can be seen as a good war for the American home front is the stimulation of its economy.* (The key words in the topic sentence that best reflect the main point of the argument are 'stimulation of the economy'.)

Unit 5 Techniques for developing your writing

Practice Activity 5.1 (pp 114–16)

1. First example Sentence [3] because it is not a relevant business example.
2. a) sexualised by the media; b) Any one of these:
   - Detail: doctors in the front row, nurses in the back. Significance: existence of a hierarchy in the medical profession
   - Detail: doctors are males, nurses are female. Significance: nursing a feminine profession
   - Detail: doctors with medical equipment; nurses with non-technical equipment. Significance: nurses are handmaidens to assist doctors
   - Detail: nurses wearing short dresses. Significance: perception of nursing as a sexualised profession
3. a) INCIDENT; b) Sentences [2] [3] [4]
4. 2. TEXT; 3. DETAIL 4. TEXT [5]. DETAIL
5. a) Theme: 'innovation in arrangement'
   b) 3 examples of innovation: Mahler, Shostakovich, Stravinsky
   c) 'a good illustration of'; 'another notable example'

Practice Activity 5.2 (pp 118–19)

1. S2 CLASSIFICATION; S4 PURPOSE; S5 EXAMPLE; S6 CONTRAST; S7&8 CLARIFICATION
2. S2 FUNCTION; S3 COMPONENTS S5 COMPARISON
3. a) one-sided concept; b) CLARIFICATION
   c) Words indicating clarification: Sentence [2] 'this means'; Sentence [4] 'In other words'; d) OPINION

Practice Activity 5.3 (p 123)

Sample answer

One of the Expert Advisory Group's most significant recommendations is the Universal Child Payment, which favours a return to universal welfare ideologies. It recommends that the Government implements a universal Child Payment to be made available to all families with children under the age of six. It argues that universal child payments is a viable method of providing governmental assistance, as shown by the success of such schemes in other countries. The Group believes that the government has an important role in ensuring equal opportunities and a sense of well-being. These recommendations contrast significantly with the neo-liberal view of the government in the 1990s, which promoted ideals of personal individuality and self-reliance. Instead of providing universal welfare assistance, it believed in minimal state intervention and targeting only low-income families was fiscally more viable and sustainable.

Practice Activity 5.4 (pp 126–7)

1. 1. leads to; 2. Is associated with; 3. Consequently; 4. result in; 5. could affect; 6. correlation exists; 7. could have an impact
2. a) competition; b) earning ability; c) standard of living; d) a threat to economic livelihood of citizens
3. In developing your cause-effect paragraph from notes, make sure that your sentences are complete and all missing grammatical items (articles, verbs) are added. In addition, check that your use of cause-effect language is adequate and is not limited to commonly used cause-effect markers (leads to, affects, causes).

Practice Activity 5.5 (pp 131–2)

1. a) Sentence [1] describes purpose and specific content
   Sentences [2] [3] [4] [5] interpret the data
   Sentences [6] [7] comment on the data's significance and limitation
   b) Some evaluative expressions: positive relationship; clear evidence; slight drop
2. Sample data description to accompany HAZOP chart
   Suggested answer (showing the three-skills approach to data commentary)

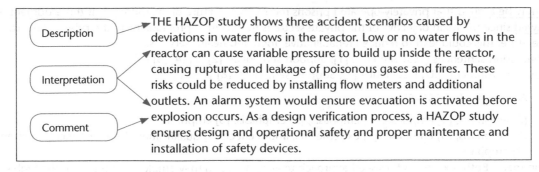

THE HAZOP study shows three accident scenarios caused by deviations in water flows in the reactor. Low or no water flows in the reactor can cause variable pressure to build up inside the reactor, causing ruptures and leakage of poisonous gases and fires. These risks could be reduced by installing flow meters and additional outlets. An alarm system would ensure evacuation is activated before explosion occurs. As a design verification process, a HAZOP study ensures design and operational safety and proper maintenance and installation of safety devices.

Labels pointing to the text: Description, Interpretation, Comment

Part IV Presenting a point of view: argumentation

Unit 2 The issue and thesis statement

Practice Activity 2.1 (pp 140–2)

A. 1. a) No (too vague); b) other view: sentences [2] and [3]; c) student's view: sentences [4] and [5]; d) Thesis sentence [6]
   2. a) No (Context: provide some information about the Meiji period and its significance with regard to modernisation and its inclination towards western developments); b) other view: there is some evidence of western developments; c) student's view: the imitations were temporary and limited in scope; d) Sentence [5] states the thesis
   3. a) No (Context: provide some explanation of its relevance to business success); b) other view: entrepreneurs are born with traits – cannot be taught; c) student's view: some skills can be taught; d) YES: Sentence [6]

B. 1. Clear thesis, Uses emotive language (false, greatly)
   2. Vague thesis (what is the contrast opinion?), uses personal pronouns
   3. Vague thesis, emotive language (should not)
   4. Repeats word from the question, vague thesis (repeating 'good' from the question is not useful), uses emotive language (good, bad, total sense)

Unit 3 Structuring the argument

Practice Activity 3.1 (pp 145–6)

1. Paragraphs [1] and [2]
2. Paragraphs [3] [4] and [5]
3. Organisational method: separate/block
4. However
5. No

Unit 4 Building the argument

Practice Activity 4.1 (p 148)

[1] Another [2] Therefore, Consequently [3] However [4] Furthermore, In addition, [5] As a result, Consequently, As a consequence

Practice Activity 4.2 (pp 152–3)

1a. There is no denying that technology can enhance business practice and give companies a competitive advantage. However, without skilled staff, a favourable and effective information system plan, businesses are unlikely to benefit from modern technologies.
1b. Women are clearly participating in more paid work, but the fact is they are also retaining responsibility for the unpaid domestic work, which indicates that women are in reality working much more than their husbands.

1c. It may be argued that privately-operated prisons reduce expenditure of tax money, but this argument is flawed since the main objective of the private sector is to maximise profitability. In the prison context, therefore, this could lead to reduced rehabilitative, food and health services.

2. Concession sentences (YES) Sentence [1]; Support sentences: [2] [3] [4] [5] [6]
   Counter-argument (BUT): Sentence [7]; Support sentences: [8]]9] [10]

Practice Activity 4.3 (pp 155–6)

1. a) [2] emphasis; [3] emphasis; [4] emphasis; [5] emphasis; [6] emphasis
   b) [2] emphasis; [3] emphasis; [4] extreme/maximum effect; [5] qualification; [6] emphatic; [7] extreme; [8] emphasis

Comment: Both texts use a thesis-led approach to argument and may employ intensifiers at the high end of the scale of intensity more than the discussion-led approach.

2. a) Delete 'very' OR Write a new sentence: The harmful effects from second-hand smoking is lower in open areas.
   b) Remove 'essentially'
   c) Remove 'greatly' (this word is also informal and emotive).
   d) Remove 'safely' and 'basically'
   e) Remove 'commonly' and 'potentially' OR Write a new sentence: The argument concerning technology is that it is not authentic and does not enhance the music.

Comment: It is best to avoid intensifiers that are vague, over-used and subjective and replace with more concrete and active verbs or adjectives.

Practice Activity 4.4 (p 160)

[1] are not; [2] may be; [3] cannot be; [4] is possible; [5] could be acquired; [6] can be; [7] is

Unit 5 Argumentative essays for study

Essay 1 (p 164) 1. Paired; 2. Yes; 3. Yes, but: frequent use, Intensifiers: frequent use, Modal verbs: some use.
Essay 2 (p 167) 1. Paired; 2. Yes; 3. Yes: frequent use, Intensifiers: limited use, modal verbs: frequent use.
Essay 3 (p 177) 1. Paired; 2. Yes; 3. Yes, but: some use, Intensifiers: limited use, Modal verbs: limited use.
Essay 4 (p 174) 1. Separate; 2. Yes, but strategy: limited use; Intensifiers: some use, Modal verbs: limited use.

Part V Putting it all together

Essay 1 (p 181) 1. Paired; 2. Yes; 3. Uses film vocabulary/techniques; 4. Yes. Refers to films; 5. Yes; 6. specific examples, comparison
Essay 2 (p 184) 1. Division; 2. Uses specialised terms; 3. Yes; 4. topic focus; end sentence; 5. Yes; 6. Yes
Essay 3 (p 188) 1. Division; 2. Gives specific examples/details; 3. Last 2 short quotes; 4. Overuse of 'indeed', informal language ('battle with tradition'; 'took it further'); 5. Yes. Consistent reference to avant-garde style; 6. examples, comparison, visual analysis
Essay 4 (p 191) 1. Division; 2. theory of standardisation and false needs; 3. T4; 4. Repeats key words; 5. Yes
Essay 5 (p 195) 1. Logical enquiry; 2a. New paragraph for new topic focus; 2b. Industrial age; 2c. Modern households; 3. author tag and reporting verb; paraphrase followed by citation; 4. No; 5. Yes; 6. Yes
Essay 6 (p 199) 1. Division; 2. No; 3. Yes. Theory followed by case; 4. No; 5 Yes. Shows awareness of case study methodology
Essay 7 (p 203) 1. Logical enquiry; 2. Yes; 3. Yes, shows awareness of inconclusive findings/evidence; 4. Separate method would be clearer, considering the complexity of the content. Combining the criterion and measurement/decision could make the paragraph too long.

A classification of instruction verbs and their meaning

1. Verbs requiring display of **knowledge** of concepts

analyse	break something down to its parts and examine each part methodically and in detail
define	give the exact nature, scope or meaning
describe	give accurate details about something or someone
outline/list	give a summary or main features
identify/state	express a fact or requirement clearly and precisely

2. Verbs requiring demonstration of **understanding**

account for/explain	make an idea clear by describing it in more detail or by giving reasons
compare and contrast	show similarities and differences (NOTE: Used on its own, 'compare' refers to similarities and/or differences.)
discuss	write about a topic in detail by examining it from different perspectives
summarise	give a brief statement of the main points

3. Verbs requiring **knowledge application**

apply/draw on	use (theories, models, other people's ideas) as a resource to explain opinions/ decisions/conclusions
illustrate/show	make something clear by using examples or figures
examine/explore	use a questioning approach to look closely at something
interpret	explain information as having particular significance
relate	show or describe the connection between ideas
synthesise	combine ideas from different sources to form a new understanding of theory (opposite of 'analyse')

4. Verbs requiring **evaluation** (includes justification, persuasion)

appraise/assess/evaluate	estimate the value, quality or ability of someone or something
argue/debate	give reasons or evidence in support of an idea, action, or theory, typically with the aim of persuading others to share one's point of view
comment on/reflect	express an opinion or reaction
critique	evaluate (a theory or practice) in a detailed and analytical way
justify/prove	give reasons or examples to demonstrate how or why something is true
review/consider	think carefully and deeply about something, typically before making a decision; examine a subject closely
survey	look carefully at a range of ideas so as to appraise their significance to a subject area

5. Verbs requiring **knowledge creation** or generation and research skills

construct	form an idea or theory by bringing together various concepts, typically over a period of time
design	create a system or method of doing something; decide on the look and functioning of a building or other object, typically by making a detailed drawing of it (in the Physical Sciences)
formulate	create a strategy or method
propose/suggest	put forward an idea

The language of description

Points of reference in a space or on your canvas:

The purpose of a visual description is to draw the reader's attention to the image and then move the reader's eye across the painting or space in a logical manner. Knowing how to refer to position and location points is helpful for this purpose:

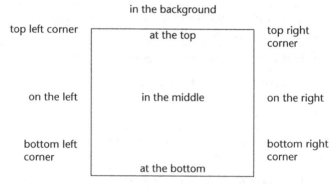

Concrete use of language

As a student of the visual arts, you are likely to be provided with adequate visual vocabulary but here is a quick summary.

Visual elements	Adjectives
Line	horizontal, vertical, diagonal, bold, soft, flowing, crisp, clear, sharp, thin, thick
Colour/hue/tone	subtle, bold, vibrant, strong, warm, cool, complementary, light, dark, pale, earthy
Texture	smooth, rough, fine, coarse, uneven
Shape	geometric, curvaceous, angular, circular, round, square, an A-frame, U-shaped slab, an I-beam
Form	two-dimensional, three-dimensional, bulky, solid, static
Space	white space (airy, spacious), dark space (cramped), open, closed spaces

Tense and voice

Describing visual elements	Use present simple:
	The painting <u>shows</u> a solitary figure at a lake. (active voice) The statue <u>is made</u> of stone. (passive voice)
Describing activity	Use present simple progressive:
	The two men <u>are looking</u> up at the sculpture from their low viewing angle.
Describing historical context	The sculpture <u>was completed</u> in 2000. (passive voice; past simple)

Verbs (according to function)

Existential verbs	Categorising/ compositional verbs	Connecting verbs (passive)	Locating verbs (passive)	Reporting verbs (active)
is/are	has/have consists of comprises is made up of contains covered with coated with	is attached to is connected to is mounted on is bolted to	is located in is enclosed in is surrounded by is suspended from	show represent illustrate demonstrate reflect

Expressing dimensions

Pattern A (is + measurement + adjective)	Pattern B (has + an/a + noun + of + measurement)	Pattern C (a/an + measurement + adjective + noun)
X is 30 km wide, 80 km long	X has a width of … a length of	a 90 m tall beam
X is 90 m high, 20 m deep, 6 cm thick	X has a height of … a depth of … a thickness of	X is a 90 m tall beam

The English Articles

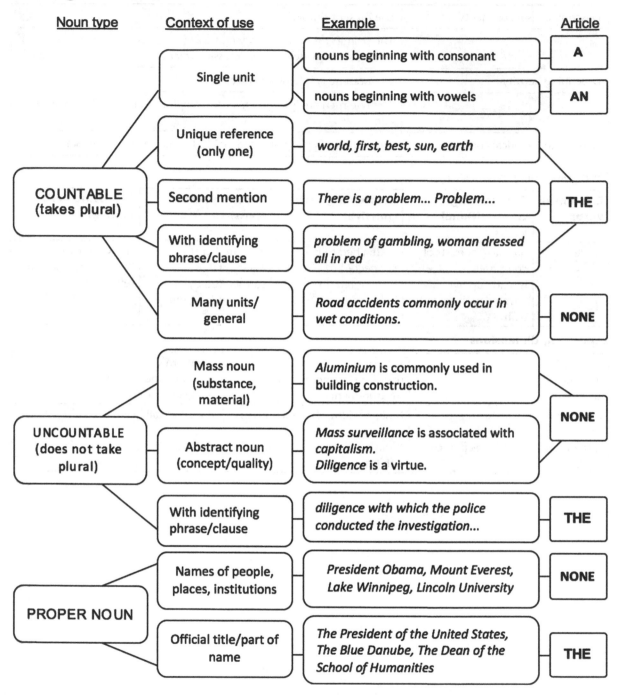

Noun type	Context of use	Example	Article
COUNTABLE (takes plural)	Single unit	nouns beginning with consonant	A
		nouns beginning with vowels	AN
	Unique reference (only one)	*world, first, best, sun, earth*	THE
	Second mention	*There is a problem... Problem...*	THE
	With identifying phrase/clause	*problem of gambling, woman dressed all in red*	THE
	Many units/ general	*Road accidents commonly occur in wet conditions.*	NONE
UNCOUNTABLE (does not take plural)	Mass noun (substance, material)	*Aluminium* is commonly used in building construction.	NONE
	Abstract noun (concept/quality)	*Mass surveillance* is associated with *capitalism.* *Diligence* is a virtue.	NONE
	With identifying phrase/clause	*diligence with which the police conducted the investigation...*	THE
PROPER NOUN	Names of people, places, institutions	*President Obama, Mount Everest, Lake Winnipeg, Lincoln University*	NONE
	Official title/part of name	*The President of the United States, The Blue Danube, The Dean of the School of Humanities*	THE

The English prepositions

Single-word prepositions	about, across, after, along, around, at, before, behind, beside, by, down, during, for, from, in, inside, into, of, off, on, onto, out, over, round, since, through, to, toward(s), under, until, up, with, without
Two-word prepositions	ahead of, apart from, because of, close to, due to, except for, instead of, near to
Three-word prepositions	as far as, by means of, in accordance with, in addition to, in front of, in spite of, in terms of, on behalf of, with reference to.

FUNCTION
Prepositions express different relationships of meaning between two parts of a sentence.

USE
Some prepositions can be used to express different relationship meanings.

POINT OF TIME	about, after, at, by, during, for, from, in, over, past, throughout, until
PURPOSE/REASON	Search *for* gold, thank someone *for* their support
PLACE/DIRECTION/MOVEMENT	*in* London, *at* the traffic lights, travel *from/to*, drive *through* a tunnel, drive *past*
MANNER (OF BEHAVIOUR)	treat *with* kindness, answer *without* hesitation, work *in* silence, work *by* themselves
MEANS (INSTRUMENT)	travel *by* car, write *with* a pen, work *without* a plan
QUANTITY/AMOUNT	*for* twenty dollars, buy *in* bulk
STATE/CONDITION	*in* good health/difficulty/conflict/harmony

IDIOMATIC USE
Refers to the use of certain prepositions after verbs, nouns and adjectives

After certain VERBS:	account *for*, consist *of*, depend, provide *for*, contribute *to*, relate *to*
After certain NOUNS:	Impact *on* impact/effect *on*, success *in/of*, difference *between*,
After certain ADJECTIVES:	according *to*, based *on*, capable *of*, composed *of*, interested *in*

TIP Check in a good dictionary or concordance such as www.just-the-word.com

The English tenses

The aim of the chart is to help you see how the different verb tenses are placed in relation to time and status or aspect, so that you can manage tense and aspect shifts more successfully. [Notice the changes in the endings of the base verb 'try' according to what time or status is expressed.]

TIME OF ACTION		PAST [tried]		PRESENT [try/tries]	*FUTURE [will try]
ASPECT/ STATUS OF ACTION					
Past action <u>completed</u> before another past action	**PAST PERFECT** [had tried]				
Action that has <u>just completed</u> or its effect continues into the present			← **PRESENT PERFECT** [has/have tried] →		
Action <u>in progress</u> at a given time	**PAST PERFECT PROGRESSIVE** [had been trying]	**PAST PROGRESSIVE** [was trying]	**PRESENT PERFECT PROGRESSIVE** [has/have been trying]	**PRESENT PROGRESSIVE** [is/are trying]	**FUTURE PROGRESSIVE** [will be trying]

*Other ways of expressing future time: e.g. I [am going to] Paris next year, I [may/might] stay for two weeks.

APPENDIX C A glossary of some grammatical terms

Abstract noun. A noun used to describe a quality, an idea or experience rather than something physical, e.g. *intelligence, safety, kindness.*

Adverb. A word which gives more information about a verb, adjective, adverb or phrase.

Adverbial. A word which adds information about a situation such as the time of the action or its frequency.

Auxiliary verb. One of the verbs *'be'* is/are/was/were, *'have'* has/had, *'do'* does/did, used to add extra information to a main verb e.g. *is walking, has made, does match.* There are also modal auxiliary verbs, e.g. *can/could, will/would.*

Base form. The form of a verb which has no letters added to the end and is not a past form, e.g. *walk, go, have.* In English, the base form changes according to tense and time.

Clause. A part of a sentence which contains a subject and a verb. A main clause (also known as an independent clause) can exist as a separate sentence, e.g. *She is a professional artist.* A subordinate clause depends on the main clause for its meaning, e.g. *who specialises on portraits.*

Concrete noun. Refers to entities which can be observed or measured. *See* **Abstract noun.**

Conjunction. A word which connects words, phrases, or clauses in a sentence.
Coordinating conjunctions or coordinators e.g. *and, but, so, for, nor, or* join units with equal grammatical status. Subordinating conjunctions or subordinators e.g. *although, so, because, as, when, before, after, if* join subordinate clauses to main clauses.

Consonant. In English writing, consonants are represented by the letters *p, b, t, th, d, k, g, ch, j, y, s, sh, z, f, v, w, l, r, h, m, n, ng.*

Countable noun. A noun that has a singular (one) and a plural form (more than one), e.g. *cat/cats; foot/feet.* Also known as Count Noun. *See* **Uncountable noun.**

Definite article. Grammatical name for *the,* which is used with a noun to indicate that it is specific and known to speaker/writer and listener/reader. *See* **Indefinite article.**

Indefinite article. Grammatical name for *a/an* to express non-specific meaning (any one) or 'a single unit'.

Irregular verb. A verb which indicates past tense in different way from regular *-ed* ending, e.g. *take-took-taken.* *See* **Regular verb.**

Logical connectors (also known as 'transitions' or 'discourse markers'). Words which show the transition of ideas between sentences and paragraphs.

Modal. A verb used with the base form of another verb to express possibility, obligation, prediction, or deduction, e.g. *can, could, may, might.*

Noun It is most often the name of a person or thing, e.g. a word like *oil, memory, robot,* which can be used with an article.

Personal pronoun. One of a group of words to refer to three classes of people: first person e.g. *I, we, my, our, us, me, my, mine;* second person e.g. *you, your;* third person e.g. *it, he, she, they, him, her.*

Object. A word or phrase which is directly affected by the action of the verb in a sentence, e.g. *The Prime Minister planted* a native tree. *See* **Subject.**

Object complement. A word or phrase which adds meaning to the object of a sentence, e.g. *They elected* him (object) president. (object complement)

Parts of speech. Classification of words in English: nouns, pronouns, verbs, adjectives, adverbs, prepositions, conjunctions, interjection.

Phrase. A group of words which is not a complete clause. *See* **Clause.**

Plural. A grammatical form used to refer to more than one person or thing, e.g. *engine/engines; industry/industries.* *See also* **Singular.**

Pronoun. A word used instead of a noun to name someone or something e.g. *he, she, they, them, our, you, your.* *See* **Personal pronoun.**

Proper nouns. Personal names, e.g. *John,* institutions and place names e.g. *Auckland, Princeton University.*

Relative pronoun. Used to link a relative clause at the head of the noun phrases, e.g. *who, whom, whose, which, that.*

Relative clause. A subordinate clause which gives more information about someone or something in the main clause, usually introduced by *who, which, that, whose*.

Regular verb. A verb which changes according to tense and aspect using conventional *-ed* ending for Past Tense and *-ing* ending for progressive aspect, e.g. walk→walked→walking. *See* **Irregular verb**.

Sentence fragment. An incomplete sentence, missing a key clause element that is either a verb or subject, e.g. *Students who study abroad.*

Simple sentence. A sentence with one clause expressing a single idea.

Singular. A grammatical form used to talk about one person, thing, etc., or about an uncountable quantity or mass. *See also* **Plural**.

Subject. The first element of a sentence which identifies the topic or theme of the sentence. *See* **Object**.

Subject complement. A word or phrase which adds meaning to the subject of the sentence, e.g. *The prime minister's speech was inspiring*.

Uncountable noun. A noun which has only singular form, e.g. *money, furniture, equipment, information, rudeness, research.* Also known as Noncount Noun. *See* **Countable noun**.

Verb endings. Denote time and tense. Present form *-ing*; Past form (*-ed*). Denote singularity and plurality e.g. The student tries→ The students try.

Verb to be. E.g. *is, are, was, were, will be, would be. See also* **Auxiliary verb**.

Voice. Refers to the form of a verb to show the relation between a subject and the action. Active voice – emphasis on the subject performing the action (He *designed* the product). Passive voice – opposite of active voice (The product *was designed* by him.)

Vowel. The main English vowels are *a* (pronounced as 'ah'), *e* (pronounced as 'eh'), *i* (pronounced as 'e'), *o* (pronounced as 'or'), and *u* ('oo'). English vowels are not always pronounced the way they are represented in writing. For example, 'put' and 'cup' are pronounced differently. 'Umbrella' is pronounced with the 'uh' sound, and 'university is pronounced with the consonant sound 'y', sounding like 'yuniversity'.

Word order. Refers to the way different elements in a sentence are put together. Some common examples of wrong word order:

1. Misplaced adverbs: **Also, he created most of the designs* → *He also created most of the designs*; He has applied for the position already → He has already applied for the position.
2. Misplaced phrases/clauses: **The engineer was specifically selected for the project* with the most experience → *The engineer with the most experience was selected for the project.*

Index

9781352003758